RESEARCH IN
THE HISTORY OF
ECONOMIC THOUGHT
AND METHODOLOGY

Volume 6 • 1989

RESEARCH IN THE HISTORY OF ECONOMIC THOUGHT AND METHODOLOGY

A Research Annual

Editor: WARREN J. SAMUELS
Department of Economics
Michigan State University

VOLUME 6 • 1989

 JAI PRESS INC.

Greenwich, Connecticut   *London, England*

CONTENTS

REVIEW ESSAYS

LIST OF CONTRIBUTORS

Peter J. Boettke

Department of Economics
Oakland University
Rochester, Michigan

Bruce J. Caldwell

Department of Economics
University of North Carolina
Greensboro

A. W. Coats

Department of Economics
Duke University
Durham, North Carolina

Kenneth Dennis

Department of Economics
University of Manitoba
Winnipeg, Canada

William M. Dugger

Department of Economics
DePaul University
Chicago

Richard A. Gonce

Department of Economics
Grand Valley State University
Allendale, Michigan

Wendell C. Gordon

Department of Economics
University of Texas
Austin

James P. Henderson

Department of Economics
Valparaiso University
Valparaiso, Indiana

William S. Kern

Department of Economics
Western Michigan University
Kalamazoo

Brian J. Loasby

Department of Economics
University of Stirling
Stirling, Scotland

John Lodewijks

Department of Economics
University of New South Wales
Kensington, Australia

Edythe S. Miller

Littleton, Colorado

John R. Presley

The Banking Centre
Loughborough University
Loughborough, England

Salim Rashid

Department of Economics
University of Illinois
Champaign-Urbana

Peter Rosner

Department of Economics
University of Vienna
Vienna, Austria

Malcolm Rutherford

Department of Economics
University of Victoria
Victoria, Canada

Larry Samuelson

Department of Economics
Pennsylvania State University
University Park

Nina Shapiro

Department of Economics
Drexel University
Philadelphia

J. Ron Stanfield

Department of Economics
Colorado State University
Fort Collins

Georg Winckler

Department of Economics
University of Vienna
Vienna, Austria

EDITORIAL BOARD

ACKNOWLEDGMENTS

The editor wishes to express his gratitude for assistance in the review process and other consultation to the members of the editorial board and to the following persons:

Jeff Biddle	*Philip Mirowski*
Sheila Dow	*D. E. Moggridge*
William Dugger	*Salim Rashid*
John E. Elliot	*Malcolm Rutherford*
D. W. Hands	*Allan Schmid*
B. J. Loasby	*Nina Shapiro*
W. E. Mason	*Peter Wiles*

HERBERT SIMON'S HUMAN RATIONALITY

Brian J. Loasby

The sixty papers included in the two volumes of Herbert Simon's *Models of Bounded Rationality* (1982) constitute, in the author's (1:xviii) words, "a reasonably complete collection of my economic works that have not been published elsewhere in book form." In this paper, which has been developed from a review (Loasby 1985), written for the *Economic Journal*, I propose to use this collection as a single body of evidence to illuminate Simon's view, not just of economics, but of the human situation—a view which is remarkably coherent, if incomplete, and very different from the predominant economic culture. It is always dangerous to consider a set of pieces published over a period of more than forty years without reference to their temporal sequence; but neither in his general nor in his sectional introductions does Simon suggest that he has discarded any of his earlier ideas. There are some qualifications and some changes of emphasis, but not many even of these. In appraising Simon's work, time does not seem to be impor-

Research in the History of Economic Thought and Methodology,
Volume 6, pages 1-17
Copyright © 1989 by JAI Press Inc.
All rights of reproduction in any form reserved.
ISBN: 0-89232-928-9

1

tant: as we shall see, that statement bears more than one interpretation. This attempt to summarise and comment on what, to use his own terminology, one might call Simon's decision premises may help us to understand not only his own work but also the reaction—or lack of reaction—to it by economists of various persuasions.

I. COMPLEXITY AND PRAGMATISM

Let us start with an article of 1971 which bears a characteristic title: "Designing Organizations for an Information-Rich World" (2:171–85). Here Simon argues forcefully that plentiful information will not resolve the difficulties which we face in trying to behave reasonably. The abundance of information accentuates the scarcity of our means of handling it. Although we must attempt to recognise externalities and interdependencies, we must also recognise that "the dream of thinking everything out before we act, of making certain we have all the facts and know all the consequences, is a sick Hamlet's dream. It is the dream of someone with no appreciation of the seamless web of causation, the limits of human thinking, or the scarcity of human attention" (2:180). That the complexity of our environment, natural and artificial, extends far beyond the bounds of our rationality is the central fact with which Simon has been trying to deal throughout his career. One obvious consequence is that we must expect to make mistakes, sometimes serious mistakes. "The world will always remain the largest laboratory, the largest information store. . . . Of course it is costly to learn from experience; but it is also costly, and frequently much less reliable, to try through research and analysis to anticipate experience." In other words, don't expect too much from any model—and don't claim too much either.

Nevertheless, there is no need to worry. "We must assume, as mankind has always assumed, that a reasonable allocation of our limited attention and powers of thought will solve the crucial problems facing us at least as fast as new ones arise" (2:181). Before turning to the implications of this assumption, let us consider for a moment the parenthetical comment—"as mankind has always assumed." As an assertion about human history, this is obviously false; but it tells us a great deal about Simon. First, it demonstrates that his recognition of the central fact just emphasised is matched with a central belief; a belief in the capacity of human reason (and perhaps, like Einstein, in the fairness of God) which is so fundamental that Simon simply assumes that it must be shared by all reasonable men. That belief sets unrecognised bounds to his own rationality: and it may serve to remind us that our own systems of thought almost certainly contain basic elements which we have just never thought of as open to question. Second, such an assertion could hardly have been made by someone who is deeply interested in history: Simon looks back only to draw the lessons of immediate experience, and then quickly forward to the next problem. Third, he is a pragmatist, who gives little attention to philosophical issues. As with Oliver Edwards, who (in Boswell's *Life of Johnson*) had often tried to be philosopher, cheerfulness is always breaking in.

Life is a succession of problems, to be tackled successively. It appears to embody no grand theories. Nevertheless, the challenge of new problems, and their successful resolution, makes life an intellectual adventure (2:132). I am reminded of a saying by Charles Suckling (a research chemist who became General Manager, Research and Technology, in I.C.I.) that "the best things we can leave to our children are unsolved problems." If this is to be a message of hope, then we must assume that we can solve crucial problems as fast as new ones arise— but preferably not much faster.

Simon's central assumption implies an interest in processes rather than equilibrium, though since all models are incomplete representations of the phenomena to which they are applied, equilibrium concepts may be used on occasion. It implies a system view, which is in some respects almost the opposite of that taken by general equilibrium theorists. First, the overall system is not to be regarded as complete: there are transactions across its boundaries which are not fully modelled. Second, the behaviour of this overall system is explained in terms of the aggregate behaviour of its subsystems, each of which is explained in turn by the aggregate behaviour of its own subsystems; there is no attempt to relate overall system performance directly to its basic elements. Third, the usual problem addressed is the ongoing management of the system in response to extraneous data, rather than the calculation of equilibrium states or equilibrium flows. Finally, the problem of system management often (especially for Simon) causes interest to be focussed, not on the "real world" elements—the usual variables of economic models—but on the organisational arrangements and decision routines by which these variables are handled.

A combination of these last two elements is implied by the title of Simon's essay "From Substantive to Procedural Rationality" (2:424–43): instead of seeking to derive from axioms and data the values which would be ascribed to the relevant variables by an optimal decision, attention is turned to the processes by which decisions might be made. The complexity of the decision environment places optimality beyond reach, and often beyond definition; what is sought is a feasible procedure for achieving satisfactory results, and ways of checking on experience as a possible guide to doing better.

This concern for effective means of handling complexity sometimes leads Simon to argue that the progress of management science permits increasing centralization of decision-making, in partial replacement of the market; and that since this centralization allows us to handle more interactions, it will improve the quality of decisions (2:61–2). In a talk to town planners, he reminds his audience that what happens in a city depends on the behaviour of its citizens, who have no intention of surrendering their freedom of action to those who have been given "certain very limited powers to modify the design" (2:52); but he does tend to be absorbed by the technology of information processing and the challenge of the conscious design of institutions. What preserves him from the advocacy of any kind of system of central planning is his continuing conviction that all our technical advances still leave far too much beyond the bounds of our rationality for that to be a sensible way of organizing our affairs. We need rather to look for means of coupling together partial decision rules—for example through the price mechanism; or even sometimes to content ourselves with securing "compatibility requirements," so that one decision procedure will not produce results which actually impede the effectiveness of another (1:191).

Loose coupling of partial systems (which is exemplified in Cyert and March's (1963) analysis of organisational behaviour) implies a set of objectives rather than any kind of single objective function, however complicated. What we do not find is a recognition of the potential value of incompatible systems: insistence on compatibility may prevent certain kinds of exploration which do not fit in with present ideas or present practices. But Simon does not consciously envisage the intellectual adventure of solving human problems as a competitive discovery procedure—though this is clearly what it is, even in several areas of pure science. Though he favours a competitive economy, he does not explain why. Neither entrepreneurship nor spontaneous organisation are significant concepts in Simon's work.

Whether the fundamental cause of the difficulties which we face is to be found in our inadequate ability to cope with complexity or because at least part of the future is unknowable is not an issue which he ever raises. Unlike Shackle, he is not very interested in such philosophical questions. His continuing fascination with chess, computers, and artificial intelligence suggests that he believes the cause to be complexity; although, as we shall see later, he recognises the indeterminacy of interdependent decisions, he does sometimes give the impression that we do live in a fully defined system, if only we had the wit to understand it. But his understanding of computers and of artificial intelligence do not give him any hope that we shall ever acquire the wit fully to understand complexity; and perhaps his interest is attracted by the belief that there are more usefully solvable problems in complexity than in ignorance. (Neoclassical economists, in his view, too often make their problems soluble by making the solutions useless.) He has no expectation of constructing a comprehensive system, no ideals to match those of many physicists or economists. His business is piecemeal social engineering.

II. OPTIMISATION

In some respects he appears very conventional. He is an enthusiast for mathematical analysis, and welcomes the increasing mathematisation of the social sciences. He is obviously pleased (2:3) at his success at translating into mathematical form the theory of group interaction proposed by the sociologist G. C. Homans (2:33–42), to which he applies the standard economic method of deriving comparative static equilibria. At the end of an article entitled "Some Economic Effects of Technical Change," after acknowledging the unrealism of the models presented, he offers an argument which we might expect to hear from another author. "If such models have no other value, they are of use in permitting a precise statement of the Malthusian hypothesis, and an examination of the conditions under which that hypothesis holds" (1:305). (In what ways this examination might by useful he does not say.) However he insists that mathematical social science should be applied mathematics: the language of mathematics should be used to say something about its nominal subject matter, and not merely about the language itself. Logical coherence is no substitute for empirical validity (2:209).

Neoclassical methods are justified, he argues (1:xix), if the assumptions which are made are not too far removed from the real world to invalidate the conclusions (a question to be settled by examining the assumptions, not, as with Friedman, the conclusions) and if the data required are obtainable and the computations feasible. When he judges that these conditions are met, he has had no hesitation in using neoclassical techniques. Indeed, a study undertaken in the late 1940s of the likely impact of nuclear power on U.S. national income (1:307–353) anticipates both the methods and the results of the "new economic history"—the methods in comparing the projected nuclear economy with an optimally-adapted non-nuclear economy, and the results in the conclusion that in a world full of alternatives nothing actually matters very much.

More instructive is his attitude to the extensive collaborative work which he undertook on production scheduling and inventory control, in which optimisation techniques were freely applied to quadratic cost functions which were acknowledged to be false. He makes no use of Friedman's arguments, to which he strongly objects elsewhere (2:369–71). The use of false assumptions is justified on two grounds: first, they make the problem manageable, by requiring managers to supply relatively few estimates—and those not needing to be very accurate—which can be used in fairly straightforward computations (2:386–8); second, as is argued in some detail (1:202–11), each is a reasonably good approximation to the likely truth within the range of variation to which the decision rules are meant to apply. It is this reasonable approximation which, he asserts (2:371), is far more significant for the acceptability of data than the significance which statisticians emphasise. The limits of acceptability may then be tested by sensitivity analysis, which sometimes assures us of the robustness of our conclusions, and at others warns us of their vulnerability to estimates which have no sure foundation (1:264).

As Simon (2:486) has observed, this work has had an ironical sequel; one of his collaborators, John Muth, impressed by their success in calculating apparently-optimal actions from the expected values of probability distributions, proposed that such expected values, each derived from the relevant economic theory, should be taken as the basis of rational decisions. To Simon, of course, the optimising procedure which they had devised was itself an example of satisficing, not to be generalized without detailed examination: the optimisation of artificially-simplified models is not a good strategy for solving problems in chess (2:414). But even if we can assume that the world supplies us with probability distributions which allow us to make unbiased forecasts (and that the cost of obtaining the necessary information does not render the acceptance of possible bias optimal), the derivation of rational decisions from rational expectations is straightforward only if the loss function is quadratic (as was assumed for the original study). "Unbiased estimation can be a component of all sorts of rational and irrational behaviour rules" (2:438).

If Simon is skeptical about the merits of rational expectations, aggregate Cobb-Douglas production functions are dismissed with scorn. The apparent evidence in favour of such functions and of their success in predicting labour's share of output is declared to be vitiated by faulty econometric method (1:444–54): "these results are a statistical artifact without economic significance" (1:405). "The data say no more than that the value of product is approximately equal to the wage bill plus the cost of capital services" (1:454); and since the latter explanation is adequate and simpler, it should be preferred (1:458). In making this recommendation, it has to be said that Simon reveals a failure to understand the purpose of Cobb-Douglas functions—or indeed of production functions as a class; Simon's preferred explanation is very far from adequate for the issues which neoclassical economists deem important. We shall return to this issue at the end of this paper.

Aggregate production functions are under some suspicion because of the dangers of aggregation. These dangers engendered a spirited and notorious dispute between Cambridge, England and Cambridge, Massachusetts; but the reluctance of the disputants to look beyond the problems of capital aggregation suggests that the dispute was ideological, and not empirical—perhaps the reason why Simon seems never to have referred to it. The plausibility of aggregation and decomposition in the analysis of complex systems is an obvious issue for him to investigate, and it is no surprise to find him giving his paper on this subject in this collection a very high place among "scientific publications of which I am proud" (1:404). It is no surprise, either, to find that it is a technical inquiry into a practical problem, not a philosophical discussion (1:411–41). In *The Sciences of the Artificial* (1969), he is less technical, but still emphasises the practical issues.

The great bulk of economists still do not appear to find the issues of aggregation and decomposability of either practical or philosophical importance, even though they are central to the present confusion over what used to be called macroeconomics. Simon's own analysis no doubt helps to buttress his belief in our ability to solve problems at least as fast as they are created; but though he recognises the practical importance of the varying speeds with which different interactions take effect, nevertheless for one who prefers process to equilibrium as an organising principle, he seems to have very little sense of the significance of time in human affairs. Compare his writings with those of Marshall, Shackle, or the later Hicks, and one is immediately conscious of a great difference in attitude and style.

III. RATIONALITY

With the increasing focus on choice, rationality has become almost the distinguishing characteristic of economic analysis; but it is rationality in a sense not recognised in the other social sciences. Simon points to the contrast with psychology. "It is only a slight exaggeration to say that what an economist or statistical theorist regards as a 'rational decision process' is what a psychologist might regard as 'habitual behaviour'; while what a psychologist regards as 'rational choice', an economist would refuse to regard as 'rational' at all'' (2:383). But economists have great difficulty in pursuing rigorously their rational programme—though they are often unaware of the difficulties. Neither the objectives nor the limiting conditions within which economic agents optimise can themselves be derived on the rational principles which the economist wishes to use. Boundary conditions must be imposed—and often they are imposed unconsciously. But the analysis of constrained optimisation implies a shadow price for each constraint, and the fully rational optimiser would redefine his problem to include the optimisation of these constraints. The standard specification of the economic problem, with resources, technology and preferences all given, is necessarily an exercise in bounded rationality, whatever its practitioners may think, and the decision—if it is a decision, and not the result of unconsidered habit—to pose the problem in this form cannot be explained by optimisation, whatever recourse may be had to search costs and the economics of information. It also excludes some of the most important questions, as economists as different as Marshall and Schumpeter well realised.

The current fascination of many theorists with the concept of games is surely due in part to the delusion that the rules of whatever game is being modelled have the same status that such theorists implicitly (though dubiously) accord to natural laws. But we might remember that the game of Rugby football was created by a player of association football who broke the rules; and more-or-less orderly revision of the rules is not uncommon in sport. (Some revisions, such as the introduction of the tie-break in lawn tennis, result from a redefinition of system boundaries.) Professor Shackle has frequently drawn attention to the limitations imposed on the applicability of game theory by its exclusion of surprise; these limitations are characteristically underrated because only by placing all surprises out of bounds can theorists preserve the rationality of the players. Simon is well aware of the fallibility of human decisions, and of our ability to generate unexpected problems: yet surprise is not a concept which belongs in his pattern of thought.

Even with no surprises, as is well known, rationality may prove an elusive goal. The search for rational solutions to the oligopoly problem can probably continue for as long as anyone thinks it worthwhile. The Cournot model, which has come back into favour in recent years, does possess a quasi-rational equilibrium (reached by an irrational process); but, as Simon (2:216) observes, it does not achieve fully-informed rationality, since if one agent were correctly to predict the others' decision rules, then he could do better by changing his own. The unpalatable fact is that it is impossible to define an equilibrium of interdependent optimising agents unless "we can assume that not more than one participant is unlimitedly clever in predicting the reactions of the other participants to his behaviour" (2:217). Simon here anticipates Coddington's (1975) dictum that there can be at most one omniscient being.

The case is actually stronger than Simon realizes. He appears to accept (2:215–6) that the assumptions of perfect competition, however empirically dubious, do allow every economic agent rationally to treat the actions of every other in the same way that he is supposed to treat the conventional "givens" of the environment—"as some kind of responsive or unresponsive mechanism." But as G. B. Richardson (1960) has shown, this is not so: even in a perfectly competitive economy, the consequences of any one person's action depend on the actions of others. The familiar cobweb theorem, whatever its deficiencies in other respects, is enough to demonstrate that the usual assumptions of perfect competition are not enough to guarantee even the (unconsciously bounded) rationality which is sought.

Determinate solutions are attainable by the axiomatic method only for problems which have been defined by nonrational constraints. Fully-rational optimisation within limits arbitrarily defined is one response to the unavoidable phenomenon of bounded rationality; as Simon makes clear in many places, this is sometimes a perfectly satisfactory response (and, I would add, often one useful component of a satisfactory response). The other response is to accept limits, not on the definition of the problem, but on the rationality of the procedure used to cope with it. It is the second approach which is characteristic of the study of organisational behaviour (which is to be distinguished sharply from almost everything that economists call industrial organisation or the theory of the firm) and of the work of psychologists on human decisionmaking; and it is in the study of organisations and in psychology that Simon has primarily sought to improve our understanding of the ways in which human beings may solve problems at least as fast as new ones are created.

IV. INSTITUTIONS

If actions are to be based on reason—not, of course, to be demonstrably optimal in the way that economists would like—then the knowledge requirements must be reduced. Decomposability of the systems within which decisions are made is a principal means of reducing these requirements; and one particularly important kind of decomposability is that which allows the actions of other people to be tolerably well predicted most of the time by the patterns of behaviour which correspond to their rôles. Economies are stabilized by their institutions, in the widest sense of that word: by the recognisable sets of decision premises which are embodied in the rôles and conventions of the social (including of course the industrial) system (2:390–91). Although Simon does not go so far, his position is compatible with that of G. B. Richardson: the atomistic and anonymous competition beloved of economic theorists imposes information requirements which are impossible to satisfy; though it may, under certain assumptions, be formally compatible with a general equilibrium, it has no means of achieving or maintaining coherence. The perfectly competitive model is not appropriate for an enquiry into the working of a competitive economy.

The contrary idea, that the predominance of programmed behaviour is necessary for the combination of coherence and originative choice, is not without its supporters; among economists, we may point, in addition to Simon and Richardson, to Schumpeter (1934), whose theory of development cycles depends on the ability of innovators to base their novel calculations on the routines of the circular flow—when the routines are thrown into confusion by innovation, the innovators find that they have destroyed the conditions of their own success—and also to Kirzner (1973), whose entrepreneurs profit from the persistence in error of their less alert contemporaries. Perhaps more significant is the similar position taken by some of those who have approached the problems of human knowledge more directly, through the philosophy of science. It is well known that both Kuhn and Lakatos argue that scientific rationality is bounded; it may be less widely realised that Popper, though rejecting the idea that paradigms or research programmes prevent wider thought, affirms that the process of scientific enquiry can only be carried out within a framework which, for a time, must be placed beyond the bounds of rationality. He even begins his *Logic of Scientific Discovery* (1972, 13), by observing that scientists have an important advantage over philosophers of science in their ability (almost always) to work within an already-defined problem-situation. That rational decisionmaking is easier in a substantially-programmed environment is precisely what Simon argues (2:390).

The stability of institutions is therefore, as Simon points out (2:391) a critical issue—though one that he deals with, as a general problem, somewhat inadequately. (He is not, as was noted, much bothered about general problems; he has, of course, given much attention to the question of stability within formal organisations.) Practitioners of institution-free economics are not likely to pay much attention to what they have decided to ignore; but the consequences of their neglect can be dangerous. It is not surprising, for example, that such economists have found it hard to discover any significant costs of inflation—even those who are most insistent that we must follow a monetary policy which will avoid (or cure) it. This failure gives us no reason for confidence in their policy prescriptions, whatever they may be. Leijonhufvud's (1975) anger was thoroughly justified.

Whereas Richardson's inquiry into the possible institutional framework for rational decision focussed on relations between firms, Simon's attention has been concentrated on formal and informal organisation—following Barnard (1938) in giving attention to the link between the two. (Both these research strategies rely on the decomposability of a multi-level system.) Organisational structures and the relationships which develop within them, determine rôles (2:308), each of which is to be understood (2:345) as "a social prescription of some, but not all, of the premises that enter into an individual's choice of behaviours." The prescription of some of the decision premises assists prediction by others who need a reasonable basis for their own decisions; that not all are prescribed leaves room for the exercise of reasoning power, and the making on occasion of novel choices. In addition to decision premises, organisations store information, and the contents of both stores change with experience (2:441); indeed, "a technology exists largely in the minds of its labour force" (2:144).

This view of organisations has been effectively developed by Nelson and Winter (1982), who draw attention to the difficulty of defining precisely the content of any individual's knowledge and of any organisation's capabilities (or programmes), and explain how institutions drift over time. This drift, as successive events are construed by individuals in terms of their own interpretative frameworks (Kelly, 1963), can help to stabilise institutions through adaptation; it may also undermine them, if the expectations of interdependent groups diverge—and that is not impossible, even if (which is unlikely) they are all exposed to the same set of phenomena.

Nelson and Winter also develop Simon's (2:397) observation that "the interdependence of organisation units is a strong force towards conservatism"; each unit has a strong interest in preserving the stability of its environment in order to facilitate the formation of confident expectations, and that implies a reluctance to disturb established decision programmes among its neighbours. Organisations may be stable because their members fear that they will not prove resilient. There is thus a strong tendency to try to fit innovations into existing systems; and indeed we see that innovations which require extensive reconstruction of existing institutions meet with great resistance and are accomplished only slowly, if at all. They may succeed only by circumventing existing structures and developing in new locations or in new industries. Schumpeter's emphasis on the necessarily destructive consequences of creativity can be justified in Simon's terms; so, in a different way, can Marshall's emphasis on the cumulative importance of incremental change, occurring in a large population of freely competing firms, each with its own established customers and competitors, but each with its own slightly idiosyncratic set of decision programmes, which facilitates particular and localised sorts of beneficial adjustments.

V. PERCEPTION AND THEORY

In considering the rôle of institutions we should recognise (even though he himself does not) the warning implicit in Simon's (2:306) insistence that "the decision-maker's information about his environment is much less than an approximation to the real environment. . . . In actual fact the perceived world is fantastically different from the 'real' world." Because of the limitations of the human brain, selection and distortion are inevitable both in perception—the acquisition of information—and inference—the processing of the information acquired. Although Simon (2:307) insists that the filtering which takes place is an active process, he does not go on to point out that this process necessarily implies the imposition of a conjectural framework as a means of selection and interpretation. This is mildly surprising, not only because of his substantial interest in psychology, but also because he observes (2:391) that for any individual decisionmaker "the 'facts' on which he acts obtain their status as facts by a social process of legitimation, and have only a very tenuous and indirect connection with the evidence of his senses."

He appears to imply that such a social process is necessarily beneficial when he claims (2:399) that the need for stable expectations makes it "more important, in some circumstances, to have *agreement* on the facts than to be certain that what is agreed upon is really fact. Hence we often find that the procedures for fact finding and for legitimating facts are themselves institutionalized." The processes of social legitimation of facts are certainly important, and their neglect by economists a source of serious error; but Simon seems to have no sense of the potential fragility of the structures based on such "pretty, polite techniques." The stability and resilience of institutions, and of the expectations which they support, remains problematic. Leijonhufvud's (1973) "corridor hypothesis" still awaits development, even within its original macroeconomic context. But Simon must be given full credit for recognising that such stability ought to be—though it is not—a central concern of economics.

The significance of institutions is not diminished by the increasing availability of information. Greater information makes more acute the need to economise on attention, and increases the significance for decisionmaking of the means of economising. Information-processing systems are of no value unless they are net absorbers of information (2:175). Among the most efficient information-processing systems is science, which exploits the redundancy of facts in a world which appears to obey natural laws by substituting the laws, which are few, for the facts, which are very many. "With each important advance in scientific theory, we can reduce the volume of explicitly stored knowledge without losing any information whatsoever" (2:178). Thus scientific advance simplifies our problems. "To become a research chemist should involve less learning today than it did fifty years ago, because physical chemistry and quantum mechanics have provided such powerful tools for organizing facts, and indeed making them derivable from theory" (2:142).

Organisations have theories too, sometimes set out in highly organised principles of corporate strategy, sometimes the result of imposing simple structures on their past record. The research director of a chemical business which had lost money trying to develop self-assembly furniture, for which they produced only the bulk filler, not the surface laminates, defined his research strategy thereafter as "no more bloody flat things." This was certainly an efficient information-processing rule. But Simon does not explicitly consider the processes by which organisations acquire and amend their theories; nor do Nelson and Winter, though they do focus on the issue of knowledge within organisations. None of them recognise that theories (or any other information processing system) may impose misleading patterns. There can be no way of guaranteeing that an active filtering process will not lead its users astray; and to argue that no-one will persist in error (a proposition which can itself be misleading) is not sufficient reason to pay attention only to those situations in which no errors are made. Simon's own failure to recognise the possibility of faulty decisions arising from misleading theories is particularly striking when we recall that his criticism of conventional economics is precisely that the theoretical filters which it employs are inappropriate for many of its purposes. Unfortunately, his analyses of information processing are not founded on any adequate theory of the growth of knowledge.

VI. SIMON VS. NEOCLASSICAL ECONOMICS

Simon fails to use his own (incomplete) theories of institutional conservatism and data-absorption to explain the resistance of the great bulk of economists to his own ideas. His own explanation (2:401) is one of the weakest elements in the book. "Now I learned that behaviour was of interest to economists . . . only if it had important implications for matters of policy at the level of the economy, or at least of the industry." The proposition that the prime concern of economists is economic policy, primarily macropolicy, is an active filter which destroys more information than it absorbs.

Let us apply a little of Simon's analytical apparatus. Economists, like other people, face the problem of information overload, and they recognise the value of science in making "facts derivable from theory." What, then, could possibly be better than the well-developed structure of microeconomics—"deductive theory which requires almost no contact with empirical data—once the underlying assumptions are accepted or verified—to establish its propositions" (2:321)? Although Simon (2:476) points out that Occam's razor is double-edged, so that the "much stronger assumptions . . . about the human cognitive system" which are required for theories of utility or profit maximisation than for satisficing might by deemed a disqualification, succinctness is likely to be a far more powerful argument for anyone conscious of the need to absorb information. It is indeed an argument which Simon employs himself to justify the use of such theories on the occasions when he deems them appropriate.

In moving from models of fully-informed optimisation to models of bounded rationality, one accepts increasing complexity in the specification of the decision procedure: moreover, complexity is not the only cost: "At each step we have gained realism, but lost certainty" (2:235). Perfect competition "is an essential condition for unambiguous prediction of behaviour from the classical assumptions of economic rationality" (2:339). These two observations are intended as criticisms of conventional economics; but they may also be used as a defense. The bounded rationality of the analyst leads him to use models which generate clear outcomes. The certainty may have been false, but its disappearance is still perceived as a loss.

Moreover, let us remember that "it may be more important to have agreement on the facts than to be certain that what is agreed upon is really fact." Agreement on the "fact" that the established structure of economics is broadly appropriate for the purposes of economists is important for permitting economists to work within an agreed framework, and therefore to work (in some sense) more effectively. Economics is a fairly well-ordered intellectual adventure, in which problems can be solved as fast as new ones are created, as long as the structure is protected by its interdependencies. The interdependence of economic theories, mutually reinforced by their derivation from a small set of ideas and assumptions, provide them with an armour which is not easily penetrated. It is this interdependence which protects Cobb-Douglas production functions and allows Occam's razor to be deployed in their defense—and in defense of every other part of the structure in turn.

This application of Simon's own arguments needs to be supplemented by the philosophical argument—which is actually a psychological argument—supplied by Adam Smith (1980) and by Shackle (1967). A single, apparently well-integrated theory is much more comfortable than a set of partial theories which are not readily commensurable; for it not only provides a means of accommodating all phenomena, but does not leave one in any doubt about the relationship between the particular explanations which are employed on different occasions. If we rely on a cluster of theories which clearly do not fit together very well, then the more sensitive we are to the problems of the human condition, the more concerned we are likely to be that such obviously incomplete theories may be inadequate or misleading—and therefore unreliable as a basis for expectations and for decisions. Even if we can quiet our doubts by pretending to more assurance than we feel, nevertheless contemplation of the future brings, in Shackle's (1967, 288) words, "the uneasy consciousness of mystery and a threatening unknown."

It is perhaps the most remarkable feature of Simon's work that it appears to be the product of a man who is prepared to face the unknown without a general theory, but with a faith that, despite the bounds on their rationality, human beings can display enough flexibility and imagination to recognise and to solve their problems fast enough to maintain, and even to improve their situation. If his faith is justified, few people will have done more to help us realise it.

ACKNOWLEDGMENT

This paper is also being published, with minor changes, in Loasby, B J (1989), *The Mind and Method of the Economist*, Aldershot: Edward Elgar.

REFERENCES

Barnard, Chester I., (1938) *The Functions of the Executive*. Cambridge, Mass.: Harvard University Press.

Coddington, A., (1975) "Creaking Semaphore and beyond." *British Journal for the Philosophy of Science*, 26, 2.

Cyert, R. M. and March, J. G., (1963) *A Behavioural Theory of the Firm*. Englewood Cliffs, N.J.: Prentice-Hall.

Kelly, George A., (1963) *A Theory of Personality*. New York: Norton.

Kirzner, I. M., (1973) *Competition and Entrepreneurship*. Chicago: University of Chicago Press.

Leijonhufvud, A., (1973) "Effective Demand Failures." *Swedish Journal of Economics*, 75, 1. Reprinted in A. Leijonhufvud, *Information and Coordination*. New York and Oxford: Oxford University Press, 1979.

Leijonhufvud, A., (1975) "Costs and Consequences of Inflation." in G. C. Harcourt (ed.) *The Microeconomic Foundations of Macroeconomics*. London: Macmillan. Reprinted in A. Leijonhufvud, *Information and Coordination*. New York and Oxford: Oxford University Press, 1979.

Loasby, B. J., (1985) Review of H. A. Simon, *Models of Bounded Rationality*. *Economic Journal*, 95, pp. 796–99.

Nelson, Richard R. and Winter, Sidney G., (1982) *An Evolutionary Theory of Economic Change*. Cambridge, Mass.: Harvard University Press.

Popper, K. R., (1972) *The Logic of Scientific Discovery*, 6th impression. London: Hutchinson.

Richardson, G. B., (1960) *Information and Investment*. Oxford: Oxford University Press.

Schumpeter, J. A., (1934) *The Theory of Economic Development*. Cambridge, Mass.: Harvard University Press.

Shackle, G. L. S., (1967) *The Years of High Theory*. Cambridge: Cambridge University Press.

Simon, H. A., (1969) *The Sciences of the Artificial*. Cambridge, Mass.: MIT Press.

Simon, H. A., (1982) *Models of Bounded Rationality*. Cambridge, Mass.: MIT Press.

Smith, A., (1980) " History of Astronomy." In W. P. D. Wightman (ed.), *Essays on Philosophical Subjects*. Oxford: Oxford University Press.

ASPECTS OF AUSTRIAN ECONOMICS IN THE 1920s AND 1930s

Peter Rosner and Georg Winckler

After 1918 most of the political and ideological controversies in Austria were reduced to a fight between Marxist-socialists and antisocialists including conservatives, liberals and German nationalists. The fierce political controversies hindered academic discussions among political opponents that had been possible before the war.[1] In this situation there was a strong demand for a great ideologue against socialism who could work out uncompromising basic principles of liberal economics. Ludwig von Mises having published his highly original *Theorie des Geldes und der Umlaufmittel*[2] in 1912 filled this demand. As a Privatdozent (later with the title of professor extraordinarius) at the University of Vienna, he could not make a living out of teaching and publishing, but worked at the Chamber of Commerce. Nevertheless Mises could exert great academic influence through his private

Research in the History of Economic Thought and Methodology,
Volume 6, pages 19-30
Copyright © 1989 by JAI Press Inc.
All rights of reproduction in any form reserved.
ISBN: 0-89232-928-9

seminar in which Martha St. Browne, Gottfried von Haberler, Friedrich A. von Hayek, Fritz Machlup, Oskar Morgenstern, Paul Rosenstein-Rodan, Karol Schlesinger, Richard von Strigl, and others participated (Browne 1981; Haberler 1981).

Mises's liberalism was of interest to the Chamber of Commerce because to Mises liberalism primarily meant antisocialism. The protectionism of the Chamber of Commerce, an institution "dedicated mainly to the administration of quotas, clearing agreements, tariffs etc." (Steindl 1984) did not disturb Mises as much as the socialist-dominated trade unions did. With his 500-page pamphlet against socialism (Mises 1922) he did not only serve political interests but also set the stage for theoretical economic research between the wars.

The main message of this book is that there exists no possibility for a compromise between socialism in its extreme form of a centrally planned economy and pure capitalism.[3] According to Mises, socialism has already won the fight since everybody accepts public regulation of private property, social reforms etc.[4] The task of the liberal academic is therefore to analyze pure capitalism, to show its advantages in a scientific way. By drawing a *theoretical* line between a society with unlimited use of private property, and all other societies, he shifted the attention away from historical analyses and argued against the political hopes that had been put into economic and social reforms. Such analyses and hopes were then prevalent in the economic literature in Germany (the tradition of the Verein für Socialpolitik).

Mises paved the way for an abstract analysis of a pure capitalist society. This explains why Mises could become the head of the Austrian school after 1918 and gain international reputation, although not he but the members of his private seminar mostly took part in the theoretical disputes from the 1920s to the 1940s.

The main contributions of the Austrians to the progress of economic discourse can be found in the methodological investigations, in canvassing the importance of expectations and the informational role of prices, and in the theory of business cycles.

I.

Apart from being a brilliant pamphleteer and an organizer of a scientific discussion, Mises's main theoretical work was his interpretation of economics as a science in *Grundprobleme der Nationalökonomie* (Mises 1933). This book can be seen first as a continuation of Menger's discussion with the German historic school, since Mises wanted to show that without theory not even one sensible question can be asked in an empirical investigation. But secondly, the book served as a clarification for the argument within the Austrian school that since there is no way to solve the problem of induction, economic laws cannot be discovered by empirical research, only by a priori reasoning (Mises 1933, 9). This a priori concept of economics did not only separate pure theory from the then current historically and institutionally oriented research, it also separated pure theory from certain ideas of Menger, which were prominent with F. Wieser and Hans Mayer, the successor of F. Wieser as professor ordinarius at the University of Vienna, and adversary of Mises within the Austrian school.

According to Menger and Wieser, economics is an empirical science, which is based on empirically testable assertions about wants and needs of the individual. To Menger needs and wants are given by the nature of man (Menger 1871, 32) and his cultural development (34). Different wants can be distinguished as differently cultivated basic needs. Refinement of wants has to be seen in the context of cultural progress, which Menger mentions again and again.

Once Menger's optimism about cultural development is put aside, and only the subjective valuations of individuals in a given environment are considered to be the sole basis for a theory of value, psychology is the appropriate foundation for economics as an empirical science (Wieser 1884, 34; 1889, 8). According to Wieser, the individual has different needs, all of which he wants to satisfy (see also Cuhel 1907); they are different in quality, different in intensity. A scale of satisfaction for each want can be objectively constructed and the degree of desire measured (Wieser 1924, 26; Mayer 1924).

It is clear that the idea of some kind of measurability of desires can serve as a basis for government intervention: If there exists a scale on which the desirability can be measured, it must be possible to state which wants have to be satisfied first. Wieser himself spoke of "healthy" and "degenerate" needs (Wieser 1924, 22) and considered economic theory as a basis for social reform (preface).

Mayer did not go so far, yet in his arguments against the Lausanne School (Mayer 1922; esp. Mayer 1932) he still claimed that abandoning the quest for "causal-genetic" price theory based in psychology is tantamount to giving up the search for an economic theory. However, Mayer thought something like "utility" did not exist; only different needs exist. Nobody can evaluate the relative importance of differences in needs. The law of the equalization of the weighted marginal utilities (Second Law of Gossen) has to be rejected as tautological and, therefore, as fruitless for empirical research (Mayer 1922, 170 ff). As a result of this rejection Mayer destroyed the fundamentals of modern economic theory, which are based on a *coherent* demand theory. The only way left would have been a measurement of cardinal utilities, an idea, which was not completely alien to Wieser. Mayer did not go this way; perhaps he felt that such a theory could serve as a basis for all kinds of central economic calculation and state intervention.[5] He remained sterile and is (justly) forgotten.[6]

It is clear that such concepts cannot be accepted by a true-hearted liberal and antisocialist as was Mises. He considered Wieser's idea of the possibility of calculation with marginal utilities as a contradiction of the basic elements of a subjective theory of value (Mises 1940, 193), and, therefore, tried to cut off all psychological bases of economics. He disentangled Austrian economics from all cumbersome reasoning about the "true" origin of demand. It is merely a convention in Mises's view, when economists talk about "desires" and "needs" as a basis for individual choice, and, therefore, a pleonasm to talk about "rational" acting. In the view of Menger and Wieser rationality is an empirically meaningful concept, since one can ask if somebody acts rationally according to his (empirically observable) needs (Menger 1871, 85). To Mises, however, if someone acts, the economist has to consider it as rational, since everything else needs introspection into the mind of somebody else.[7] The science of economics is therefore not the science of the economy, but of economic acting, that is the science of human action.

II.

Against his own intentions, Mises opened the Austrian school to the general equilibrium theory. He, as most of the Austrians, was against the use of mathematics, but within his concept of economics, it was possible to work on pure theory.

Besides personal reasons,[8] Mises, Morgenstern, and the other Austrians rejected the concepts of the Lausanne School, because of a fundamental methodological difference: The Austrian program—to conceptualize everything from pure individual decisions—could not be brought in line with the auctioneer, the central agent of Walras. The Austrians put all the emphasis on individual plans being carried out independent of the existence of an equilibrium. This "non-tâtonnement'' process may lead—and the Austrians supposed it did—to an equilibrium. This equilibrating process was regarded as the main justification for capitalism. The hero of the Austrian school was the capitalist as an arbitrageur but not—as in the Marx-Schumpeter tradition—as an organizer of production. The capitalist discovers and exploits opportunities of trade. To restrict economic analysis to the question of the existence of equilibrium seemed like playing Hamlet but leaving out the Prince. That this process gave a basis for calculation by all individuals was already stressed in Mises's pamphlet against socialism.

Within the Mises branch of the Austrian school, an important step toward the critique of the general equilibrium analysis was two publications by Oskar Morgenstern (Morgenstern 1928; 1935). Two problems permeated them. The first is the mutual interdependence of human actions. Since any individual changes by his or her actions the circumstances of others, everybody has to consider the others' reactions and their results provoked by his or her action. This problem later became the "game-theoretic" problem of strategic interdependence.

The second problem emerges from the analysis of the importance of expectations in an equilibrium. For an action to be in equilibrium, the results of the action have to be consistent with the expectations when the action was planned. According to Morgenstern, the concept of general equilibrium stipulates the equilibrium of each individual action and, because individuals have expectations, thus implies perfect foresight. Morgenstern challenged the logical coherence of this concept: Perfect foresight presupposes an almost omniscient individual, however the omniscience of individuals make problems of strategic interdependence insolvable; since any individual's action depends on the actions of others, nobody can start any action before the others have done so. This dilemma of the Sherlock Holmes-Moriarty type leads to general despair. One cannot, according to Morgenstern, even think of perfect foresight in a logically meaningful way. He offers no solution. To have no expectations concerning the behavior of others is no acceptable alternative to him. But he makes proposals for further research: How does the forming of expectations affect the stability of the equilibrium? It was Morgenstern himself, together with John von Neumann, who later developed ideas for the solution in their book *Theory of Games and Economic Behavior* (Neumann and Morgenstern 1943).

The problem of the omniscient economic agent was also prominent with Hayek. He put a theoretical basis to the ideological prejudices of

Mises, namely that of the superiority of free enterprise economy over a planned economy. This was important because the arguments had to be refined to challenge Barone's or Lange's ideas of competitive social-ism (Hayek 1935; 1940). In *Economics and Knowledge* Hayek redefines the empirical context of economics as a theory of human ac-tion. To him, general equilibrium analysis is not pure tautology, inso-far as the "real" process of acquisition and communication of knowl-edge is taken into consideration.

Connected with the point of acquisition and communication of knowledge, is an interpretation of the idea of changing data: It is not important whether "objective" data change, only the divergence be-tween the actual and expected outcome has to be considered. This fits perfectly into the concept of Austrian subjectivism.

The condition of equilibrium, therefore, does not require perfect foresight of omniscient individuals but only compatibility of the indi-vidual plans. Whereas the pure theory of equilibrium simply states that the individual plans are mutually consistent—and can therefore not distinguish between capitalist and socialist economies—economic analysis according to Hayek should inquire, how the compatibility of individuals plans are brought about. He claimed to have an answer to this problem: It is the division of knowledge and, in his later article "The Use of Knowledge in Society" (Hayek 1945), the impossibility to overcome the division of knowledge through any central agent. It is rather the capitalist as arbitrageur who pushes the economy toward equilibrium. The relevant knowledge not only consists of prices, but of special circumstances of particular markets. Hayek did not prove his assertion and his idea was lost for quite a while.

In the seventies, however, when informational problems in the Walrasian general equilibrium analysis and in the Keynesian aggregat-ive theory were rediscovered, Hayek's arguments became prominent again.

III.

The Austrian school between the wars, especially Hayek, became known in the international discussion due to their contributions to the business cycle theory.

Their position seemed to be extreme in the international context, yet not so in Austria for two reasons. Firstly, the great inflation between October 1921 and August 1922, during which prices rose by 7,000 percent, was regarded to be a catastrophe by all groups of society.[9] There was hardly anyone in Austria who dared to propose inflationary measures. The idea of a balanced budget was prominent even with the Austrian social democrats, even while approximately 30 percent of the industrial labor force were unemployed. To ease the circulation of money was considered evidently harmful. Secondly, especially the adherents of the Austrian school feared that by inflationary measures the existing stock of capital was consumed because of lack of savings. This fear was fed by the belief that the political and economic breakdown in Austria after World War I, being accompanied by the realization of longstanding socialist demands (e.g., eight-hour working day, unemployment benefits, paid holidays, shop steward, etc.), had led to a severe impediment to capital accumulation.[10]

Reading the books of the Austrians written between 1929 and 1934 must give the impression that the most important problem for Austria was that the boom—especially the overexpansion of investment credits—might get out of control.[11] What made their books and articles academically important was the fact that the Austrians saw the necessity to integrate the research on cycles into pure economic theory and not to draw conclusions only from empirical research. The polemics of the Austrian theory of cycles were directed against the arguments of Foster and Catchings, against the use of the Harvard Barometer and the results of the Konjunkturforschungsinstitut in Berlin in both theoretical and political arguments. Especially regarded as useless was Fisher's effort to estimate a true index of change of prices as an indicator of the change of the money value unless it could be proven that a constant price level is of specific importance for individual decisions (Hayek 1931, 4). Hayek challenged this idea by developing his concept of "neutral money."

Central to Hayek is that an expansion of the money volume changes the *relative* price of future goods against present ones. This price has a double meaning. It is the rate of interest for assets and the relative price of investment goods against consumption goods. "Neutral money" is that amount of money for which the money rate of interest equals the "natural" rate of interest. Note that to Hayek money is not neutral in the usual sense. He regards the effects of changes in the quantity of money on the price level as of secondary importance.[12] This *classical* idea, which can also be found in Mises's book on money, seems strange in the Austrian context.

Mises's theory of money, which greatly influenced Hayek's argument is a direct challenge to the ideas of the "quantity theory." In the

Austrian spirit and as a continuation of Menger's theory of money, Mises put the emphasis on the subjective valuation of money and other means of payments. Something like the "quantity of money" or the "velocity of circulation" are only statistical aggregates and do not exist in the mind of individuals. Only through income and distribution effects does the quantity of money affect the level of prices and the level and direction of economic activity. To analyze this, one has to look at the individual demand for money, and then the effects of variations in the demand for money can be estimated. It seems that this concept is more in line with Keynes's monetary ideas than with the world of Hayek's *Geldtheorie und Konjunkturtheorie* or *Preise und Produktion*. Keynes's concept of the marginal efficiency of capital, with its dependence on subjective estimations of future earnings, and his theory of liquidity preference fit better into a subjective theory than the mechanical use of the concepts of the quantity of money, velocity of circulation, and roundaboutness of production processes as shown by Hayek in his famous triangles. Although Hayek pays tribute to Mises's concept of money (Hayek 1931, 4), he wrote a monetary theory of business cycles without individual demand for money, without expectations, and without subjective valuations. The only importance of money in his aggregate theory is that due to the false monetary policy (in *Preise und Produktion*) it can induce a overly roundabout process of production. This in turn necessitates a painful reshortening of the roundaboutness.[13] This does not mean that Hayek did not see the importance of expectations for the business cycle. But whereas for Keynes, changing expectations could alter the equilibrium level of economic activity, Hayek's notion of an economic equilibrium is independent of expectations: The expectations of the entrepreneurs can cause them to invest too much or too little compared to the savings, but by these investments the equilibrium level of economic activity is not changed (Hayek 1939). Only decisions concerning the consumption/saving ratio can change the equilibrium level of investment.

The problem of the relation of saving and investment and the connection of this problem with the supply and demand for money and financial assets was worked out by Fritz Machlup (1931). His argument was directed against two articles by R. Reisch, a former president of the Austrian Central Bank, in which Reisch claimed that speculation at the stock exchange requires too much money and therefore has deflationary effects on the real economy. Machlup challenges this idea by distinguishing between capital as a means of production and capital as a result of an individual act of saving (Kapitaldispositionen). Increased real investment, induced by increased saving, may cause a crisis, if savings are not tied in long term financial assets. Machlup does not consider a structure of interest rates to match supply and demand for different assets. According to him increased short term saving reduces the (unique) rate of interest and thus stimulates investment above that level, which can be sustained through long term saving. However, if short term savings are absorbed at the stock exchange, increased short term saving does not create false signals for real investment; the deflationary effect of speculation at the stock exchange enhances the stability of the economy.

APPENDIX: THE AUSTRIANS
AND EMPIRICAL RESEARCH

Mises and his followers were not only pure theoreticians with an antiempirical scientific program, they actually were the founding fathers of systematic empirical research in Austria. Although Mises questioned the usefulness of empirical research again and again, he convinced the government, the Austrian Central Bank, the Chamber of Commerce and the socialist-dominated Chamber of Labour in 1926 to set up an independent economics research institute, the Österreichische Institut für Konjunkturforschung. The first director was Hayek, until he went to London (1931); the second, Oskar Morgenstern, until he was forced to leave Austria in 1938. It is not clear what the reason for this activity was; probably it was important that in Austria at that time hardly any jobs for economists existed. Additionally, the institute had the option of giving jobs to visitors from all over the world. Some brought with them the ideas of the then-rising Keynesianism.

The institute started to collect data in a systematic way, to analyze the data with the means of modern statistics[14] and to publish the results in a monthly bulletin.[15] Apart from this work, the institute advanced theoretical research by publishing a series of books: Beiträge zur Konjunkturforschung. Most of the books mentioned in the last section of this article were published in this series.

According to their program, Hayek and his collaborators never tried to draw theoretical conclusions from the empirical research. However, implicit theoretical statements are to be found again and again in their forecasts of the level of economic activities.

It is interesting to note that through 1930 up to the middle of 1931 the institute hoped the easing of the money markets would put an end to the depression. Only later did their statements on current events began to fit into their theory. So it was recommended that costs had to be reduced to overcome the crisis. It was probably the banking crisis in 1931 that made it clear to the members of the institute that the easing of money markets would not bring about an end to the depression but would create new problems.

NOTES

1. Besides Mises, Böhm-Bawerk had as students in his seminar, among others, Otto Bauer, the leading figure of socialism in Austria between the wars, and Rudolf Hilferding, who became famous with his "Finanzkapital" and was twice Minister of Finance for the Social Democrats in the Weimar Republic. Böhm-Bawerk published a critique on "Das Kapital" (Zum Abschluß des Marxschen Systems, 1896), to which Hilferding answered with a rejoinder (Böhm-Bawerks Marx Kritik).

2. "Theorie des Geldes und der Umlaufmittel" (Vienna 1912, second edition 1924, English translation 1934). This book did not get the attention it deserved.

3. Later on is his "Kritik des Interventionismus" (Vienna 1929, English translation New Rochelle, 1977), he qualified his argument, He drew a line between interventionism and socialism, but tried to show that the former leads to the latter. Again there is no compromise.

4. While Mises was busy writing against socialism, J. Schumpeter served as Minister of Finance in a coalition government of Social Democrats and conservatives who had on their program the socialization of certain industries.

5. Otto Neurath, a member of the Böhm-Bawerk seminar, considered utility analysis as a basis for central planning (Neurath, 1923). He worked as the head of the planning department in the short-lived Munich Räterepublik in 1919. Later he tried to convince the Social Democrats in Austria to introduce central planning.

6. For Hayek on Mayer, see Hayek, 1937, p. 34.

7. In this context Mises refers to Sigmund Freud (Mises, 1933, p. 33): According to Freud even the neurotic acts rationally. Mises felt sympathy for Freud because Freud was never accepted by the establishment of the University, as was the case with Mises (Mises 1978, 23).

8. One reason was that, besides Karol Schlesinger, who was a banker by profession, none of the school had any mathematical training. General equilibrium analysis had no steady contact with the Mises seminar. It was Oskar Morgenstern who organized this contact. See also Weintraub, 1983.

9. The farmers, the industrialists and the industrial workers suffered least during the inflation. The white collar workers, the professional groups and the creditors to the state (Kriegsanleihen) were the main victims. The relative position of different social groups must have changed dramatically during this period, and this may have been one of the reasons of the tragic political situation of Austria between the wars.

10. Mises wrote in a leading daily newspaper a highly favorable comment on a book, called "Der Selbstmord eines Volkes," by Siegfried Strakosch, which tried to show dramatically how the country is ruined by these social changes (Mises, 1923).

11.   An indicator of the *deflationary* process is the monthly wage bill in Vienna, which fell from 158 Mill. Schillings in 1929 to 89 Mill. Schillings in 1934.

12.   Mises saw an important distributional effect of inflationary processes, away from the groups with high rates of savings.

13.   What does too much roundaboutness mean? The Austrians somehow had the idea—and this idea can also be found in Mises's book on money—that at each moment of time there exists a technically given amount of consumer goods (Subsistenzfonds), which can only be enlarged within short time at the cost of existing capital goods. The crisis is therefore due to the disproportion between the production of consumption goods and investment goods in relation to the planned division of income between consumption and saving. Hayek, Mises, and Machlup thought that people were consuming too much and therefore destroying the stock of capital (the index of sales of consumer goods fell from 119 in 1929 to 80 in 1934; see also Erich Schiff 1933).

14.   Gerhard Tintner and Abraham Wald worked in this institute for some time.

15.   Monatsberichte des Österreichischen Instituts für Konjunkturforschung.

REFERENCES

Browne, Martha Steffy, (1981) "Erinnerungen an das Mises-Privatseminar," in Wirtschaftspolitische Blätter, 28.Jg 110–118.

Cuhel, Franz, (1907) "Zur Lehre von den Bedürfnissen, Theoretische Untersuchungen über das Grenzgebiet der Ökonomik und Psychologie," Innsbruck.

Haberler, Gottfried, (1981) "Mises' Privat Seminar," in Wirtschaftspolitische Blätter, 28.Jg 121–125.

von Hayek, Friedrich August, (1929) "Geldtheorie und Konjunkturtheorie," Wien.

————— , (1931) "Preise und Produktion," Wien.

————— (ed.), (1935) "Collectivist Economic Planning," London.

————— , (1937) "Economics and Knowledge," *Economica*, 33–54.

————— , (1939) "Price Expectations, Monetary Disturbances and Malinvestments," in Hayek "Profits, Interest and Investment," London, 135–156.

————— , (1940) "Socialist Calculation: the Competitive Solution," *Economica*, 125–149.

————— , (1945) "The Use of Knowledge in Society," *American Economic Review*, XXXV, 519–530.

Machlup, Fritz, (1931) "Börsenkredit, Industriekredit und Kapitalbildung," Wien.

Mayer, Hans, (1922) "Untersuchungen zum Grundgesetz der wirtschaftlichen Wertrechnung," Zeitschrift für Volkswirtschaft und Sozialpolitik, NF 2 1–23.

————— , (1924) "Bedürfnis," in Handwörterbuch der Staatswissenschaft, 4.Auflage, Bd. 2, 450–456.

————— , (1932) "Der Erkenntniswert der funktionellen Preistheorie," in Mayer, Fetter, Reisch, eds., 'Die Wirtschaftstheorie der Gegenwart,' Vol. 2, Wien, 197–239.

Menger, Carl, (1871) "Grundsätze der Volkswirtschaftslehre," Wien.

Mises, Ludwig von, (1912) "Theorie des Geldes und der Umlaufmittel," Wien.

————— , (1922) "Die Gemeinwirtschaft: Untersuchungen über den Sozialismus," Wien.

————, (1923) "Das österreichische Problem," in *Neue Freie Presse*, March 2.

————, (1927) "Kritik des Interventionismus," Wien.

————, (1933) "Grundprobleme der Nationalökonomie," Jena.

————, (1940) "Nationalökonomie, Theorie des Handelns und Wirtschaftens," Genf.

————, (1978) "Erinnerungen," Stuttgart/New York.

Morgenstern, Oskar, (1928) "Wirtschaftsprognosen, eine Untersuchung ihrer Voraussetzung und Möglichkeiten," Wien.

————, (1935) "Vollkommene Voraussicht und wirtschaftliches Gleichgewicht," in *Zeitschrift für Nationalökonomie*, VI, 337–357.

Neumann, John von, and Morgenstern, Oskar, (1943) "Theory of Games and Economic Behavior," Princeton.

Neurath, Otto, (1923) "Geld, Sozialismus, Marxismus," in *Der Kampf*, XVI, 283–288.

Schiff, Erich, (1933) "Kapitalbildung und Kapitalaufzehrung im Konjunkturverlauf," Wien.

Steindl, Josef, (1984) "Reflections on the Present State of Economics," unpublished manuscript, Wien.

Weintraub, Roy E., (1983) "On the Existence of a Competitive Equilibrium: 1930–1954," *Journal of Economic Literature*, March, 1–39.

Wieser, Friedrich v., (1884) "Über den Ursprung und die Hauptgesetze des wirtschaftlichen Werthes," Wien.

————, (1889) "Der natürliche Werth," Wien.

————, (1924) "Theorie der gesellschaftlichen Wirtschaft," Tübingen.

J. M. KEYNES
AND D. H. ROBERTSON:
THREE PHASES OF COLLABORATION

John R. Presley

I. INTRODUCTION

Academic interest in the working relationship between Keynes and
Robertson has, not surprisingly, focused upon their disagreements
over the writing of *The General Theory* (J. M. Keynes 1936). While
not disputing that the period from 1931–5 was the most productive and
relevant period in the formulation of 'Keynesian Economics,' such a
focus does disguise the close and substantive collaboration which existed between Keynes and Robertson throughout the 1920s and to a
lesser extent from 1910–15. The purpose of this paper therefore is to
redress the balance, to examine the ebb and flow of ideas between
them which culminated in such major books as *Banking Policy and*

Research in the History of Economic Thought and Methodology,
Volume 6, pages 31-46
Copyright © 1989 by JAI Press Inc.
All rights of reproduction in any form reserved.
ISBN: 0-89232-928-9

The Price Level (BPPL) (D. H. Robertson 1926) and *The Treatise on Money* (TM) (J. M. Keynes 1930). The *GT* was the finale in Keynes' presentation of his macroeconomic thinking, but certainly not his only major contribution; although it could be argued that the *GT* was not totally consistent with what Keynes had written before, nevertheless his earlier work with Robertson and others, did have some bearing upon the *GT* and to that extent is important. The *GT* represented the end product of over a quarter of a century of Keynes' thoughts on macroeconomic theory, and it was upon this solid foundation that the *GT* was constructed. Clearly for Robertson, as will be seen in the final section here, the *GT* was an inadequate ending to their collaborative efforts; for Keynesian economists it symbolized the beginning of a totally new approach to macroeconomics and unfortunately this led to a relative neglect of what had gone before. Yet one is reminded of Hicks' comment on the *GT*:

> the effect on Mr. Kaldor's mind, as well on as on my own, of the *GT* has been profound; but we have each of us been led, sometimes consciously, sometimes unconsciously, through Keynes to Robertson (J. R. Hicks, 55).

Equally, as the following pages demonstrate Hicks could have argued that he was led back to the pre-*GT* Keynes who shared much common ground with D. H. Robertson from 1910 to 1930.

The paper is divided into three parts. Section one looks at the period of early collaboration 1910–15; section two examines the more significant period of joint work from *Money* (D. H. Robertson 1922) and *The Tract on Monetary Reform* (TMR) (J. M. Keynes 1923) through to *TM*; section three considers their conflict over the drafts of the *GT* and Robertson's reaction to it. The paper concentrates throughout upon their work in the area of macroeconomic theory and policy.

Robertson devoted most of his working life to the study of industrial fluctuation but wrote also on many topics of mutual interest to Keynes. Although the impression of academic disagreement will be given in section three here, it must be stressed at the outset that they shared common views on many topics outside of macroeconomic theory; there was little dispute over policy, over the consequences of World War I or the return to the Gold Standard, all controversial issues of their day. Indeed in essence there was a fourth phase of collaboration in the post war period when Keynes and Robertson worked together at Bretton Woods. Although this gave little opportunity for reconciliation over the *GT*, it did nevertheless show the strength of their like-mindedness on the international monetary order (R. F. Harrod, ch.XIII).

II. TEACHER AND STUDENT 1910–15

This is the most neglected period of their working relationship and rarely merits recognition in contemporary literature, yet in terms of its significance for the evolution of their respective theories it is very important.

Keynes became Robertson's Director of Studies at Trinity College, Cambridge in 1910 when Robertson transferred from the Classics to Economics tripos. Keynes was seven years older than Robertson; he graduated from Cambridge in Mathematics in 1905. By 1912 Robertson had gained a first in the Economics tripos and two years later was able to submit a thesis on industrial fluctuation which earned for him a Trinity Fellowship. Their relationship during this period was very much one of student and tutor. Robertson was required to submit essays to Keynes. These essays (some of which survive) are "rather remarkable for a young man whose knowledge of economics was at first derived from reading Marshall's *Principles* and the *Wealth of Nations* during the previous summer vacation" but they are on "standard Marshallian topics (e.g., theory of rent) and have no relevance to later work, especially industrial fluctuation".[1]

Their major early collaborations concerned the drafts of *A Study of Industrial Fluctuation* (*Study*) (D. H. Robertson 1915). Robertson's thesis impressed Keynes as a "most brilliant and important contribution to the subject" (J. M. Keynes 1975, 1). Despite this, Keynes was not prepared to support it fully as an explanation of the trade cycle, although he did remark "your work has suggested to me what appears at first sight a superb theory about fluctuations" (J. M. Keynes 1973a, 1).

This "superb theory" was presented at the Political Economy Club's meeting on 3 December, 1913 in London. In many ways this was the first step towards Keynes' *TMR*, although it specifically addressed the question of the responsibility of bankers for industrial fluctuations.[2]

Keynes' paper exhibits a number of interesting features. First, it rejects the type of over-investment theory associated with Robertson's *Study* on the grounds that it contains two invalid suggestions; that more capital can be invested than exists and that more investment is made than is profitable. Keynes proceeds to uphold the "real saving" doctrine (see later) and counteracts the second suggestion by an appeal to the facts. Secondly, Keynes distrusts the monetary explanation of the cycle which emphasises the fluctuation in bank credit as the cause of cyclical movements. This, at that time, was associated with both Fisher and Hawtrey. Consequently Keynes had to provide an alternative explanation and this is found within the behaviour of the banks.

Resources in any period are either spent, saved or "suspended", that is either held in the banks or hoarded. Investment is financed from two sources, from that part of existing resources saved by individuals or from part of the "suspended" resources made available by the banks for investment. It is the second source which promotes a tendency to over-investment during the upswing of the cycle: "If no one who directs capital operations could obtain funds except by inducing someone who had saved them to place them with him, clearly investment could never in a period exceed saving. . . . The machinery of banking, however, permits this". Banks allow those who invest to "encroach on the community's reserves of free capital." (J. M. Keynes 1973a, 9).

Robertson was not sufficiently persuaded by this paper to make fundamental revisions to his *Study* before publication. He was more preoccupied than Keynes with the causes of the upturn in the cycle. These were the real factors promoting the initial change in investment, not those which caused over-investment to take place and the downturn to follow. Keynes did however accept that the growth of more profitable investment opportunities through invention and the opening up of new territories (and changes brought about by, for example, wars) could stimulate investment. This approach is totally consistent with the *Study* and was indeed the major feature of the real over-investment theory put forward by Robertson. Robertson in 1915 chose also to stress the role of agricultural change in encouraging a burst of investment out of depression. For Robertson there were more fundamental causes of over-investment than those isolated by Keynes. Over-investment was inherent in the capitalist system of production; the nature of capital goods, their indivisibility, their long gestation period and the consequent uncertainty which surrounded the investment process were central to the generation of too much investment and the downturn.

Although Keynes had based his approach in no small degree upon the drafts of the *Study*, Robertson, in turn, had a reciprocal obligation to Keynes, acknowledged in the published version of the *Study* and in later work. Keynes' paper exhibits some characteristics which

Robertson was to develop later in *Money* and in *BPPL*; in particular, one can recognize the embryo of the forced saving thesis which Robertson was to elaborate more comprehensively in the concepts of automatic and induced ''lacking'' in *BPPL*. Keynes believed that saving and investment need not be equal; during a boom investment would exceed voluntary saving, the deficiency being accounted for by the ability of the banks to transfer ''suspended'' resources to investment. In the *Study* Robertson wrote ''to the latter (Mr. J. M. Keynes) I owe more than it would be possible to acknowledge.'' (D. H. Robertson 1915, xx). Undoubtedly, Keynes had helped refine Robertson's thesis, although there is little to support this claim either in correspondence or within the text of the *Study*. What is evident, however, is the partial acceptance in the *Study* of the ''real saving'' doctrine advocated by Keynes in 1913.

In this the amount of saving which can finance investment is equated with the accumulated stocks of consumer goods. This is consistent with Robertson's desire to get behind the monetary veil to the real determinants of the cycle in the *Study*. This contrasts with the approach of, for example, Tugan Baranowski where savings were equated with loanable funds rather than with the real stock of consumer goods which allow an economy to divert a larger proportion of its resources to investment.

It would be incorrect to claim that Keynes was the only influence upon Robertson in this respect for he had, by 1913, already discovered a more lucid account of the ''real saving'' doctrine in the work of Marcel Labordère (1908) and also in a summary of Spiethoff's theory (W. Mitchell 1913). Nevertheless he did thank Keynes for furnishing him with the understanding that crisis could be caused by too rapid a utilization of the stock of consumer goods in the process of redistributing production more towards capital goods (D. H. Robertson 1915, 171). But clearly Robertson was less convinced by this argument than Keynes: ''he is, I think, mistaken in conveying the impression that the relapse of investment is always due to the physical impossibility of maintaining it upon the existing scale'' (D. H. Robertson 1915, 171). Of more importance to Robertson, over-investment is defined not in relation to the supply of real saving but in terms of the inadequate demand for capital goods relative to their supply at the peak of the cycle. Indeed the crisis could occur even where the stock of consumer goods was relatively high.

Keynes' exposure to the *Study* did not persuade him of the virtues of public finance at that stage and certainly there was no reference to

Robertson's *Study* in this respect in his later writings on fiscal measures. D. H. Robertson had been very supportive of public spending as a cure for depression; this was a natural consequence of the over-investment theory of industrial fluctuation which he presented.

Unemployment was the direct result of a deficient demand for capital goods and the solution therefore lay in "an artificial elevation in the demand for constructional goods" (D. H. Robertson 1915, PT II, Ch.IV). He did not claim any originality for this policy cure, accepting the similar recommendation of the Minority Report of the Poor Law Commissioners which had preceded the *Study*. Public works policies in a depression became a persistent recommendation by Robertson throughout his lifetime. He was the strongest critic of the so called "Treasury View"; as for Keynes, his advocacy of fiscal measures did not really appear until 1924 (P. Lambert 1969).

Of course the over-investment theory was indicative of one major characteristic of Robertson's work which Keynes was later to appreciate. The emphasis upon the lumpiness of investment, the long gestation period and the indivisibility of the production process, as well as the role of invention, innovation and agricultural change in the *Study* led Robertson to have little respect for Say's Law and the associated, so-called "classical" disposition to see an automatic movement to full employment in a capitalist economy.

Keynes was later to write "I regard Mr. Hawtrey as my grand parent and Mr. Robertson as my parent in the paths of errancy" (J. M. Keynes 1973b, 202). It was Robertson who had persuaded him to stray from the classical fold. Later, in *BPPL*, Robertson was to enlarge upon this continuous failure of a capitalist economy to achieve the objective of full employment.

He chose to distinguish between appropriate and inappropriate fluctuations; it was the objective of society to get rid of inappropriate fluctuation caused by errors of optimism and pessimism on the part of businessmen, or by monetary overexpansion or contraction. But to try to avoid "appropriate" fluctuations was tantamount to preventing economic progress; industrial fluctuation was inevitable: "out of the welter of industrial dislocation the great permanent riches of the future are generated" (D. H. Robertson 1915, 254). It is this view of the capitalist economy expressed by Robertson in 1915 and remaining with him throughout his life, which goes some way to explaining his lack of acceptance of the approach within the *GT*. Robertson believed a static economic equilibrium was never attainable; economic life was continuously changing and the analysis undertaken by economists must reflect this.

One can also observe no great preoccupation with the price level in the *Study*; Robertson was primarily concerned with industrial fluctuation, with cycles in real output. Economists are accustomed to applauding Keynes for shaking off the shackles of the classical obsession with the price level; he was to do this in 1936, Robertson had done it in 1915 surprisingly under the influence of A. C. Pigou (D. H. Robertson 1915, ix, 1948).

Keynes' 1913 paper on industrial fluctuation, brief as it was, could not have incorporated all of Robertson's main points in the voluminous drafts of the *Study*. Keynes' paper was not a policy paper and indeed Keynes did not write a substantial piece on economic policy until *TMR* (D. Moggridge and S. Hawson 1974, 227–9). *TMR* however took the stance of his 1913 paper, blaming industrial fluctuation on the poor bankers and consequently recommending monetary, not fiscal policy; there is little evidence to suggest that it had been influenced significantly by the *Study*.

III.   INTO THE 1920s: CARRYING THE FLAG FORWARD

In 1947 Robertson looked back on the pre-war period and declared: "In the early 1910s and again in the 1920s I did do a bit of scrambling towards the frontier (of economic thought), firmly roped to the man of genius (Keynes) who has perished there. Sometimes, I venture to think, I was even a little bit in front of him; but in the end he went on beyond me and it is my belief—an unpopular one, I know, but I cannot help it—that he got a bit off the track and set the flag in places where it is not destined to rest."[3] Although many would dispute the strength of Robertson's contribution to the study of industrial fluctuation, few would deny that the *Study* and *BPPL* did represent significant departures from what had gone before, particularly in the British literature.

The 1920s are remarkable for the spirit of cooperation which existed between Robertson and Keynes and the sharp contrast with their relationship in the 1930s. Their two minds worked in similar directions throughout the period until the final version of *TM* was published and the first major sign of academic disagreement appeared. Reading Keynes', *Collected Writings*, volume XIII, it is difficult to disentangle

the sources of the many original ideas which they put forward in the
1920s. They acted as a stimulus to each other, I suspect in the role of
equal partners at least until *BPPL* [although this may not be a widely
accepted view] (J. Leith and D. Patinkin 1977).

Their major objective in the 1920s was to elaborate upon their
earlier discussions of trade cycle theory; more specifically they were
attempting to integrate interest rate theory and saving/investment analysis into the theory of industrial fluctuation. For Robertson the focus of
his work was upon the role of banks in the cycle; this reflected what he
saw as an overemphasis upon the importance of monetary forces in the
trade cycle: "far more weight must be attached than it is now fashionable to attach to certain real, as opposed to monetary or psychological,
causes of fluctuation" (D. H. Robertson 1926, 1). In this he was
arguing against the extreme position of Hawtrey ("the trade cycle is a
purely monetary phenomenon") (R. G. Hawtrey, 141) and the less extreme view of Keynes' *TMR* that the initial disturbance in the price
level may be the result of non monetary causes but that it should be
counteracted via monetary policy (J. M. Keynes 1923, 38).

Keynes and Robertson worked very closely on four books in this
period, *Money, TMR, BPPL* and *TM*; none appeared under joint au-
thorship though clearly the published acknowledgements and correspondence indicate the tremendous debt they owed to each other in
their respective publications (J. R. Presley 1978, Part II). A typical
example of this joint effort can be gained by a more thorough examination of *BPPL*. This will also serve as a prelude to establishing why
their later conflicts over theory were so painful, since much of
Robertson's displeasure over the drafts of the *GT* stem from their departure from the approach of *BPPL*.

Alongside the *Study*, *BPPL* ranks as Robertson's most important
contribution to economic theory. Its publication followed long correspondence between Keynes and Robertson which by May 1925 had
resulted in almost total agreement on its contents.[4] In the preface
Robertson wrote: "I have had so many discussions with Mr. J. M.
Keynes on the subject matters of chapters V and VI and have rewritten
them so drastically at his suggestion, that I think neither of us now
knows how much of the ideas therein contained is his and how much is
mine" (D. H. Robertson 1926, 5). That Keynes accepted the fundamental arguments within *BPPL* is confirmed by correspondence.
Keynes wrote: "I like this latest version though God knows it is concise" (J. M. Keynes 1973a, 39). He regarded chapter V as
"splendid—most new and important. I think it is substantially right

and at last I have no material criticism. It is the kernel and real essence of the book'' (J. M. Keynes 1973a, 40).

It is instructive to examine what Keynes was agreeing with in *BPPL*. The major objective of *BPPL*, as the title suggests, was to formulate guide lines for banking policy over the course of the cycle, particularly in relation to the desired behaviour of the price level. The real over-investment theory of the *Study* was the acceptable starting point; *BPPL* sought to develop cycle theory by establishing the role of monetary forces in exaggerating cyclical movements and consequently the function of banking policy in avoiding such inappropriate fluctuations. Its approach was in marked contrast with the *GT*. Robertson employed dynamic analysis, a step by step approach. He believed that it was imperative to recognise the time lags which existed in the relationships between economic variables; indeed he saw the differences portrayed in time lags in competing theories as often the major expression of differences between theories (J. R. Presley 1978, 154). The application of ''period analysis'' in *BPPL* led Robertson to present a very complex view of the nature of savings over the cycle. Saving was disaggregated; it did not consist merely of voluntary savings; indeed Robertson was to incorporate his own terminology. Saving became ''lacking'', this could be automatic or induced, long or short; he then talked of ''splashing'' and also of ''stinting'' which again had their own subdivisions, and so the Robertsonian concept of saving emerged (J. R. Presley 1978, Part II). Saving was, in turn, related to the behaviour of the price level, the monetary system and the finance of investment.

What all this amounted to was a dynamic theory of forced saving, an extension of the type of theory which had been propounded before in ''classical'' literature (B. Corry). It had however one special ingredient, a remarkable one which, in fact, was contributed by Keynes. This was a concept of ''induced lacking'' (J. R. Presley 1986). The idea that those on fixed incomes may be ''forced'' to save in a situation where prices were rising was not new in 1926. That individuals may be ''induced'' to save was however given much greater emphasis in *BPPL* than in previous work.

In defining induced lacking Robertson wrote: ''induced lacking occurs when, the same process that imposes automatic lacking on certain people having also reduced the real value of their money stocks, these people hold off the market, and refrain from consuming the full value of their current output, in order to bring the real value of their money stocks up again to what they regard as an appropriate level'' (D. H. Robertson 1926, 61). In an appendix Robertson also attempts to employ induced lacking in an attempt at "stability analysis". Surprisingly it was Keynes who prompted Robertson to recognize this real balance effect. In May 1925 he wrote of a situation in which money supply and prices were increasing: "no position of equilibrium can be reached until someone is induced to replenish his hoard, i.e., to do *some new* hoarding out of current income. It is only when this occurs that new short lacking is provided.

This inducement to effect new hoarding comes about, in general, in one of three ways:

1.   The real deposits of the public may fall to a highly inconvenient low proportion of their real income, so that they prefer to do new hoarding so as to raise them, rather than to maintain their current expenditure at its previous level (J. M. Keynes 1973a, 36–7).

2.   Inflation may effect a redistribution of current real income into the hands of people whose incentive and ability to hoard is greater than those from whose it is taken.

3.   A higher bank rate may increase the incentive to hoard" (J. M. Keynes 1973a, 36).

The first bears a strong resemblance to the real balance effect. In the same letter Keynes also writes on the redistributional effects of inflation and the effects on inflationary expectations of an increase in money supply and prices. Both arguments were subsequently utilized by Robertson in *BPPL*.

To summarize, without doubt Keynes and Robertson were almost as one over the contents of *BPPL*. Keynes clearly had a major share of the credit for its originality. As such Keynes made no objection to its dynamic approach, he was happy to accept its theory of forced saving and indeed was prepared to assist in its elaboration. He made no fundamental criticisms of the disaggregated nature of Robertson's saving analysis, nor of Robertson's persistent classification of fluctuations into those which were appropriate and those which were inappropriate; that appropriate fluctuation (continuous disequilibrium ?) was desirable in the interests of economic progress remained a central feature of *BPPL* as it was in the *Study*.

The drafts of *TM* exhibited much of the analysis of *BPPL* until as late as August 1929. (Keynes had begun *TM* in 1924.) By that time Keynes was still content in a draft of chapter 23 to incorporate the forced saving thesis (J. M. Keynes 1973a, 104–8). But this was omitted from the published version in 1930. This about turn by Keynes brought with it differences with Robertson in the definitions of savings and investment, in the nature of saving over the cycle and ultimately in the appropriate banking policy.

TM was the beginning of totally different approaches by Robertson and Keynes to the analysis of economic fluctuations. They had gone forward together throughout the 1920s, but now their paths were to diverge, not so much on policy issues but on the theoretical justification of the policies which they both advocated.

The partial breakdown in their working relationship was disguised by their correspondence. Keynes thought that *TM* would "get through the criticisms of Robertson . . . without serious damage" and indeed believed that *TM*: "owes a great deal to him" (J. M. Keynes 1979, 2). Robertson described *TM* as "marvelously full of new meat . . . I think the whole book VII, most of which is new to me, splendid" (J. M. Keynes 1973a, 202). But at the same time he was resistant to large parts of it (J. M. Keynes 1973a, 21–2).

Much later he attacked Keynes for his conformity with the traditional approach in *TM*, particularly on the question of monetary stabilisation. (He believed that Keynes was calling for price stabilisation.) In *BPPL* he had proposed that banking policy might promote instability in the price level in order to facilitate the creation of credit necessary to finance both working and fixed capital over the trade cycle.

Although both *BPPL* and *TM* recognise the inequality of saving and investment over the course of the cycle, Robertson did not see excessive saving as a cause, but a symptom of depression (D. H. Robertson 1934, 650–66). The debate in the *Economic Journal* which followed the publication of *TM* has the outward appearance of a dispute over the definitions of saving and investment. It was however much more fundamental than this. Robertson was unhappy that Keynes had failed to evolve the view of the economic system he had put forward in *BPPL*, a discontent which was to grow with the drafts of the *GT*.

IV. WORKING OUT THE GENERAL THEORY AND AFTER: UNPRODUCTIVE COLLABORATION?

The period from 1931 onwards has justifiably gained most attention from historians of Keynesian economic thought in recent years. It would be fruitless simply to reiterate what has gone before; this section therefore makes a general comment on the working relationship of

Keynes and Robertson in this period and secondly attempts to explain why Robertson was so critical of the *GT*.

The current literature reveals two popular interpretations of the period 1931–6. D. Patinkin concludes from his study of Keynes' writing of the *GT* that: "the received version of the transition from the *Treatise* to the *General Theory* assigned too large a role to the discussions of the "Cambridge Circus", and correspondingly too small a one to the criticisms of such individuals as Hawtrey, Robertson and even Hayek" (J. Leith and D. Patinkin 1977, 6). The received version, of course, is associated with the excellent work of D. Moggridge who has been largely responsible for collecting and editing Keynes' papers and correspondence. Moggridge writes: "Ralph Hawtrey and Dennis Robertson were even further outside the inner circle (Cambridge Circus). Although their comments may have been formally correct on occasion, they appear to have had little effect on the final product, except in cases where they either echoed points raised by others in close sympathy with the whole exercise or where Kahn and Joan Robinson . . . commended their criticisms to Keynes" (J. Leith and D. Patinkin 1977, 68).

As far as Robertson is concerned, my inclination is towards Moggridge's interpretation of this period. Robertson only attended, at most, one meeting of the Cambridge "circus." He was the first to see drafts of the *GT* outside of the "circus" but in response to them he complained to Keynes: "a large part of your theoretical structure is still to me almost complete mumbo-jumbo!" (J. M Keynes 1973a, 506). Offended by this remark and upset by critical comment from Robertson on the drafts, in March 1935 Keynes broke off the debate with Robertson and only minor correspondence then took place between them. It is a fair interpretation therefore that during this period Robertson had very little of a positive nature to offer Keynes for the *GT*.

There is however a further important point to be made. Keynes had been moving towards the *GT* through *TMR*, *BPPL* and *TM*; admittedly the final contents of the *GT* had been worked out from 1931–35, but the pre-1931 period was also important in providing Keynes with a foundation from which to build this *GT*. The contention here is that Robertson was as influential as anyone in creating that foundation. Keynes, as we saw earlier, regarded Robertson as his parent leading him from the classical fold. Together they had conducted their debate in the 1920s in terms of saving and investment, although the definitions employed of saving and investment differed significantly from those of the *GT*. Keynes was already, by 1931, prepared to recognise the possible inequality of saving and investment over the cycle; he had been exposed to Robertson's belief in public spending policies as a cure for unemployment and this followed logically from Robertson's view of a deficiency in demand for capital goods as a cause of depression. Robertson also had continuously stressed the importance of investment in the economic system and the causes of its volatility as the source of macroeconomic fluctuation. Neither by 1931 had any great respect for Say's Law. The *GT* was also to lay stress upon investment, although through the multiplier process. The Cambridge School, with Robertson as a leading member, had also conducted its analysis of monetary factors in terms of the real cash balance approach. It preferred to look at the demand for money rather than "money on the wing." Keynes also chose this approach in the liquidity preference theory. Hence Keynes did depart from the "classical" fold in the *GT*, but he was already being encouraged to do so before 1931 by Robertson (and also by R. G. Hawtrey) and this clearly had its implications for the writing of the *GT*. Given this encouragement by Robertson to rebel against the "classical" approach, one may be surprised by his negative reaction to the *GT*. There are however two major reasons for this:

1. Keynes was keen to present the *GT* as a revolution in economic thought; Robertson had always viewed his own work as evolving from the work of Cambridge economists, past and present. Like many within Cambridge he believed that "its all in Marshall" and always saw his work on industrial fluctuation as extending theories within the Cambridge School. He believed that Keynes had given too little credit to the work of Marshall and Pigou in influencing the *GT* and was far too content in being critical of what had gone before.

Robertson always upheld that there was an element of truth in all theories and that they should not be dismissed too lightly. He gave considerable effort to showing that substantial pieces in the *GT* could be traced back to classical and Cambridge writings.

Keynes was upset by this and accused Robertson of always retreating to his mother's womb (the "Cambridge School") while he had been able to shake himself free of it.

2. Probably of more weight than (1), Robertson was deeply disappointed with the *GT* because it did not evolve out of their joint work in the 1920s, particularly *BPPL*. He clearly felt that his own approach in *BPPL* was superior to that of the *GT*. He later wrote: "not only did

Keynes fail to acknowledge what had gone before, but many aspects of his work which had not gone before represented erroneous argument rather than economic truth.''[5] The *GT* was too simplistic in approach. Robertson objected to its use of comparative statics and also its failure to disaggregate. His attack upon the multiplier process was typical of his view of the *GT* through the eyes of *BPPL*. The instantaneous equilibrium it brought about, the equality of investment and voluntary saving, disguised for Robertson the true nature of the economic system. It ignored the time lags which were apparent in the real world, it failed to take account of the accelerator and above all it treated the finance of investment via voluntary saving as unproblematical. In this manner the *GT* dispensed with much of the analysis of *BPPL* which had been primarily concerned with the complexities of the saving process and the problem of providing finance for investment over the trade cycle.

But this was for Keynes the advantage of *GT*; he had regarded *BPPL* as too complex and far too difficult to understand (J. M. Keynes 1973a, 39–40). The *GT* was an attempt to present a view of the functioning of the macroeconomic system which could be understood by a larger audience. Robertson had never been in a position where *BPPL* had been widely accepted. Despite its relevance, its contents defied the understanding of the vast majority of its readers.

V. SOME CONCLUSIONS

The paper has attempted to view the working relationship between Keynes and Robertson before 1940 as three distinct phases. In so doing it has avoided the inclination to concentrate upon the later period during the writing of the *GT*. Clearly the relationship between these two eminent economists was much closer not only for 1910–15 but more importantly for the 1920s than it was in the 1930s. It has attempted to demonstrate the existence of a much longer gestation period for the *GT* than one gathers from contemporary literature. While not suggesting that the pre-1931 period deserves equal treatment, it was nevertheless productive in carrying economics forward beyond the classical system and there were few economists more pioneering in this respect than Keynes and Robertson.

ACKNOWLEDGMENTS

I would like to thank Professor S. R. Dennison and Professor T. Cate for assistance on this paper. I am also grateful to The Wincott Foundation, The British Academy and the Economic and Social Research Council for providing grants to support my research on Sir D. H. Robertson. The paper was presented at the History of Economics Society Conference at George Mason University, April, 1985.

NOTES

1. Letter from Professor S. R. Dennison to the author dated 16 March 1985.
2. The precise title was: "How Far are Bankers Responsible for the Alternatives of Crisis and Depression?" (J. M. Keynes, 1973, p. 2).
3. An address by D. H. Robertson to the Conference of Economics Teachers, Oxford, 4 January 1947 titled: "The Frontiers of Economic Thought." The brackets are mine.
4. The only minor difference by May 1925 was over real hoarding and new short lacking, which Keynes regarded as identical. Robertson in fact accepted Keynes' stand point in the published version of *BPPL* (J. M. Keynes, 1973a, p. 38).
5. Letter from D. H. Robertson to Professor T. Wilson, dated 31 October 1953.

REFERENCES

Corry, B., (1952) *Money, Saving and Investment in English Economics 1800–50*, Macmillan, London.
Harrod, R., (1951) *The Life of John Maynard Keynes*, Macmillan, London.
Hawtrey, R. G., (1919) *Monetary Reconstruction*, Longmans, London.
Hicks, J. R., (1942) "The Monetary Theory of D. H. Robertson," *Economica*, New Series 9–10, Feb.
Keynes, J. M., (1923) *The Tract on Monetary Reform*, Macmillan, London.
Keynes, J. M., (1930) *The Treatise on Money*, Macmillan, London.
Keynes, J. M., (1936) *The General Theory of Unemployment, Interest and Money*, Macmillan.
Keynes, J. M., (1973a) *The Collected Writings of John Maynard Keynes Vol XIII*, Macmillan, for the Royal Economic Society, London.
Keynes, J. M., (1973b) *The Collected Writings of John Maynard Keynes Vol XIV*, London.
Keynes, J. M., (1979) *The Collected Writings of John Maynard Keynes Vol XIX*, London.
Lambert, P., (1969) "The Evolution of Keynes' Thought for the Treatise on Money to the General Theory," *Annals of Public and Cooperative Economy* Liege, pp. 1–21.
Labordère, M., (1908) "Autour de la Crisis Americaine de 1907," *Revue de Paris*, 1 Feb.
Leith, J. and Patinkin, D., (1977) *Keynes, Cambridge and the General Theory*, Macmillan, London.
Mitchell, W., (1913) *Business Cycles: The Problem and its Setting*, Burt Franklin, New York.
Moggridge, D. and Hawson, S., (1974) "Keynes on Monetary Policy 1910–46," *Oxford Economic Papers*, Vol 26, No 2, July, pp. 227–34.
Presley, J. R., (1978) *Robertsonian Economics*, Macmillan, London.

Presley, J. R., (1986) "Keynes and the Real Balance Effect," Manchester School
    Spring.
Robertson, D. H., (1915) *A Study of Industrial Fluctuation*, P. S. King and Son Ltd.,
    Westminster.
Robertson, D. H., (1922) *Money*, Cambridge Economic Handbook, Cambridge.
Robertson, D. H., (1926) *Banking Policy and the Price Level*, P. S. King and Son
    Ltd., Westminster.
Robertson, D. H., (1934) "Industrial Fluctuation and the Natural Rate of Interest,"
    Economic Journal, December, pp. 650–6.

SYMPOSIUM ON AUSTRIAN AND INSTITUTIONAL ECONOMICS

INTRODUCTION

Warren J. Samuels

In the summer of 1981 I prepared a paper on some characteristics and thematic elements apparently held in common by economists of the Austrian and Institutionalist schools. The paper was presented in November 1981 at the Southern Economic Association annual meeting. The genesis of the project was my perception that once one conceptually factored out certain obvious ideological, methodological and substantive differences, there seemed to be significant common subject-matter and much parallel substantive content. The important point was to factor out the ideological differences. At any rate, I received several very perceptive responses, both affirmative and deeply critical, from friends to whom I had sent copies for their reactions and at the SEA session. Given the ideological, methodological and substantive differences, I was not surprised by the diversity of response, and I was pleased at their quality. Because of the pressure of other, higher-priority research projects and also because I wanted to give myself more time to think about the issues involved in treating the similar-

Research in the History of Economic Thought and Methodology,
Volume 6, pages 49-51
Copyright © 1989 by JAI Press Inc.
All rights of reproduction in any form reserved.
ISBN: 0-89232-928-9

ities and differences between competing schools of thought, I delayed indefinitely any revision of the paper.

In late 1985 Peter Boettke submitted his paper, "Evolution and Economics: Austrians as Institutionalists" for consideration for publication in this research annual. He had had access to a copy of my earlier paper. Reports from readers were generally enthusiastic but typically requested a more thorough and deeper treatment of the subject of the relationship between the two schools.

I wrote Boettke that both of us had been down the same path, that to do the job right requires a much longer and much more complicated and also much more subtle paper, more likely a book. I also pointed out that while the problem of differences between the two schools is difficult enough, much more difficult is that of areas of agreement because these take on differing significances due to their being nested in different larger theories and approaches. If both schools accept point A, point A still means something different to both because it is ensconced within different paradigms. Thus even to identify the areas of agreement one has to identify the differences in nuance due to the larger nesting.

I then suggested to Boettke the possibility of publishing both papers together with invited responses, taking advantage of different points of view but with the obvious disadvantage of not producing a single complete integrated viewpoint, however subject to criticism it might be. He agreed and this symposium was generated.

It is not my intention to affirm Peter Boettke as a definitive representative of Austrian economics; nor is it to proclaim my own position on and in institutional economics. I shall let my past (and future) writings and JEI editorship speak for themselves, other than to say that I consider myself an eclectic institutionalist especially (but not completely) of the John R. Commons variant of institutionalism. As for Boettke, the Austrian who did in fact write the paper, he too represents one wing of a fractured school. This is indicated, for example, by his statement that "the Austrian claim that 'history has no place in praxeology' seems to me to be in error. In their explicit defense of praxeology Austrians have perhaps misrepresented their own work. At the time Mises wrote he took it for granted that economists were well informed about history, so in his reaction against both the historicist and positivist he might have overstated the insulated foundationalism of praxeology" (Boettke to Samuels, March 21, 1986).[1] Indeed, Austrian economics, sometimes referred to as neo-Austrian economics, while it has enjoyed something of a resurgence (financed in part by conservative foundations), has evidenced considerable intramural conflict. Different Austrians surely would have produced quite different alternatives to Boettke's paper, as indeed different institutionalists would have written quite different papers from mine, as can be seen below.

Which brings me to the strategy I sought to employ in designing this symposium. Given the use of Boettke's and my papers as the basis for comments, I sought to enlist three groups in roughly equal proportions: Austrians, institutionalists, and historians of economic thought and methodologists who appeared to have a close and deep familiarity with both bodies of thought. Invitations were accepted by fifteen and declined by several. If all fifteen had produced comments there would have been a roughly equal balance among the three groups. Unfortunately the lowest compliance rate was among the Austrians: they are in fact, alas, conspicuous by their complete absence. On the basis of a recent discussion with one of the absent Austrians, I can report that he attributed his failure to produce a comment to two things: his general overcommitment and the press of other projects (which I can understand) and his lack of familiarity with the institutionalist literature (which I find discouraging, particularly inasmuch as this person has recently widely affirmed the desirability of greater communication between schools of economic thought).

The symposium thus consists of the initial two papers, ten commentaries thereon presented in alphabetical order by author, and separate responses to the comments by Boettke and myself.

NOTE

1. Boettke also wrote that "It is more than a coincidence that some of the leading Austrian thinkers have interesting intellectual connections with thinkers in both the historical and institutional camps. For example, Mitchell was responsible for and wrote the introduction to the English version of Wieser's *Social Economics*. Hayek studied with Mitchell in the early 1920s. Lachmann was a student of Sombart. Rothbard wrote his Ph.D. under Dorfman. You wrote the introduction to Wieser's *The Law of Power*. Moreover, I believe that the interconnectedness is even deeper than 'influence.' Mark Perlman has argued that there are interesting similarities between Hayek's recent work in *Law Legislation and Liberty* and Commons's *Legal Foundations of Capitalism*."

AUSTRIAN AND INSTITUTIONAL ECONOMICS:

SOME COMMON ELEMENTS

Warren J. Samuels

> When men observe two things to be in some respect similar, they are wont to
> ascribe to each what they have found to be true of the other, to the neglect of
> that in which they differ.
>
> —Descartes, *Rules*

The objective of this paper is to identify certain characteristics and elements of thought and analysis which arguably are common to both Austrian and institutional economics.

Such an objective likely will displease certain people in both schools of thought. They will consider the task either impossible of fruition or undesirable. Let me state as clearly and directly as I possibly can that it is *not* my intention to either reconcile or make compatible the two schools' competing views of economic reality and of the proper man-

Research in the History of Economic Thought and Methodology,
Volume 6, pages 53-71
Copyright © 1989 by JAI Press Inc.
All rights of reproduction in any form reserved.
ISBN: 0-89232-928-9

ner of its study. It is my sole intention to identify common characteristics and, especially, elements of thought and analysis. In addition, it is
not my intention here to create, reinforce, or take positions on schisms
and tensions within each school. (I shall return to the heterogeneity
problem in a moment.) The sole genesis of the research leading to this
paper resides in my reading of the works of Austrian-school economists and finding ideas and lines of reasoning seemingly sympathetic
to some of those articulated in the literature of institutional economics.

Such a venture is not unique, notwithstanding enormous relevant
differences between the two schools. Jurgen Herbst (1965, 130–131),
for example, has reported Henry W. Farnam's (1908) study which
found a not insignificant number (or percentage) of economists who
stressed the resemblances rather than the contrasts between ''Professor
Bohm-Bawerk's Vienna school of marginal utility economists'' and
the German historical school. More recently, E. Streissler and W. Weber (Hicks and Weber 1973, 228) have stressed the historical dimension of Carl Menger's work and further noted the ''interesting parallels
between Menger and Commons.'' In different directions, Ludwig M.
Lachmann (Dolan 1976, 217ff.) has compared the points of agreement
and disagreement between Austrian and neo-Ricardian schools, and
Richard B. McKenzie (1980) has attempted at least that between neoclassical and Austrian schools. (McKenzie also attempted ''a partial
reconciliation'' of what appeared to him as two competing world
views. Presumably not all Austrians—or neoclassicists—agree with all
the terms of his reconciliation. From a typical institutionalist perspective, neoclassical and Austrian world views appear, of course, to be
very close.)

As I will summarize shortly, there are important, if not fundamental
differences between Austrian and institutional economics. But that fact
does not preclude the possibility that there can be some congruence in
the ideas of otherwise differing schools of thought. In my view (Samuels 1974), the meaning of the doctrines or theories of one school can be
interpreted in the terms of both its devotees and its rivals; and that, as a
consequence, meaning can be contemplated in terms of the matrix of
issues and positions formed by the juxtaposition of, and partial conflict
and convergence among, rival schools of thought. Quite different, indeed, rival schools of thought can share points and positions. The
meaning (for each) of a point shared with another is likely to differ
between the relevant schools because of differences in their respective
larger systems of thought, a factor which, notwithstanding the

commonality, enables (further) differentiation between them and a third school which does not share the point.

Part I will summarize certain important differences between Austrian and institutional economics, aspects of which also will be alluded to in the following part. Part II will summarize certain characteristics and elements of thought and analysis apparently shared by Austrian and institutional economics.

Before going further, I want to make the following points. First, an initial common characteristic, it seems to me that each school has tended strongly to define itself vis-à-vis neoclassical economics. Some similarities between the thought and analysis of Austrian and institutional economists thus may derive from the psychodynamics of a common opposition to neoclassical economics (although each also has elements in common with neoclassicism, Austrian economics likely more so than institutional economics). Other similarities between Austrian and institutional economics may derive from the nature of the real world as they commonly see it. Still others may be only coincidental.

Second, another initial shared characteristic, each school is markedly heterogeneous. The heterogeneity of belief within each school often is as great, seemingly, as the differences between schools (although the substantive issues differ). Apropos of this heterogeneity let me make the following points: There is heterogeneity of economic doctrine, of methodology, and of policy analysis. There actually is a spectrum of developmental possibilities characteristic of each school. There is heterogeneity as to the meaning of the classic literature in each school. There are more or less clear rival factions within each school. There are both philosophical absolutists and relativists within each school, positions often coupled with differing attitudes within each school as to doctrinal purity and eclecticism. There are both sophisticated and vulgar formulations of the ideas of each school (and it not always possible readily to distinguish between them). Accordingly, finally, there are problems of identifying membership in each school: who is a, or who is a "true," as contrasted with a "deviant," Austrian and institutionalist; and whether a particular work of a member of a school belongs within its literature.

Third, although there are many important points of difference between the two schools (see Part I) and these differences, as noted above, are important to the total meaning of the juxtaposition of the two schools, I will concentrate in Part II on the commonalities with only minimal attention to differences of nuance, etcetera, consequent to the differences and conflicts. While, following the epigraph from Descartes, I want to avoid exaggerating the commonalities in contrast to the differences, I do want to explore the commonalities, a course in part justified by the fact of obvious and indeed well-known differences. Furthermore, I will state the common points in a manner intended to facilitate their identification as common points rather than to emphasize related differences, although in some cases I will exemplify the complex relation between similarities and differences by indicating something of the impact of the differences. Generally I will avoid questions as to whether a commonality or difference is a matter of degree or of substance, recognizing nonetheless that commonalities (for example) may be limited and perhaps sometimes superficial vis-à-vis the related differences. I certainly do not want to obscure the differences either within each school or between the two schools. But neither do I want here to emphasize them. Thus I generally will state the points in my own terms—influenced by my reading, to be sure, but trying to avoid the often stylized language of some practitioners of each school—and will avoid citations to the supporting literature precisely because I do not want to be read as taking positions here in disputes within each school. Every statement, then, carries with it the caveat *pro tanto*.

Fourth, I will abstract from the question of wherein Austrian and institutional economics supplement and conflict with each other insofar as that involves going beyond the iteration of differences and commonalities. I also will largely abstract from questions of differences between doctrine and practice on the part of practitioners. As for the relative importance of the similarities and differences, that largely is a matter of point of view. There is no reason why different assessments could not exist: Some may feel that certain differences are so fundamental that the common elements are swamped; others, that certain common elements are so important as to render the differences nugatory; and still others may have mixed views, for example, at different levels of abstraction or on different issues, some of whom may feel no compulsion to reach any conclusion as to conflict, convergence, and supplementarity. At the very most, this paper is one institutionalist's view of the elements common to Austrian and institutional economics, given the differences between the two schools.

I. SOME DIFFERENCES

It would not be difficult to secure agreement among Austrian and institutional economists that there are important, perhaps fundamental, differences between the orientation and work of the two schools. It is more than likely, however, that there would be interesting if not significant differences among individuals' respective formulations of the differences. For present purposes, let me identify the following.

First, there clearly is a difference as to the central problem of economics as self-perceived by the two schools: The central problem of the work of the Austrian economist is tracking the logic of choice involved in the allocation of resources through the exercise of subjective valuation by individual economic actors in the market. To the institutionalist, the central problem is the interplay of technology, market, and institutions as they contribute to the organization and control, and evolution, of the economic system (understood to include more than the market) in which individuals and subgroups act. Along with this difference go numerous others, for example, the Austrian concentration of analytic attention upon rational calculations pursuant to subjective valuations and preferences, in contrast to the institutionalist concentration of attention upon nonrational (nondeliberative) behavior and social (methodological collectivist) forces informing individual subjective valuations and preferences. But the actual work of both Austrian and institutional economists does in fact encompass both methodological individualist and methodological collectivist elements and both the play of choice in markets and the working out of problems of organization-and-control and institutional and systemic evolution and adjustment. Doctrinally, or officially, however, their respective definitions of their central problems differ quite fundamentally. Much the same can be said with regard to the scope of variables brought to bear on common analytical problems: Doctrinally, the institutionalist range is wider than the Austrian; in practice, the gap is not nearly as large as one might think from an examination of doctrine or particular pieces of writing.

Second, there clearly is a difference(s) with regard to the respective attitudes of the two schools concerning capitalism. Austrian economists tend strongly to be pro-market and to be interested in constructing the best possible intellectual case for the market. (Some Austrian economists have been more open, neutral, and positive [rather than normative] than others, but they are the exception.) Austrian economists tend to identify the market in terms of the traditionally existing forms of capitalism. Institutional economists tend neither to limit their imagination of markets to traditional forms nor to be preoccupied with the defense of the market system. On the contrary, some institutionalists often are critical of the market and/or capitalism. Some are, or try to be, open, neutral, and positive in their analysis. Some are

concerned with the disjunctions and contradictions between the received images of the market and capitalism and the reality of extant
market, capitalist systems (for example, with regard to the concentration of power and industry domination of government), as well as
problems of market failure, so-called. Some desire different institu-
tionalizations of market capitalism, that is, a different power structure,
being less critical of the system per se than of its present institutional
and power structures. Austrians, accordingly, tend to see institutionalists as interventionists and egalitarian, and institutionalists tend to see
Austrians as principally interested in creating a system of rationalization which will finesse problems and issues deemed important by the
institutionalists and which will indirectly support the existing hierarchic structure of society. One reason why Austrian economists—notwithstanding their formal declarations about methodological individualism, subjectivism, and the logic of choice—also often elaborately
discuss problems of the organization and control, and evolution, of the
economic system, derives from their interest in the market as a system
of order. One reason why institutionalists analyze the working of markets and private choice is that at least some of them favor the market
but neither blindly nor fanatically. Another reason is that many appreciate the important roles of markets and private choice alongside other
institutions and forces.

Thirdly, the difference between the Austrian preoccupation with order as principally a spontaneous result of the market and the
institutionalist emphasis on nonmarket processes of securing order, legal foundations of the market, power play throughout the economy,
and analytical problems of differential weightings (as well as forma-
tions) of preferences, involves the fact that the two schools also disagree as to the necessity or utility of going beyond individual subjective
valuation and choice to structural considerations governing whose
preferences count. Institutionalists tend to follow longer causal or explanatory chains of reasoning, including the factors and forces governing the formation and weighting of individual subjective preferences. Another way of expressing part of this is that Austrian
economists tend to focus on choice within opportunity sets and institutional economists on the formation of opportunity sets and the preferences to which choice gives effect. Thus, institutionalists tend to pay
attention directly and explicitly to the formation, operation, and consequences of the property-power structure of society. Nonetheless, some

Austrian economists have devoted considerable positive as well as normative attention to these larger considerations of order going beyond the pure theory of choice and markets.

Fourth, whereas Austrian economists denigrate the meaningfulness and utility of macroeconomics, preferring to concentrate on the microeconomics of aggregative conceptions (money, inflation, unemployment), institutionalists, while not necessarily wedded to Keynesian or Post Keynesian analysis, tend to accept the field of macroeconomics as legitimate and, often at least, to consider important the variables stressed by macroeconomics, particularly by certain Post Keynesian varieties. Institutionalists accept the macroeconomic conceptions that aggregate income determination is an analytically separable problem (whatever its interdependence with resource allocation, individual choice, and power structure and whatever the problems of aggregating in subjective terms) and that analysis of aggregative forces can yield insights which are not, or not so readily, achieved through microeconomic analysis. Also, most institutionalists want no part of the conservative counterrevolution against Keynes and macroeconomics the leaders of which have included Austrian-school economists.

Fifth, whereas Austrian economists denigrate the state, institutional economists consider it fundamentally important to study the actual nature and operation of the state (government, legal system, politics) as a basic choice process inextricably intertwined with the operation of markets. Some institutionalists, of course, see the state as a positive institution for socioeconomic reform, in part because of their (more important) stress on the systematic importance of the state. (On a related point in common, see Part II.)

Sixth, the two schools have markedly different theories of value. The Austrians focus on subjective valuations of economic goods in markets. The institutionalists focus on the values ensconced in the working rules governing the organization and control of the economic system, the allocation of scarcity (or sacrifice), and the access to and use of power (rights) in the market. Once again, insofar as the Austrian is concerned with the market as a system of order, such values cannot be excluded. And institutionalists are not beyond analyzing market forces qua market forces insofar as they are interested in resource allocation, or, for example, the interaction of resource allocation, power structure, and so on.

Seventh, whereas Austrians stress the market as the allocative mechanism, institutionalists stress the institutions and power structure which form and operate through the market as the real allocative mechanism.

Eighth, Austrian and institutional economists clearly disagree as to what is value- or ideology-free and what is laden and resonant with ideology in each other's work.

Ninth, although the actual work of both schools is in fact a combination of deduction and induction (as well as paradigm articulation and development), Austrian economists emphasize a priori deductivism and institutional economists emphasize various versions of empiricism as well as the use of logic as such. Institutional economists may be more open formally to methodological diversity and certainly are generally pragmatists, but Austrian practice is more complex than their formal statements would lead one to believe (as is also true of the formal methodological pronouncements of some institutionalists). Still, institutionalists do not reject empirical falsification (although they see severe limits to it; see below) as do the Austrians; and institutionalists do not (as do the Austrians) consider economic laws deduced from certain axioms to be "apodictically" true. Actually, there are considerable differences within each school as to the status of quantitative, econometric, and formal mathematical work and the precise epistemological status of verification per se.

These are substantial differences, differences sufficiently important and often emotional enough to make one's blood boil. But it should be clear, too, that the attempt to articulate the differences involves very fine points in common. Certainly, at least, one should be wary of letting stylizing or aphoristic language obscure actual diversity and complexity. One can state the differences in such absolutist and exclusivist terms as to seem to suggest that the two can have nothing to do with each other. One also can state the differences in a meaningful manner more reflective of practice than doctrine, to permit sophisticated rather than vulgar appreciations of the differences to be seen. For differences there are, and they are both important and not to be overlooked.

II. COMMON CHARACTERISTICS AND ELEMENTS OF ANALYSIS

Three characteristics common to Austrian and institutional economics already have been noted: that each tends to define itself, in part, in terms of its contrast with neoclassical economics; that each is internally heterogeneous, so that there may be perceived several branches of Austrian and of institutional economics, each group with similarities and differences; and that tendencies toward both philosophical absolutism and relativism exist within each. Let me identify certain other common characteristics.

Members of both schools tend to have the belief or attitude that, vis-à-vis neoclassicism, they are outsiders within the economics discipline. There also is a touch of paranoia associated with this attitude.

Members of both schools have tended to devote much attention to establish and articulate their respective distinctive identities. To a large extent this has substituted for the possibly more creative work of applying and extending, rather than rehearsing with new twists, the received corpus of beliefs and knowledge. Perhaps as a consequence, both schools comprise more a paradigm than a fully detailed body of particular theories, although there are many of the latter in the work of each school.

There is some mutual suspicion, if not active or passive dislike, between the two schools, although there also are friendships as well as cordial, professional relations. In part, this is due to strong ideological differences and what amounts to a struggle for disciplinary space, or breathing room, and status. As a consequence, members of each school tend to read very little if any of the work of the other school, although there are evident exceptions to this. Both tend to be critical of each others' work when the work is not ignored.

Both schools are preoccupied (relative to neoclassicism) with methodological, philosophical (including epistemological), and political-economy issues and foundations.

Each has points which, if pressed, they will acknowledge, although the points do not have a central role or position in their definition of reality and may tend to weaken or compromise the thrust of certain points stressed in their work.

Each school's analysis tend to build in certain conclusions, by giving effect to certain premises, which relate to subject-matter actually worked out in the real world through processes much more complex and open than their respective doctrines or formal models seem to permit. I have in mind the Austrian emphases on methodological individualism and rational calculation and the Veblen-Ayresian institutionalist emphases on the technology-institutions dichotomy and the logic of industrialism. There are, perhaps inevitably, elements of extreme a priorism within institutionalism as well as Austrian economics.

Not only is there considerable heterogeneity within each school, and

therefore considerable dispute within each as to the substance and epistemological meaning and status of certain theories, ideas, and lines of
reasoning, there also is in each a spectrum of more to less extreme positions on particular points the consequences of which tend to be ignored or played down in order to maintain relative harmony within
each school. This tendency does not prevent serious tensions within
each school from reaching potentially divisive levels.

Subgroups within each school tend to manifest certain common atti-
tudinal characteristics: fanaticism; overt ideology; isolationism; arro-
gance; sectarianism; and so on, including the aforementioned philosophical absolutism. Within each there also is a tendency to seek and
emphasize a single principle. Each school, however, has numerous
eclectic and open-minded individuals, although the true believers—the
faithful adherent and advocate of a singular apodictic truth—tend to be
more conspicuous or noisy.

Finally, each school seems to have included twin lines of development: one emphasizing a single overarching principle; the other, a
more complex and open analysis. Apropos the latter tendency within
each, the Austrian case involves the juxtaposition of marginal utility
and power and the institutionalists, the juxtaposition of technology and
power. Thus the work of Austrian and institutional economists dealing
with power may have more directly in common than each has with certain other members of their respective schools. To some extent, subgroups within each school have emphasized the more characteristic of
each ones' twin line of development, with great singlemindedness and
closure of doctrine, tending to filter out the other of their twin line of
development ideologically dissatisfying, dysfunctional and/or deviant
and perhaps an embarrassment.

More interesting and certainly more important are the specific lines
of analysis and points of substantive emphasis shared by Austrian and
institutional economics.

Both schools are critical of the neoclassical preoccupation with equilibrium analysis. Equilibrium analysis, particularly the emphasis on
rigorously stated orders of equilibrium conditions, is criticized by both
for its neglect of the economic process, adjustment mechanisms, and
the substantive factors and forces which produce actual economic results in a real world in which equilibrium per se is a fiction. Institutional economists may be more wide ranging in their attention to adjustment processes than Austrian economists (see below) but both are
critical of the game-playing and puzzle-solving contrivances of
equilibrium-conditioned neoclassical economists.

More affirmatively, the two schools share a preoccupation with economic process. Both envision the economic world as an emergent, evolving process. They share an interest in if not an emphasis on the processes by which outcomes in the real world are produced rather than predicting specific outcomes or the identification of precise, technical stability conditions. They thus share an emphasis or focus on process which can be seen as independent of the particular manifestations and objects of study subsumed thereunder. Needless to say, the respective specifics of process analysis differ between the two schools. Further aspects of this will arise below in other connections, but clearly the Austrian economists concentrate on market resource allocation, the play of subjective preferences, and entrepreneurial exploitation of opportunities as the meat of economic process, whereas the institutional economists concentrate on systemic and institutional evolution, technology (industrialization), rights redetermination, dynamics of power structure, and the impact of other methodological collectivist variables as the principal core of economic process. Both, in effect, envision the market as a process interacting with other institutional complexes or processes in society, rather than a static set of arrangements, although in the particular work of both schools specific variables may be deemed parametric. The aforementioned criticism of equilibrium analysis is predicated largely on the belief that the most interesting and important knowledge to be had of the economic system concerns its modes of change and adjustment, therefore its nature as an ongoing process, rather than the technical conditions of an hypothetical stable equilibrium, however aesthetically pleasing and technically determinate the latter may be.

Closely related to the emphasis on process is a shared understanding that the truly important characteristic of the economy is human action. Both schools emphasize that human action is purposive and, perhaps especially, creative. Both are critical of the image of man which they perceive ingrained in neoclassical static analysis: the individual as a lifeless, passive reactor to external stimuli. Closely related to their common positions on methodological issues, for example, their belief that social science can be modelled after physical science only with much peril (see below), the two schools seem to share largely common attitudes with regard to radical indeterminacy, uncertainty, and the entrepreneur. Needless to say, the two schools differ as to the utility of a pure logic of choice, especially its centrality and reach, but on the necessity to focus on the sentient, reasoning, and deciding human economic actor there is great agreement.

Both schools appear to agree that the future is made by mankind through human action and choice. Accordingly, they seem to share emphases on futurity, uncertainty, unpredictability, and a radically indeterminate future. As a consequence, they are very sceptical of techniques of analysis which require determinate solutions (particularly, of course, those which constrain analysis to yield stability conditions). It is this shared orientation which perhaps most markedly distinguishes the practice of Austrian and institutional economists from that of most neoclassical economists, but even so the difference is largely one of degree. There seems to be a dual or dichotomous treatment of human action in mainstream neoclassical economics: the businessman therein is both passive, powerless responder to market signals and innovative entrepreneur. However, the real-world neoclassical economist appreciates process, human purpose and choice, and radical indeterminacy. The difference lies in the normal practices of neoclassical vis-à-vis Austrian and institutional economic science—and, of course, both of the latter have been known to seek "rigorous" determinate solutions as a mode of work.

The two schools also agree that in the existing Western economic system the critical agent of change is the entrepreneur. Both emphasize the opportunity-conscious nature of the entrepreneur and the output-enhancing consequences of successful innovation. The entrepreneur is economic organizer, the change agent, not a passive responder to market forces; market forces themselves are altered by the innovative, change-creating actions of such agents. The two schools differ, however, in several respects in this matter: The Austrian economists seem to identify with the businessman-entrepreneur and to treat them as hierarchically elevated or superior; whereas the institutional economists also locate entrepreneurial-type behavior among workers, identify with the hierarchically subordinated, and are critical of institutional arrangements which locate and legitimize change agency in one social subgroup.

A further common element involves subjectivism. The Austrian economists have clearly long emphasized radical subjectivism as one of their distinguishing doctrines the reach of which goes far beyond but does begin with marginal utility analysis and its conception of human action. What seems to be less well appreciated is the institutionalist emphasis on selective perception (influenced by cultural and institutional arrangements and forces). Both Austrian and institutional economists are interested in both "objective" conditions and subjective beliefs with regard thereto as well as preferences and goals. Each considers subjectivism necessary with regard to individual tastes and goals and behavior predicated upon selective perception and other subjective (and objective) bases of action and choice. Each considers the social construction of economic reality to be important and grounded in subjective factors and forces. Although some Veblen-Ayresian institutionalists reject subjectivism for the objectivism of technology, and all institutionalists are sceptical of going too far with utility analysis, both Austrian and institutional economists seem in principle (the institutionalist more so, perhaps, in practice) to be sceptical of analytical determinations of "rational" substantive decisions and results.

The latter scepticism seems to carry over to a common critique of benefit-cost analysis. The principal points of concern tend to be the subjective and positional nature of benefits and costs and thus their inaccessibility to the analyst except on the basis of question-begging presumptive assumptions. Interestingly, notwithstanding the more typical discussions of market efficiency and Pareto optimality, there is doubt among some Austrian economists about the extreme uses of both in economics, based on pretty much the same scepticism regarding benefit-cost analysis. Institutional economists have an even wider range of limits to impose on efficiency and Pareto optimality analysis and thus a wider sense of abuses. Institutionalism as a whole does not seem to be as ambivalent on these points as is Austrian economics.

Austrian and institutional economists also seem to agree that individual preferences count—at least in the sense that only individual preferences can count (whatever their genesis and institutional involvements) and that one can study the play of individual preference-based choices in the market. The institutionalist, of course, also insists—and most if not all Austrians seemingly would concur, if only privately— that individual preferences are at least in part a social product (the Austrian being uninterested in exploring their origins). Moreover, the institutionalist is not interested in trying to legitimize market weighting of preferences (something in which the Austrian economist is vitally interested, whereas some institutionalists would attempt to influence or participate directly in the preference-formation system through providing information, etc.). Moreover, whereas the Austrian economist rejects all notions of "social" maximization, the institutionalist emphasizes both the reality of collective decision-making processes and the ineluctable problem of determining *which* individual's preferences are to count rather than others, that is, the institutional arrangements or power structure which governs whose interests count. The studied inattention to preference formation by the Austrian economist largely has been matched by relative institutionalist neglect, after but not including Veblen, of the topic as a serious and extensive research program. Thus, while both schools emphasize learning with regard to subjective valuations, that is, the acquisition of knowledge governing human action, neither has systematically investigated the actual processes of learning, the Austrian perhaps on principle and the institutionalist through outright neglect.

A further principal common element among Austrian and institutional economists has been the nature of economic order as both a conceptual and practical problem. Although largely contrary to its sometimes narrowly doctrinaire formalization of methodological individualism, Austrian no less than institutional economics has explored the problem of the organization and control of the economic system, including the subsidiary problems of freedom (or autonomy) and control, continuity and change, hierarchy and equality, power structure, and, *inter alia*, the relations between deliberative and nondeliberative social control and human action. It should go without saying that very often the substantive analyses, or emphases and operative conclusions, of the two schools differ. But, if one approaches their respective substantive work without trying to emphasize normative or ideological differences (which surely exist), one finds much substantive agreement. (Nor do all Austrian and all institutional economists share, respectively, the same normative, policy, or ideological views.) Both Austrian and institutional economists have been interested in the complexities of the analysis of economic, social, and political power and institutions, the methodological individualism of the former notwithstanding. Much more so than neoclassical economists (or most of them), Austrian and institutional economists practice political economy, denoting their interest in fundamental systemic, order, power, and institutional considerations and the processes through which they evolve, as well as their desirable characteristics.

Accordingly, for example, writers in both schools examine the economy and human action in terms of both deliberative and nondeliberative decision making: rational calculation and the combination of passion, habit, and the influence of culture and circumstance. Writers in both schools acknowledge and analyze both deliberative and nondeliberative social control. Both include an element of rationalism: Austrians emphasize deliberative individual choice and institutionalists, deliberative social control; but neither denies the real world relevancy of the other. Writers in both schools seem to agree that institutional arrangements undergo gradual change, although the

Austrian emphasizes how little they are subject to deliberative control and the institutionalist emphasizes the possibilities thereof, however limited. Although Austrians seem to be collectively ambivalent (split?) on the relative importance of deliberate design versus spontaneous growth of institutions—a question not of central concern to most institutionalists—, writers in both schools wrestle with the eternal problem of the need to subject spontaneous, organic institutions to deliberative critique and change. Accordingly, it is no accident that for positive (as well as for their respective unique normative) reasons, Austrian and institutional economists have focused—despite their typical ideological differences—on the analysis of the processes, fundamentals, origins, and consequences of legal change. In that regard, however, whereas the institutionalist emphasizes the importance of the legal bases of economic organization, structure, and performance, the Austrian minimizes the economic role of government, although their continual attention to its "proper" role and size seems to acknowledge their comprehension of its importance (also see below).

Accordingly, too, both Austrian and institutional economists, notwithstanding interests and doctrinal formulations seemingly to the contrary, also have focused on the analysis of institutions. Both seem to stress the critical role of institutions, the necessity for theories of institutional change and adjustment, and the essential, as it were, nature of institutions as superindividual schemes or habits of thought. Needless to say, differences have emerged based on ideological predispositions and varying conceptualizations of the market and of the "role" of institutions. But, again, one disinterested in ideological, policy, and normative differences can find much common analysis once the results thereof are factored out.

Another element common to both schools of thought, although discussed typically in quite different language and, of course, with considerable substantive differences, is an emphasis on coordination. Although the Austrian school emphasizes the market as the premier coordinating institution, both emphasize the role of the entrepreneur, and the institutional school (along with some Austrian economists) stress the role of (market and nonmarket) institutions generally as well as power structure. Just as a supplementary relationship between Austrian and institutional economics can be identified in terms of one's analysis of choice and opportunity costs within given opportunity sets and the other's analysis of power in the formation of opportunity-set structures, supplementariness also can be identified in terms of the Austrian view that market forces generate institutions and institutional change and the institutionalist view that institutions, form, shape, and operate through the market—in each case resulting in a larger general interdependence analysis and understanding than is normally or doctrinally central to either school. All institutions, including the market, involve individual adjustment to the actions of others, that is, the process of the simultaneous enhancement and limitation of individual freedom of action and choice in a world of scarcity of power and resources. That Austrians emphasize market determination of resource allocation and institutionalists, the institutional and power structure forming and operating through markets, should not obscure the attention each thereby gives to organization and control, coordination, and related topics and problems. The market economy looks different depending upon which coordination process one stresses (and therein lies the political, or policy, coefficient of each approach) but the understanding and explanation of how markets work (and other topics) are vastly improved by studying all relevant coordination processes.

The next common element undoubtedly will be even more surprising than some of the foregoing. It is clear that Austrian economists identify with the canons of laissez faire, minimal government, and nonintervention. It also is clear that institutional economists often are interventionist. It is further clear that most if not all Austrian economists and many if not all institutional economists share a scepticism regarding the meaningfulness of policy recommendations based upon narrow analytical tools and presumptive reasoning. What has not been so clear, however, but I think no less important, is that both schools share the policy activism of the so-called social engineer. Both are activist in prescribing either specific policies, policy rules or formulas, or constitutional-type rules. Each is activist in attempting to restructure and/or redirect society and economy as they find and perceive same in the actual world, each in their own direction. Representatives of each are involved heavily and widely, albeit with great differences within each school and especially between the two schools, in efforts to deliberatively reshape the economy. For all the Austrian economists' emphasis on subjectivism and the action of individual economic participants and antagonism to social maximization, intervention, and social engineering, they are typically ready and willing to pass judgment on existing institutional and policy arrangements and thereby to be presumptive with regard to matters which, by their doctrines and in the real world, are worked out through the interaction of economic and political actors. Institutional economists have fewer inhibitions in these matters, although some are wary of overcommitment to this or that "solution." In other words and speaking generally, notwithstanding Austrian disdain for government action and institutionalist tendencies to identify the institution of government with forces of reaction or of reform, each Austrian and institutionalist tends to have his/her own activist agenda for the state, the one ready to rationalize the agenda in terms of giving greater vent to the market, the other, in terms of permitting technological or normative imperatives to come to fruition, but each, for all practical purposes, willing to use government to pursue selectively perceived purposes and criteria. That one wants to abet the forces of the market and the other, the forces of technology, does not preclude the objective analyst from seeing two different agendas for government, not laissez faire versus interventionism.

Finally, although, as is well known, there are significant differences regarding methodology, or epistemology, there also are significant points shared by Austrian and institutional economists. Both schools stress that there are fundamental differences between physical and social sciences and therefore in the techniques properly applicable to each. Both share a concern over scientism, the improper use of science in working out solutions to social problems. Both emphasize general explanation and understanding vis-à-vis detailed prediction, in part due to the nature of the problems dealt with in economics, the level of analytical abstraction generic to the tools of analysis, and their conception of the economic process (and therefore of economic science). Both are sceptical with regard to the exaggerated claims often made for empirical verification as actually practiced in economics and to the specificity of both explanation and prediction possible in economics. Both are critical of the pretenses of great precision frequently found in neoclassical work. Neither is unalterably opposed to econometrics or applied econometrics but, for reasons given above, both are sceptical of the preoccupation with such work within the confines of the neoclassical market paradigm. Both schools are concerned about the disciplinary neglect of problems not immediately if ever suitable to quantitative analysis. Some of the reasons for these concerns and scepticism are given above in connection with other common elements. Overall, institutional economists likely are more amenable to econometric work than the Austrian, who often oppose such work on the basis of the noncomparability and therefore nonaddibility of subjective experiences, but both are doubtful, for example, of the wisdom of ignoring or finessing conceptual and practical limits to measurement, such as in the identification and measurement of capital stock. As for their differences, for example, Austrians are critical of the pragmatism, eclecticism, and behaviorism often found in institutionalist work (some institutionalists do not like eclecticism either); and institutionalists are critical of the Austrian practices of extreme a priorism and drawing conclusions as ostensibly a matter solely of logic, as preventing the posing of critical questions regarding the precise substance of general concepts, such as liberty and property, especially in areas of obvious conflicts among liberties and among property rights. Finally, it is obvious that Austrians are strongly deductivist and institutionalists strongly empirical (although not necessarily quantitative empiricists). But, to one who sees all disciplinary work as inevitably varying combinations of deduction and induction, this difference (as well as others) may appear somewhat superficial and misleading and certainly should not obscure relevant points in common.

III. CONCLUSION

I want to note that considerations of design, space, readability, and ignorance prevent me from indicating every possible or necessary qualification appropriate to every topic discussed above. Nor have I tried to mold the foregoing discussion to the views of any particular Austrian or institutional economist. I have tried to minimize reiteration of qualifying considerations otherwise appropriate to both topics and individuals. I also have stressed certain differences in order to sharpen the focus on the precise nature and limits of agreements. As an institutionalist I neither fully agree with all institutionalist work nor fully disagree with all Austrian work. Rather than solely represent my own views (which, of course, nonetheless inescapably govern my perceptions and judgments), I have tried to represent typical Austrian and institutionalist positions.

It is very important to recognize that both schools are heterogeneous. The Menger-Wieser attention to considerations of power, independent of the creation and refinement of the case for the market and of the analysis of the logic of choice, is one historical bridge between the two schools. Institutionalists differ with regard to the technology-institutions dichotomy and the feasibility and desirability of strengthening a competitive market *vis-à-vis* economic planning. Thus, heterogeneity leads to interests in common between schools which, in the case of particular individuals, may temporarily transcend conflicts within each school.

I think that members of each school have much to learn from each other—insofar as practitioners from each school are interested in learning how the economy operates rather than revelling in ideological and political roles.

There also is much to learn about the practice of high priest and social engineering by those interested in the sociology of economics as a professional discipline, the development of economics, and deep issues of societal evolution.

Some or much work in both schools constitutes largely reiteration, with marginal variations and novel product differentiation, of already established ideas. Too little work in each school is truly new.

Both schools, after almost a century of existence, continue to seek their respective identities. It may be a surprise to many that their identities have a good bit in common. Showing that does not prove their more-or-less joint case against the perceived limits and/or excesses of neoclassicism, but it is interesting to the idly curious and may be informative with regard to the processes of development of the history of economics.

ACKNOWLEDGMENTS

The author is indebted to Richard Gonce and Abraham Hirsch for suggestions.

REFERENCES

Farnum, Henry W., (1908) "Deutsch-amerikanische Beziehungen in der Volkswirtschaftslehre," in *Die Entwicklung der deutschen Volkswirtschaftslehre im 19. Jahrhundert, Festschrift fur Gustav Schmoller*, Leipzig, Vol. I, pp. 25–29.

Herbst, Jurgen, (1965) *The German Historical School in American Scholarship.* Ithaca: Cornell University Press.

Lachmann, Ludwig M., (1976) "Austrian Economics in the Age of the Neo-Ricardian Counterrevolution," in Edwin G. Dolan, ed., *The Foundations of Modern Austrian Economics.* Kansas City: Sheed and Ward.

McKenzie, Richard B., (1980) "The Neoclassicists vs. the Austrians: A Partial Reconciliation of Competing Worldviews," *Southern Economic Journal*, July, *47*, 1–13.

Samuels, Warren J., (1974) "The History of Economic Thought as Intellectual History," *History of Political Economy*, Fall, *6*, 305–323.

Weber, W., and E. Streissler, (1973) "The Menger Tradition," In J. R. Hicks and W. Weber, eds., *Carl Menger and the Austrian School of Economics.* Oxford: Oxford University Press.

EVOLUTION AND ECONOMICS:
AUSTRIANS AS INSTITUTIONALISTS

Peter J. Boettke

I. INTRODUCTION

In 1898 Thorstein Veblen asked; "Why is Economics Not an Evolutionary Science?" Veblen raised a pertinent and interesting question, but to what extent has his methodological plea been recognized by the profession? Though there has been a chain of economists since Veblen who have accepted the label "institutional" or "evolutionary," this paper will argue that the "Austrian" School, which is usually viewed as the antithesis of Institutional Economics, has in actuality consistently applied an evolutionary perspective in their analysis. Although the evolutionary perspective in the Austrian tradition can be traced back to Carl Menger, it can be said to have reached its most advanced level of articulation in the work of F. A. Hayek. The main purpose of this paper is to show a certain methodological common ground be-

Research in the History of Economic Thought and Methodology,
Volume 6, pages 73-89
Copyright © 1989 by JAI Press Inc.
All rights of reproduction in any form reserved.
ISBN: 0-89232-928-9

tween Veblen and the modern Austrians and to demonstrate that the
Austrian criticisms of neoclassical economics are firmly grounded in a
Veblenian appreciation of institutional and historical factors in eco-
nomics.

It is the claim of many economists that the early institutionalists
were anti-theoretical, and thus the school had no coherent doctrine. It
is often asserted that Veblen and his followers offered only ad hoc explanations of historical economic phenomena. For example, consider
the often quoted comment by Lionel Robbins that; "The only difference between Institutionalism and Historismus [Historicism] is that
Historismus is more interesting" (1952, 83). However, it will be one
of the tasks of this paper to demonstrate that much can be learned from
an inquiry into the work of institutionalists, particularly the methodological writings of Veblen.

II.   INSTITUTIONAL CHANGE
AND ECONOMIC PROCESSES

How do we define an institutional economist? It would be misleading
to suggest that he is simply one who pays attention to institutions in his
analysis of economic phenomena. C. E. Ayres in fact reacted strongly
against such an interpretation:

> As a designation of a way of thinking in economics the term "institutionalism"
> is singularly unfortunate, since it points only at that from which an escape is
> being sought. Properly speaking, it is the classical tradition that is "institution-
> alism," since it is a way of thinking which expresses a certain set of institutions
> (1962, 155–156, fn. 1).

Institutional economics is distinctive not because of the focus on institutions per se, but rather because of the insistent theme of change in the
economic process. Wendell Gordon, in his Presidential address to the
Association for Evolutionary Economics, expressed this position as
follows:

> I believe that economics should be oriented primarily to the study of the process
> of change rather than to the study of processes intended to produce equilibrium
> and maximization. . . And I believe that economics should not just assume the
> validity of the prevailing value judgments, but should concern itself with the
> process by which both individuals and institutions acquire and modify their
> values. These propositions represent basic institutionalism (1984, 369).

This recognition of and emphasis upon the concept of change is a distinctive characteristic of Institutional economics. As David Hamilton put it in his book, *Evolutionary Economics: A Study of Change in Economic Theory*:

> The institutionalist, . . . considers change to be a part of the economic process. Instead of viewing the economy as a fixed system periodically prodded into movement to a new point of non-motion, he holds that the economy is at all times undergoing a process of cumulative change, and that the study of economics is the study of process (1973, 17).

Austrians share this emphasis on change and process in economic analysis. Hayek has stated that "economic problems arise always and only in consequence of change" (1980, 82). Furthermore, he maintains "that the complex spontaneously formed structures with which social theory has to deal, can be understood only as the result of a process of evolution and that, therefore, here 'the genetic element is inseparable from the idea of theoretical sciences' " (Hayek 1973, 24).

Thus, Hayek, views the world as continually changing and, therefore, realizes that institutions are forever evolving. The role of economics as a theoretical science is seen to be primarily to understand the evolved institutions in contemporary society, to rationally diagnose their failings, and to offer positive suggestions for their revision.

III. EVOLUTION, INDIVIDUALISM AND SOCIAL ORDER

From this perspective, Hayek has tried to understand the evolution of institutions, such as the market, law and rules of conduct. He has suggested that these institutions evolve spontaneously as individuals interact. They are the result of "human action, not of human design" (Hayek 1967, 96–105). The resulting order is, "of course, not the result of a miracle or some harmony of interests. It forms itself, because in the course of millennia men develop rules of conduct which lead to the formation of such an order out of the separate spontaneous activities of individuals" (Hayek 1978, 10). Therefore, beginning with this recognition of the spontaneous ordering of activity in social interactions, Hayek, and Austrian economists in general, seek to understand the ongoing evolutionary processes in which institutions change.

Beginning with this evolutionary perspective, Hayek's approach is similar to that proposed by Thorstein Veblen. Veblen called for economics to be an evolutionary science. He said it must be a "theory of process, of an unfolding sequence" (1919, 58). Veblen later asserted:

> [A]n evolutionary economics must be a theory of a process of cultural growth as determined by the economic interest, a theory of cumulative sequence of economic institutions stated in terms of the process itself (1919, 77).

What determines an evolutionary economics? It is the inclusion of the changing human agent. He is the driving force in economic action, and his actions must be the subject matter of the science if the science is to be considered evolutionary. Veblen stated this concisely:

> It is in the human material that the continuity of development is to be looked for; and it is here, therefore, that the motor forces of the process of economic development must be studied if they are to be studied in action at all. Economic action must be the subject-matter of the science if the science is to fall into line as an evolutionary science (1919, 72).

This emphasis of Veblen's on economic action is quite similar to the Austrian suggestion that economics is a praxeological science. It might be thought that Austrians and institutionalists are diametric opposites, the former insisting like neoclassicism on methodological individualism, the latter insisting as vigorously on holism, i. e., the focus on social wholes instead of isolated individuals. However, Austrians would support Ayre's statements that, "All economic behavior is equally social in character. No economic act or function is uniquely physical (let alone spiritual) or uniquely determinative of all the rest— not motives or consumption or anything else" (1962, 95).

The Austrian's methodological individualism is not that of the standard neoclassical micro text. Rather, it is characterized by radical subjectivism. Austrians do not deny that acculturation determines much of the individuals preferences.[1] As Rothbard has said; "To say that only individuals act is not to deny that they are influenced in their desires and actions by the acts of other individuals, who might be fellow members of various societies or groups. We do not at all assume, . . . that individuals are 'atoms' isolated from one another" (Rothbard 1970, 435, fn. 6).

The atomistic view of man can be labelled "naive" individualism. Similarly, a position that considers social wholes as given without attempting to trace them to their connection to individuals choices and values represents "naive" holism. In between these two polar positions we find the positions of "sophisticated" individualism and holism. These positions are rather close to one another and it is here where we find the commonality between Veblen and the Austrians.[2]

The "sophisticated" individualist or holist focuses on the individual economic actor because it is at the level of the individual that meaning can be attached to human action. From this understanding of human action the theorist is able to understand and thus explain the origin and evolution of institutions, such as the market, law and the rules of conduct (see Lachmann 1971). "Methodological individualism, far from contesting the significance of such collective wholes, considers it as one of its main tasks to describe and to analyze their becoming and their disappearing, their changing structures, and their operation" (Mises 1966, 42).

The study of evolving institutions is recognized as extremely important to understanding the processes of social interaction. In order to really see what is going on the economist must focus attention on the relationship between the individual human agent and economic institutions. As Warren Samuels has noted, from this perspective the theorist in the Austrian tradition envisions "the economic world as an emergent, evolving process" (1989).

IV. VALUE, CHOICE AND ECONOMIC INTERACTION

Veblen recognized the unique contribution of the early Austrian economists in this regard. "The entire discussion of marginal utility and subjective value as the outcome of a valuation process," he says, "must be taken as a genetic study of this range of facts" (1919, 73). Although Veblen criticized the Austrians "faulty conception of human nature," which he took to be hedonistic, this was a misinterpretation (see Jaffe 1976, 521, cf. 79–80 below). Furthermore, much has changed in the Austrian tradition since Veblen wrote.[3] Mises, in fact, attacked both Menger and Bohm-Bawerk for not understanding the full implications derived from the subjective theory of value. "The problem arises," Mises argues, "not so much from imperfections of theory, . . . as from stylistic faults in the presentation of it, which do not detract from the thought, but only from the writings in which it was expounded" (1981b, 167). Therefore, Mises reformulated the presentation of value theory with the consistent application of subjectivism in mind (see Mises 1980, 51–62).

Institutionalists and Austrians agree that because we live in a world of uncertainty and imperfect knowledge, the economic process cannot be explained by static equilibrium models.[4] The economic process is dynamic. It is initiated as a result of the original errors of its participants. The process consists of systematic plan changes generated by the information that flows from market activity. "The market process emerges as the necessary implications of the circumstances that people act, and that in their actions they err, discover their errors, and tend to revise their actions in a direction likely to be less erroneous than before" (Kirzner 1979, 30). Signals such as prices, profits, and interest rates are seen as vital coordinating factors. Therefore, if the economist wants to understand the complex phenomena of social interaction, he should be critically concerned with identifying the institutional factors which promote or disrupt the signaling process.[5]

Hayek completely agrees with institutionalists that, as Stanfield put it, "the central question of institutional or social economics" is; "how is the economy instituted in society and what are the implications of alternative institutional arrangements?" (1983, 604). Hayek also studies the evolving processes in the market, and the institutional arrangements affecting these processes. The goal of much of his work has been to discover the institutional environment that facilitates the spread of information for the greatest possible plan coordination. However, he is always mindful that perfect coordination is never attainable. This is where he is in fundamental disagreement with neoclassicism, which insists that economic analysis concentrate on end or equilibrium states.

> The statement that, if people knew everything, they are in equilibrium is true simply because that is how we define equilibrium. The assumption of a perfect market in this sense is just another way of saying that equilibrium exists but does not get us any nearer an explanation of when and how such a state will come about. It is clear that, if we want to make the assertion that, under certain conditions, people will approach that state, we must explain by what process they will acquire the necessary knowledge (Hayek 1980, 46).[6]

To take the relevant bits of information as given is to beg the question of how knowledge is dispersed in the economic process. In effect neoclassicists fall "back on the assumption that everybody knows everything and so evade any real solution of the problem" (Hayek 1980, 51). If we want to render the evolutionary process intelligible in terms of human action, we must go beyond these models which assume away the very possibilities of change. Hayek is, in this respect, proposing a distinctively Veblenian methodology.

The Austrian opposition to static equilibrium theorizing can be traced to the founding of the school by Carl Menger. Max Alter (1982, 149–160) pointed out that although neoclassical economics is often traced back to Jevons, Walras, and Menger, there are important differences among these three. Menger, unlike either Jevons or Walras, emphasized the role of time in analyzing processes of change. As Menger stated:

> The idea of causality, . . . is inseparable from the idea of time. A process of change involves a beginning and a becoming, and these are only conceivable as processes in time. Hence it is certain that we can never fully understand the causal interconnections of the various occurences in a process, or the process itself, unless we view it in time and apply the measure of time to it (1981, 67).

Menger held, as Alter showed, that "[n]ot metrication or measurement but understanding of the essence of economic phenomena is the task of exact theory" (1982, 157).

However, when Alter attempts to explain the differences that arise between Menger and neoclassicals because of the role of time, he fails to articulate the distinction with regard to value theory. Instead, Alter emphasizes that Menger and neoclassical economists are in agreement, both stressing "[s]tatic human nature, methodological individualism (or its related concept, an atomistic view of society and social processes), and law-like behavior" (1982, 155). Alter continues by claiming that "[i]t is immediately obvious that both claim universal validity for the theory that threats individuals as optimizers; both let individuals maximize utility under the restriction of their income; the individuals display constant tastes and have a rational preference structure defined over the space of available commodities" (1982, 157).

However, in a recent response to Alter's article, A. M. Endres asserts that "Alter does not argue convincingly that Menger is preoccupied with the assumption of 'constant tastes' consonant with the standard neoclassical postulate" (1984, 898). Rather, Endres states that "[i]n examining Menger's theory of consumer behavior it becomes clear that Menger wishes to work with an assumption about consumer tastes akin to that used by U. S. Institutionalists at a latter stage in the history of economic thought" (1984, 898).

Furthermore, William Jaffe has suggested that not only is Menger's economics disequilibrium economics, but it is also in a sense social or institutional economics. Jaffe even suggests that Veblen's accusation of hedonism fits Jevons and Walras much more that it does Menger. To Menger, man is not the "lightning calculator," but rather "is a bumbling, erring, ill-informed, creature, plagued with uncertainty, forever hovering between alluring hopes and haunting fears, and cogenitally incapable of making finely calibrated decisions in pursuit of satisfaction'' (Jaffe 1976, 521).

In addition to emphasing the role of time and man's inherent fallability in the economic process, Menger also placed particular emphasis on the unintended consequences in social interaction. He held that ''the exact orientation of research'' was ''to explain the origin and functions of the unified structures [social institutions] . . . to explain how these 'real unities' have come about and how they function'' (Menger 1963, 143). He considered the following ''perhaps the most noteworthy problem of the social sciences: How can it be that institutions which serve the common welfare and are extremely significant for its development come into being without a common will directed toward establishing them?'' (1963, 146). Menger provides as empirical examples of the unintended consequences of social developments such institutions as law, language, the state, money and markets. Such importance does Menger place on the unintended evolution of such social institutions that he claims:

> The solution of the most important problems of the theoretical social sciences in general and of theoretical economics in particular is thus closely connected with the question of theoretically understanding the origin and change of ''organically'' created social structures (1963, 147).

However, we should be careful not to conclude that this renders Menger in a position of naive conservativism. Rather, Menger is ''particularly concerned that the organic view should not be interpreted to mean that rules which have developed in an undesigned manner should necessarily be regarded as superior to made or contrived law'' (Barry 1982, 33). Menger states explicitly that:

> The theory of ''higher wisdom'' of common law thus not only contradicts experience but is at the same time rooted in a vague feeling, in a misunderstanding. It is an exaggeration, carried to the point of distortion, of the true statement that positive legislation has upon occasion not comprehended the unintended wisdom in common law, and, in trying to change the latter in the sense of the common good, has not infrequently produced the opposite result (1963, 233).[7]

This emphasis on the evolution of institutions, in addition to the Mengerian emphasis on time and ignorance in economic theory, provides the foundation for later Austrians to develop their process-oriented institutionalism.

V.   PROCESS ORIENTED INSTITUTIONALISM

Hayek has severly criticized neoclassical economics from a institutionalist perspective, attacking in particular the assumptions of the perfectly competitive model (1980, 95). Hayek stresses the rivalrous aspects of competition: the attempt to gain what another is attempting to gain at the same time (1980, 96). This leads him to conclude that:

> Competition is essentially a process of formation of opinion: by spreading information, it creates that unity and coherence of the economic system which we presuppose when we think of it as one market. It creates the views people have about what is best and cheapest, and it is because of it that people know at least as much about possibilities and opportunities as they in fact do. It is thus a process which involves a continuous change in the data and whose significance must therefore be completely missed by any theory which treats these data as constants (1980, 106).

J. M. Clark, who has expressed sympathy with Veblenian institutionalism (see 1932, 105–106), was dissatisfied with the perfect competition model for reasons similar to Hayek's. His dissatisfaction stemmed from the "realization that 'perfect competition' does not and cannot exist (Clark 1940, 241). Furthermore, Clark sought to develop a definition of competition that stressed the rivalrous and thus dynamic elements of real world competitive interaction (1940, 243).

Ayres has also expressed his distain for the dynamic—static split in economic science. "Contemporary economists," he states, "maintain that the distinction is only an analytical device, but it is certainly more than that." He continues by arguing that if economist define one state "as the realm in which change is occuring and the other as a 'stationary state,' it is at once apparent that change is regarded as something of a nuisance and as an essentially transitory condition" (1962, 103).

This frustration with static theories is a common ground for evolutionary economists, Austrians and Institutionalists alike. J. R. Commons took the articulation of the economic process as the fundamental task of the economist:

> We take it that a process is more accurately described when verbs are substituted for nouns. Nouns are likely to be misleading because they give the impression of static quantities, but verbal nouns are fitted to the bargaining transactions which are none other that the process of pricing, valuing, and debting, which create, transfer, extinguish and recreate both economic quantities and the money which measures them as values. The price, the value, the debt, are each

jointly determined, if not literally created, at the point of time when the agreement transfers the ownership of the economic quantity thus agreed upon, and all
the variabilities, taken together in the sequence of time, are a process of pricing,
valuing, and debting by means of transaction (1934, 514).

A distinctive characteristic of Austrian evolutionary economics is
that it stresses the dispersion of knowledge throughout society. It is not
a theory of economic equilibrium, rather it is a theory of economic action and interaction. "The Austrian School endeavors to explain prices
that are really paid in the market, and not just prices that would be paid
under certain, never realizable conditions" (Mises 1978, 36).[8]

VI.   A THEORY OF ECONOMIC CHANGE

This emphasis on the evolutionary aspect of the economic process has
attracted accusations that institutionalists are unsystematic and anti-
theoretical in their analysis. However, Thomas Sowell (1967) has defended Veblen against charges of possessing an anti-theoretical bias.
Veblen clearly demonstrated a high appreciation of the value of theory
(Sowell 1967, 190). He did not criticize economics for not being an
evolutionary science on the grounds that economics could not control
experimentation, as can be accomplished in the natural sciences.
Rather, his criticism dealt specifically with the method employed in the
analysis of traditional economics. In addition, Veblen did not consider
data collection or "realism" to be the distinctive character in an evolutionary science. Consider Veblen's critique of the German Historical
School:

> The insistence on data could scarcely be carried to a higher pitch than it was
> carried by the first generation of the Historical School; and yet no economics is
> farther from being an evolutionary science than the received economics of the
> Historical School. The whole broad range of erudition and research that en-
> gaged the energies of that school commonly falls short of being science, in that,
> when consistent, they have contented themselves with an enumeration of data
> and a narrative account of industrial development, and have not presumed to
> offer a theory of anything or to elaborate their results into a consistent body of
> knowledge (1919, 58).

For Veblen an "evolutionary science" must be "a close-knit body of
theory. It is a theory of a process, of an unfolding sequence" (1919,
58).
    A. W. Coats (1954), though recognizing Veblen's great influence

blames Veblen for what he considers the failure of the institutionalists to develop a progressive research program. Coats concludes that "Veblen's methodological program was vague and incomplete, amounting to scarcely more than a few general indications of the direction in which he wished to proceed; and in consequence his admirers adopted widely differing interpretations of its nature and importance" (1954, 536).

However, this assessment is questionable. The Veblenian methodology, i.e., the call for economics to be an evolutionary science must be recognized as pointing in the right direction. The problems arise when Veblen himself moved away from his own methodological plea that concentrated on the "human factor" as the "motor force of the process of economic development" (1919, 71–72). Veblen abandoned this position of "sophisticated" holism, where he studied the economic life process as a cumulative change generated by the human agent, and instead, attracted by the early promise of behavioristic psychology, adopted a position of "naive" holism.[9] This rendered him unable to provide a "scientific explanation of the nature of change, producing instead a genetic (historical) account of how changes had, in fact taken place" (Coats 1954, 534).

VII. CONCLUSION

Others have pointed out the parallels between Veblen and the Austrians. For instance, David Seckler has stated:

> [A]t roughly the same time as Veblen was labouring to create a behavioristic solution to certain cardinal questions of social philosophy, [C]arl Menger was labouring to create an essentially humanistic solution to these same questions. Thus, by following out the Menger tradition of radical individualism, one can obtain a better grasp of what Veblen himself—in his humanistic inclinations— was trying to achieve. Veblen was driven to behaviorism because he felt that humanism could not adequately address certain cardinal questions of social philosophy. Menger and his followers tried to solve these same questions, within the context of humanism (1974, 9).

Austrian economists continue to work within this humanistic perspective. The theoretical framework they employ in their analysis of social interaction stresses time and ignorance.[10] The market is seen as a "telecommunication system" which generates information for plan coordination among separate individual actors. Following the

Hayekian plea that the evolutionary paradigm be a "new beginning" (1981, 176) Austrians are continuing to develop their research program.

In concluding I would like to suggest that Austrians and institutionalists have failed to communicate with one another in the past, though both schools could benefit greatly from such interaction. This failure has produced a situation where inr*itutionalists do not recognize the Austrians' evolutionary institutionalism, while at the same time the Austrian remains blind to the institutionalists' process perspective. Both schools have been able to dismiss one another's arguments without proper confrontation and, in particular, both have missed the opportunity of benefiting from an intellectual ally in their fight against the ahistorical economics of the mainstream.

ACKNOWLEDGMENTS

I would like to express my appreciation to Tyler Cowen, Jack High, Don Lavoie, Dave Prychitko, Viktor Vanberg, and the participants of the Austrian Colloquim at the Center for the Study of Market Processes, George Mason University for their instructive comments. Responsibility for any existing errors is solely my own.

NOTES

1. However, Hayek has emphasized that "the knowledge of the particular circumstances of time and place" (1980, p. 80) produces an inherent subjectivism in our knowledge. Kenneth Boulding has also stressed the importance of the role of knowledge and learning to understanding the economic process in any theory of evolutionary change. Furthermore, Boulding emphasizes the subjective element in knowledge:

> In my book, *The Image*, I have sketched what might be called an epistemological theory of behavior, pointing out that a decision is always a choice among alternative perceived images of the future. The study of decision, therefore, must concentrate on how these images of the future are derived from the information inputs of the past, as this is the only place from which they can come. That is, we have to think of our images of the future as essentially learned out of inputs from the past, and the nature of this learning process is therefore of overwhelming importance. Similarly, the utility or welfare function, which we impose over these images of the future, is likewise learned, though economists have been surprisingly unwilling to recognize this fact, perhaps because it was Veblen, who argued most convincingly, to my mind, that if we wanted to have a dynamic economics, we could not simply take preferences for granted but had to regard them as essentially learned (1966, p. 7).

Also see the work of Hayek (1967, pp. 313–317), Polanyi (1962), Shackle (1972) and Lachmann (1977) on the role of knowledge and expectations in the social process.

2.   I would like to acknowledge Don Lavoie for pointing out this distinction between "naive" and "sophisticated" individualism and holism.

3.   The earlier Austrians, Menger, Bohm-Bawerk and Wieser are accused by Veblen of being hedonistic. However, Mises building on these writers, developed a theory of praxeology, i.e., human action, in which all such hedonistic implications are eliminated. Mises asserted that man acts purposefully to eliminate uneasiness. Man acts not just to pursue happiness or material wealth, but rather to improve his state of affairs from his own point of view. Because man does not have the power to render his condition fully satisfactory, he acts to render it less unsatisfactory (Mises 1966, pp. 11–29).

4.   This claim has also been made by Shackle (1972). Also see Lachmann (1976) and (1977).

5.   See Hayek's essay "The Use of Knowledge in Society," in Hayek (1980); see also Sowell (1980) and Fink (1982).

6.   To the Austrian the equilibrium condition is nothing more than an imaginary construction. Mises states of the equilibrium concept that; "Such a rigid system is not peopled with living men making choices and liable to error; it is a world of soulless unthinking automatons; it is not a human society, it is an ant hill" (1966, p. 248). The Austrian is not concerned with the maximizing activity on the ant hill, rather his concentration is on real human action subject to error and uncertainty. "Economics is not about goods and services," states Mises, "it is about the actions of living men. Its goal is not to dwell upon imaginary constructions such as equilibrium. . . . The sole task of economics is analysis of the actions of men, is the analysis of processes" (1966, p. 357). Thus, Austrian economics does not conceive of the economy as an end state which is prodded periodically into movement. Rather, the emphasis is on action and action implies change and change only occurs in a temporal process.

7.   Hayek should also be defended from being interpreted as a naive conservative, and in fact it could be argued that Hayek is a radical.

> The proper conclusion from the considerations I have advanced is by no means that we may confidently accept all the old and traditional values. Nor even that there are any values or moral principles, which science may not occasionally question. The social scientist who endeavors to understand how society functions, and to discover where it can be improved, must claim the right critically to examine, and even to judge, every single value of our society (1978, p. 19).

8.   The emphasis on process-generated information and the dispersion of knowledge throughout the market helps explain more clearly the Austrian position on the calculation problem. All that information could not be known by one individual or group of individuals. The market generates information for plan coordination only within the process itself.

It is interesting to note that the calculation debate of the 1920s and 1930s is rarely if ever mentioned in the institutionalist literature. The impression may be that Oskar Lange answered Mises and Hayek, but to take that position would be to side with neoclassicism against institutionalism. In Lange's famous essay (1964, pp. 61–62) he accused Mises of being an institutionalist. Because of Mises's recognition of the

86   PETER J. BOETTKE

significance of institutional and historical factors in economics, Lange asserted that
Mises's argument must be rejected. Lange's answer does not consider these factors,
therefore, institutionalist are in a precarious position if they rely on Lange's critique of
the Mises/Hayek position on the centrally planned economy. For a further discussion
on the debate see Lavoie (1985).

   9. Veblen, in fact, received his first exposure to economics from J. B. Clark at
Carleton College and then later studied under William Graham Sumner at Yale. Sumner, along with Herbert Spencer, was a leading advocate of an evolutionary approach
to the social process. Some modern Austrians find that a reading of Spencer and Sumner produces important insights in the theory of evolutionary processes in social
change. Seckler (1974) suggests that Veblen was greatly influenced by these writers
when he first sketched an outline for an evolutionary economics.

   10. See O'Driscoll and Rizzo (1985).

REFERENCES

Alter, Max., (1982) "Carl Menger and Homo Oeconomicus: Some Thoughts on Aus-
    trian Theory and Methodology," *Journal of Economic Issues*, March, Vol. 16,
    No. 1, pp. 149–60.
Ayres, C. E., (1962) *The Theory of Economic Progress*, New York: Shocken Books.
Barry, Norman., (1982) "The Tradition of Spontaneous Order," *Literature of Lib-
    erty*, Summer, Vol. 5, No. 2, pp. 7–58.
Boulding, Kenneth., (1966) "The Economics of Knowledge and the Knowledge of
    Economics," *American Economic Review*, May, Vol. 56, No. 2, pp. 1–13.
Buchanan, James. *The Limits of Liberty: Between Anarchy and Leviathan*, Chicago:
    University of Chicago Press, 1975.
————— , (1977) *Freedom in Constitutional Contract: Perspectives of a Political
    Economist*, College Station: Texas A&M University Press.
Bush, Paul., (1981) "Radical Individualism vs. Institutionalism I: The Division of
    Institutionalists into 'Humanists' and 'Behaviorists'," *American Journal of Eco-
    nomics and Sociology*, April, Vol. 40, No. 2, pp. 139–47.
————— , (1981) "Radical Individualism vs. Institutionalism II: Philosophical Dual-
    ism as Apologetic Constructs Based on Obsolete Psychological Preconceptions,"
    American Journal of Economics and Sociology, July, Vol. 40, No. 3, pp.
    287–98.
Clark, J. M., (1940) "Toward a Concept of Workable Competition," *American Eco-
    nomic Review*, June, Vol. 30, pp. 241–56.
————— , (1932) "Round Table Conference: Institutional Economics," *American
    Economic Review*, Supplement, Vol. 22, No. 1, pp. 105–16.
Coats, A. W., (1954) "The Influence of Veblen's Methodology," *Journal of Political
    Economy*, Vol. 62, pp. 529–37.
Commons, J. R., (1934) *Institutional Economics*, New York: Macmillan Co.
————— , (1950) *The Economics of Collective Action*, New York: Macmillan Co.
Endres, A. M., (1984) "Institutional Elements in Carl Menger's Theory of Demand:
    A Comment, *Journal of Economic Issues*, September, Vol. 18, No. 3, pp.
    897–903.

Fink, Richard., (1982) "Economic Growth and Market Processes," *Supply-Side Economics: A Critical Appraisal*, Frederick, Md.: University Publications of America, pp. 372–94.

Galbraith, J. K., (1978) *The Affluent Society*, Boston: Houghton Mifflin Company, The New American Library Reprint, [1958].

————, (1979) *The New Industrial State*, Boston: Houghton Mifflin Company, The New American Library Reprint, [1967].

Gordon, Wendell., (1984) "The Role of Institutional Economics," *Journal of Economic Issues*, June, Vol. 18, No. 2, pp. 369–81.

Hamilton, David., (1973) *Evolutionary Economics: A Study of Change in Economic Thought*, Albuquerque: University of New Mexico Press.

————, (1981) "Ayres' Theory of Economic Progress: An Evaluation of Its Place in Economic Literature," *American Journal of Economics and Sociology*, October, Vol. 40, No. 4, pp. 427–38.

Hamilton, Walton., (1919) "The Institutional Approach to Economic Theory," *American Economic Review*, March, Vol. 9, pp. 309–18.

Hayek, F. A., (1976) *The Road to Serfdom*, Chicago: University of Chicago Press, [1944].

————, (1980) *Individualism and Economic Order*, Chicago: University of Chicago Press, [1948].

————, (1955) *The Counter-Revolution of Science: Studies on the Abuse of Reason*, New York: The Free Press of Glencoe.

————, (1967) *Studies in Philosophy, Politics and Economics*, Chicago: University of Chicago Press.

————, (1978) *New Studies in Philosophy, Politics, Economics and the History of Ideas*, Chicago: University of Chicago Press.

————, (1973; 1976; 1981) *Law, Legislation and Liberty: A New Statement of the Liberal Principles of Justice and Political Economy*, Chicago: University of Chicago Press, Vol. I, "Rules and Order," Vol. II, "The Mirage of Social Justice," and Vol. III, "The Political Order of a Free People."

Jaffe, William., (1976) "Menger, Jevons and Walras De-Homogenized," *Economic Inquiry*, December, Vol. 14, pp. 511–24.

Kirzner, Israel M., (1973) *Competition and Entrepreneurship*, Chicago: University of Chicago Press.

————, (1979) *Perception, Opportunity and Profit*, Chicago: University of Chicago Press.

Kirzner, Israel M., (1986) edited. *Subjectivism, Intelligibility and Economic Understanding: Essays in Honor of Ludwig M. Lachmann*, New York: New York University Press.

Lachmann, Ludwig M., (1971) *The Legacy of Max Weber*, Berkeley: The Glendessary Press.

————, (1976) "From Mises to Shackle: An Essay on Austrian Economics and the Kaleidic Society," *Journal of Ecomonic Literature*, March, Vol. 14, No. 1, pp. 54–62.

————, (1977) *Capital, Expectations and the Market Process*, Kansas City: Sheed, Andrews and McMeel.

Lange, Oskar., (1964) "On the Economic Theory of Socialism," in Lippincott, edited, pp. 55–143.

Langlois, Richard., (1983) "The Market Process: An Evolutionary View," *Market Process*, Summer, Vol. 1, No. 2, pp. 5–15.

Lavoie, Don., (1985) *Rivalry and Central Planning*, New York: Cambridge University Press.

Lippincott, B., (1964) edited. *On the Economic Theory of Socialism*, New York: McGraw-Hill, [1939].

Menger, Carl., (1981) *Principles of Economics*, New York: New York University Press, [1871].

————, (1963) *Problems in Economics and Sociology*, Urbana: University of Illinois Press, [1883].

————, (1892) "On the Origin of Money," *Economic Journal*, Vol. 2, pp. 239–55.

Mises, Ludwig., (1980) *The Theory of Money and Credit*, Indianapolis: Liberty Press, [1912].

————, (1981a) *Socialism: An Economic and Sociological Analysis*, Indianapolis: Liberty Press, [1922].

————, (1981b) *Epistemological Problems of Economics*, New York: New York University Press, [1933].

————, (1966) *Human Action: A Treatise on Economics*, Chicago: Henry Regnery, 3rd. revised edition, [1949].

————, (1978) *Notes and Recollection*, South Holland: Libertarian Press.

Mitchell, W. C., (1969) *Types of Economic Theory*, ed., Joseph Dorfman, New York: Augustus M. Kelley.

Nelson, R. and Winter, S., (1982) *An Evolutionary Theory of Economic Change*, Cambridge: The Belknap Press of Harvard University.

O'Driscoll, G. and Rizzo, M., (1985) *The Economics of Time and Ignorance*, New York: Basil Blackwell.

Perlman, M., (1986) "Subjectivism and American Institutionalism," in Kirzner, edited, pp. 268–80.

Polanyi, M., (1962) *Personal Knowledge*, Chicago: University of Chicago Press, [1958].

Robbins, Lionel., (1952) *An essay on the Nature and Significance of Economic Science*, London: Macmillan, [1932].

Rothbard, Murray N., (1970) *Man, Economy and State: A Treatise on Economic Principles*, Los Angeles: Nash Publishing, [1962].

————, (1977) *Power and Market*, Kansas City: Sheed, Andrews and McMeel, [1970].

Samuels, Warren J., (1981) *Law and Economics: An Institutional Perspective*, Boston: Kluwer-Nijhoff Publishing.

————, (1989) "Austrian and Institutional Economics: Some Common Elements," *Research in the History of Economic Thought and Methodology*, Vol. 6.

Seckler, David., (1975) *Thorstein Veblen and the Institutionalists*, Boulder: Colorado Associated University Press.

————, (1981) "Individualism and Institutionalism Revisited: A Response to Professor Bush," *American Journal of Economics and Sociology*, October, Vol. 40, No. 4, pp. 415–25.

Shackle, G. L. S., (1972) *Epistemics and Economics: A Critique of Economic Doctrines*, Cambridge: University Press.

Sowell, Thomas., (1967) "The 'Evolutionary' Economics of Thorstein Veblen," *Oxford Economic Papers*, July, Vol. 19, No. 2, pp. 177–198.

———, (1980) *Knowledge and Decisions*, New York: Basic Books.

Stanfield, J. R., (1983) "The Affluent Society After Twenty-Five Years," *Journal of Economic Issues*, September, Vol. 17, No. 3, pp. 589–607.

———, (1984) "Social Reforms and Economic Policy," *Journal of Economic Issues*, March, Vol. 18, No. 1, pp. 19–44.

Veblen, Thorstein., (1919) *The Place of Science in Modern Civilization*, New York: The Viking Press.

Wieser, Fredrich., (1967) *Social Economics*, New York: Augustus M. Kelley, [1914].

AUSTRIANS AND INSTITUTIONALISTS:
THE HISTORICAL ORIGINS OF THEIR SHARED CHARACTERISTICS

Bruce J. Caldwell

I.   INTRODUCTION

In the papers by Pete Boettke and Warren Samuels that serve as a common point of reference for the articles in this collection, the Austrian and institutionalist schools are compared. Though profound differences separate the two camps, the emphasis in the articles is on similarities that exist between them. Given the traditional antagonism that has been present between members of these two groups, the number of characteristics they share in common is nothing less than extraordinary. In my contribution to this collection on the Austrians and institutionalists, I will first add to the list of their similarities. I then

Research in the History of Economic Thought and Methodology,
Volume 6, pages 91-100
Copyright © 1989 by JAI Press Inc.
All rights of reproduction in any form reserved.
ISBN: 0-89232-928-9

will turn to the more important task of explaining how the institutionalists and Austrians came to share so many common characteristics.[1]

II. THREE OVERLOOKED SIMILARITIES

Both Boettke and Samuels note a number of substantive theoretical and methodological similarities in the approaches of the Austrians and institutionalists. Samuels also points out certain similarities of a more sociological nature, having to do with the way that the programs are presented and the way in which certain protagonists behave. Not all of these characteristics are positive. Intellectual isolationism, extremism masquerading as purism, an unhealthy preoccupation with methodology and the articulation of programs rather than with the extension of substantive work, paranoia in dealings with others: these hardly constitute complimentary behavioral traits. But neither author mentions various other similarities that may help to explain the presence of these negative characteristics among certain members of each camp.

It should first be mentioned that both Austrian and institutionalist economics began as national movements, in the sense that their founders were identified with particular countries. Furthermore, neither of the countries involved (Austria and the United States) had yet developed its own school of economic thought. Indeed, each was dominated by the ideas of economists from other countries: England in the case of American thought, and Germany in the Austrian case. Finally, both schools began in part as a reaction against what might be perceived as the "mainstream" of economic thinking in their respective countries.

Another common characteristic is that the reception of the ideas of each school by their respective mainstream counterparts was roughly similar. After an initial flurry of interest, both schools experienced a period in which their influence waned, and once the denouement began it was rapid in both cases. The particular paths differed slightly. Both the growth and decline of institutionalism was gradual, spanning about three decades at the beginning of this century. The Austrian experience was more apocalyptic, and it happened twice. Menger's work was initially ignored in Germany. He went on the offensive, publishing a methodological critique of historicism which led to the famed *Methodenstreit* with Schmoller. This was when the term "Austrian Economics" was coined; it was used derisively by German economists to indicate the second class status of the doctrine. A more important result of the battle was that the teaching of Austrian ideas was effectively banned in German universities by the powerful Schmoller. The Austrian's second brief moment in the sun occurred in England in the early 1930s, when Hayek was brought by Lionel Robbins to teach at the LSE. By the end of the decade, however, Austrian thought had again been left behind.[2]

A final similarity is that members of both camps were reacting not only to the prevailing economic theory of the time, but also to the political and social milieu of the countries of their origins. Significantly, the environments they reacted against were quite different. The growth of the power of the state, initially under Bismarck and in a later generation under Hitler, provided powerful motivation for the Austrians to defend the market system and forms of government in which strong constitutional constraints on the power of the state were vigilantly enforced. Institutionalism was a more populist movement which arose in part as a reaction against the unbridled growth of big business in turn of the century America, and later to the profound (and not always salutary) effects of rapid technological change on the fabric of American society.

The commonalities of experience mentioned above are not offered as excuses for the extremes of rhetoric that can occasionally be found in certain of the writings of Austrians and institutionalists. But remembering the frustrations that led to such rhetorical excesses makes them a little easier to understand.

III. THE HISTORICAL ORIGINS OF SHARED CHARACTERISTICS

Let us turn now to an examination of how the institutionalists and the Austrians came to share so many similarities in their approach to economics. As Boettke mentions, certain of these common points may be found in the writings of the originators. For example, Menger emphasized the evolution of institutions, the importance of time in economic analysis, the changeability of individual tastes, and the non-passiveness of human action, all of which are themes that institutionalists considered significant. But other similarities exist that cannot be traced to the founders of these schools, and these common points warrant explanation.

My thesis can be briefly stated at the outset. As is well known, institutionalism began as an opposition movement. Theirs was a revolt against formalism, and the opponent was the budding neoclassical research program that had its origins in the marginal revolution. Though the Austrians also began as an opposition movement (their opponent was historicism), they were co-founders of marginalism, and once that doctrine became more widely-accepted the Austrians could be considered as a part of the "orthodoxy." Their split with the mainstream was precipitated by their participation in the socialist calculation debate in the 1930s. From that time onwards, similarities between the two groups in terms of methodological critiques and in terms of positive recommendations concerning how economics should be done emerged. Just as the neoclassical program has gained coherence and unity in the subsequent decades, so have the analyses of its critics become increasingly homogenous.[3]

The marginal revolution has its origins in the independent work of Jevons, Menger and Walras in the 1870s. But it was not until the 1920s and 1930s that the work of the Austrian and Lausanne schools began to become more widely known in England. In the 1920s, visits by English economists to Mises' *privatseminar* became more frequent. In 1931 Hayek accepted the Tooke Chair at LSE, and the publication of his *Prices and Production* (1931) and the translation of *Monetary Theory and the Trade Cycle* (1933) followed in rapid succession. Significantly, Austrians at this time did not view themselves as all that different from their counterparts in other countries, as evidenced by the following statement made by von Mises in the early 1930s.

> Within modern subjectivist economics it has become customary to distinguish several schools. We usually speak of the Austrian and the Anglo-American Schools and the School of Lausanne. . . . [The fact is] that these three schools of thought differ only in their mode of expressing the same fundamental idea and that they are divided more by their terminology and by peculiarities of presentation than by the substance of their teaching (Mises 1933, 214).[4]

Indeed, as Israel Kirzner points out in a paper in which this quotation is mentioned, "the major opponents of Austrian economic theory were, in 1932, perceived by Mises not as being the followers of Walras or of Marshall, but as being the historical and institutionalist writers (as well as a sprinkling of economic theorists) who rejected marginal utility theory" (Kirzner 1988, 9–10). All of this was to be changed by the socialist calculation debate.

The debate began in the 1920s with the publication of a provocative paper by von Mises. Mises claimed that the absence of a price mechanism in a socialist economy made rational calculation under socialism "impossible." As Kirzner notes in his recent reexamination of the debate, the initial response by proponents of socialism to Mises' challenge was anything but sophisticated (ibid, 5 ff.). Most seemed unaware of the implications of the problem of scarcity for questions of choice, or of how a price system provides an allocation mechanism in the face of that problem. As a result, the initial Austrian counterattack consisted in pointing out this benefit of a market system. Such a response could as easily have been made by any neoclassical.

Later in the 1930s a more sophisticated defense of socialism was crafted by such economists as Abba Lerner, Oskar Lange and H.D. Dickinson. These authors were able to show that a general equilibrium model of the economy could be used to describe either a competitive or a socialist institutional framework. The long run equilibrium conditions obtained under competition could be duplicated in a socialist world in which managers are directed to behave in appropriate ways, e.g. to price at marginal costs. Thus Mises' claim that calculation under socialism is impossible is refuted.

It was in formulating a response to this later socialist challenge that Hayek and Mises were to alter the direction of Austrian economics. Their answer to the socialists involved a radical departure from the usual approach to economics: they rejected the usefulness of the equilibrium construct for understanding the workings of a dynamic competitive economy. In its place they put the notion of a dynamic market process.

Their rationale may be explained in the following way. Both the socialist and neoclassical camps suffered from, in Hayek's words, "an excessive preoccupation with problems of the pure theory of stationary equilibrium" (Hayek 1940, 188). By focusing on questions of equilibrium, members of both groups failed to appreciate certain essential characteristics of the market system.

One of those characteristics is the ability of markets to efficiently convey information, to coordinate the actions of many agents, all of whom hold different knowledge. The ability of a market system to solve the coordination problem became a major theme in Hayek's work, beginning with his famous article "Economics and Knowledge" and continuing in various later publications.[5] The reason that the equilibrium approach was inadequate to capture this phenomenon had to do with its assumptions concerning knowledge. Simply put, in a world in which it is assumed that all agents have perfect information, the coordination problem doesn't exist. It can be mentioned that even in the more recent literature on the economics of information no account is taken of the facts that information is dispersed (that is, different agents have different, and sometimes incompatible, information) and subjectively-held.

Mises' contribution (which was later extended in Kirzner's work on the entrepreneur) was to recognize the entrepreneurial-discovery function of markets. In a dynamic world, new knowledge is constantly coming into existence. In a world in which knowledge is dispersed, arbitrage opportunities also exist. The profit motive drives the entrepreneur to discover new knowledge, to exploit its existence, and to seek out arbitrage opportunities when disparities in knowledge occur. Only a dynamic account of a rivalrous market process is capable of identifying this important function of markets. There is no entrepreneur in the standard general equilibrium model. Either prices are assumed always to be in equilibrium, or some fictional agent (like a Walrasian auctioneer) is postulated to explain the adjustment process.

In developing a positive account of how a market process works, the Austrians began to use concepts that had much in common with those used by institutionalists. Equilibrium analysis was rejected and a dynamic, rivalrous process view was advocated. The passive, purposeless agent of neoclassical theory was replaced by the acting, purposeful, future-oriented agent described in *Human Action*. The entrepreneur became identified as a critical agent of change. The dispersion of knowledge and its importance for problems of coordination was emphasized. Recognition of the subjectivity of things like costs led Austrians to harbor suspicions about the efficacy of cost-benefit analysis in particular and welfare economics in general. And Hayek, in seeking those institutions that were most likely to lead to coordination of plans, turned away from economics proper towards the study of philosophy, law, sociology and other fields in which the evolution of institutional forms, their change and their growth, became a major focus of his work. All of these are similarities with the institutionalist approach mentioned by Boettke and Samuels, and all had their origins in the socialist calculation debate.

IV. SIMILARITIES IN THE CRITIQUE OF MAINSTREAM METHODOLOGY

The authors also note various similarities in the methodological critiques of the mainstream offered by both groups and in particular their mutual rejection of certain tenets of "positivism." The story here is a bit more complicated. First of all, the philosophical doctrine of positivism is not monolithic. It changed dramatically as it evolved over the course of a century from the writings of classical positivists like Auguste Comte to the work of logical empiricists like Carl Hempel and Ernest Nagel. Next, though various positivist ideas dominated the rhetoric of mainstream economists writing in the 1950s and 1960s, the actual practice of economists was at best a bowlderized version of the philosophical doctrines. During the same period, the methodological critiques of opponents like the Austrians and institutionalists were often kept at the philosophical level, with the result that many mainstream economists found them unintelligible. Finally, philosophy aside, the actual practice of mainstream economics was in fact quite different from the approaches recommended by the heterodoxy. The primary difference was the growth in the use of mathematically expressed theoretical models and the development and use of econometric estimation techniques among practitioners of mainstream economics. So to state that neoclassical economics embraced positivism, while its opponents rejected it, is really to oversimplify matters. Again, a closer look at history will help us sort the issues out.

As Professor Kirzner points out in a passage quoted earlier, in the beginning of the 1930s the Austrians viewed their enemies as being historicists and institutionalists. The Austrians rejected what they took to be an anti-theoretical bias in the methodological approaches of these groups. There were historical antecedents for their attitude towards historicism. In Menger's debate with Schmoller, the Austrian argued for the primacy of "exact theoretical" laws over "realistic-empirical" ones.[6] In a like manner, Hayek in *Monetary Theory and the Trade Cycle* stated that purely empirical explanations of the business cycle are wrong-headed. Empirical work cannot produce any new theories; standard economic theory already exists and is well-verified. All that empirical work can do is to reveal to us areas that standard theory has yet to explain fully, and to help us to make forecasts (Hayek 1933, Ch. 1). Such beliefs were in direct opposition to those of the more empirically-oriented institutionalists like Wesley Mitchell. So if we examine the methodological literature of the interwar years, the institutionalists (at least those following Mitchell) and the Austrians were indeed at loggerheads, the former group advocating a form of measurement without theory and the latter giving minimal weight to empirical work. In the intervening years, a number of changes took place that pushed the two groups closer together and separated them from the mainstream.

Recall that the transformation of mainstream thought took place on two fronts, consisting of growth in the use of mathematical modelling techniques for theoretical work and of econometric estimation technique for empirical work. The Austrians would presumably favor the former development but oppose the latter, while the institutionalists would presumably take the opposite view. But this was not the case.

The Austrians, as we have seen, rejected the use of the standard equilibrium model because they felt it did not adequately capture the dynamic aspects of the market process. As a result, though the Austrians have continued to claim that their approach is theoretical, they have consistently attacked the use of mathemtical equilibrium models by mainstream economists. The institutionalists who embraced empiricism were happy to find the growing use of empirical methods in the economic profession, but they also found themselves being criticized by econometricians like Koopmans who railed against "measurement without theory." The "institutionalist approach" in fields like labor or agricultural economics increasingly took a back seat to the neoclassical approach, which emphasized the use of formal theoretical models that were tested against data. The institutionalists responded that such an approach missed the rich diversity of economic phenomena, that such mathemtical formalism produced an "unrealistic" vision of phenomenal reality. Just as the Austrians insisted that their non-mathematical approach was actually "theoretical," the institutionalists claimed that their more holistic, pattern-modelling approach was truly "empirical" because it more accurately reflected reality. Mainstream economists who equated the term "theory" with mathematical modelling techniques and "empiricism" with econometric estimation techniques found such claims rather bizarre. But more to the point, such claims could be dismissed as "unscientific" by mainstream practitioners who thought (wrongly, as it turned out) that they were positivists and that positivism was an unimpeachable (wrong again) philosophical foundation for the practice of science. Meanwhile the attacks of Austrians and institutionalists against the positivist pretensions of their orthodox counterparts came to sound more and more alike. Though they began as methodological opposites, members of both groups found themselves united against a common ememy, and a formidable one, at that.

V.   CONCLUSION—THE ROLE OF METHODOLOGICAL WORK

I have argued that an understanding of the historical origins of the similarities of the approaches of the institutionalists and Austrians, and of their methodological criticisms of mainstream theory, makes those similarities more intelligible. How does all of this reflect on the role of methodological work in the discipline?

It is clear from what has been said above that a knowledge of the history of methodology can be very useful in understanding the present positions of various groups in economics. Though not an explicit theme of this paper, it is also true that different methodological positions often reflect differences concerning fundamental epistemological issues: differences concerning what can be known about phenomenal reality and of the best ways to represent that knowledge. Finally, it has been shown that methodological positions rarely if ever develop in a vacuum. Rather they result from complex interactions involving philosophical, sociological and political considerations in addition to those that are internal to the development of a discipline. It is my belief that a knowledge of methodology, in this broadly defined sense of the term, is extremely useful in gaining an understanding of the dynamics of the development of a discipline. That is no small role to play.

NOTES

1. I am more familiar with the development of Austrian thought than I am with that of the institutionalists. A similar excercise by someone more familiar with institutionalism would be very useful.

2. This second episode is discussed in two papers by Ludwig Lachmann (1982), (1986).

3. This interpretation, particularly the emphasis on the significance of the socialist calculation debate for the later development of Austrian thought, extends ideas found in two previous papers. See Kirzner (1988) and Caldwell (1988) and references therein.

4. This quotation is mentioned in Kirzner (1988); the author notes that, given the subsequent development of Austrian ideas, "one is tempted to describe it as an astonishing statement" (p. 9).

5. The role of this article in the evolution of Hayek's thought is explicated in Caldwell (1988).

6. An excellent discussion of this debate, in which the thesis is advanced that Menger and Schmoller differed on fundamental epistemological issues, is contained in Bostaph (1978).

REFERENCES

Bostaph, Samuel., (1978) "The Methodological Debate Between Carl Menger and the German Historicists," *Atlantic Economic Journal*, vol. 6 September, pp. 3–16.

Caldwell, Bruce., (1988) "Hayek's Transformation," *History of Political Economy*, vol. 20 Winter, pp. 513–41.

Hayek, Friedrick A., (1929) *Monetary Theory and the Trade Cycle*. Translated by N. Kaldor and H. M. Croome. N. Y.: Harcourt Brace, trans. 1933.

Kirzner, Israel., (1988) "The Economic Calculation Debate: Lessons for Austrians," *Review of Austrian Economics*, vol. 2, pp. 1–18.

Lachmann, Ludwig., (1982) "The Salvage of Ideas: Problems of the Revival of Austrian Economic Thought," *Zeitschrift fur die gesamte Staatswissenschaft*, vol. 138, pp. 629–45.

_____, (1986) Austrian Economics Under Fire: The Hayek-Sraffa Duel in Retrospect. In W. Grassl and B. Smith, eds. *Austrian Economics: Historical and Philosophical Background*. N.Y.: N.Y.U. Press, pp. 225–42.

REFLECTIONS ON THE AUSTRIAN/ INSTITUTIONALISM SYMPOSIUM

A. W. Coats

The continuing prominence and vigor of contending schools of economic thought has been one of the more distinctive features of the discipline's recent history, a feature inconsistent with the powerful pressures to professional conformity. Naturally enough, mainstream (neo-classical?) economists view these rival positions with mixed feelings—indifference, contempt, hostility, or at best condescension—either denying their significance (like the reviewer who claimed over 90 percent of economists are neoclassical, as though numbers were the relevant criterion), or dismissing them for failure to produce a viable alternative paradigm or intellectual framework.

Whether this state of affairs is peculiar to economics or characteristic of the social sciences generally and, perhaps all other intellectual disciplines (including the so-called 'hard' sciences) need not concern us here. The point is that despite the incentives to professional conformity and the belief that agreement on fundamentals is the hallmark

Research in the History of Economic Thought and Methodology,
Volume 6, pages 101-106
Copyright © 1989 by JAI Press Inc.
All rights of reproduction in any form reserved.
ISBN: 0-89232-928-9

of a genuine 'science',[1] dissident and heterodox streams of economic thought have persisted throughout most of the discipline's history and show no signs of withering away. On the contrary, there is clear evidence—which cannot be presented in detail here—that the divisions among economists are not merely surviving but also beginning to penetrate the subject's basic textbooks,[2] which have long been central agents for the preservation and dissemination of the conventional wisdom.

Broadly speaking, in methodological, doctrinal, and policy terms, economics has been in a markedly transitional and unsettled phase, both as a discipline and as a profession, during the past decade or two. To pessimistic critics the situation has been one of crisis, whereas optimistic defenders (Heller 1975; MacDougall 1974) have viewed it bravely as evidence of healthy scepticism towards received doctrine and exceptional openness to new ideas and approaches. There is, indeed, some truth in both these perspectives. Mainstream economists are nowadays generally far more conscious of the limitations of their science than in the 1950s and 1960s, and somewhat more sympathetic towards the traditional heterodox criticisms. Many are reaching into neighbouring fields for concepts, models, and research findings which can be applied to theoretical and applied problems treated earlier either as irrelevant to economics or beyond the discipline's boundaries. While economistic imperialists have been vigorously colonising problem areas hitherto regarded as belonging to other disciplinary domains, specialists in those and other cognate disciplines have been taking a sustained and intelligent interest in economists' concepts and models, even trying them out in their own fields. As yet the promise of these developments may be said to exceed the achievements—the interactions between economics and politics (Frey 1978, 1983), and between economics and psychology (Earl, 1988; Hogarth and Reder, 1987) are two conspicuous examples. Nevertheless, the portents are good.

Against this background, exploration of the commonalities and differences between two strong and durable dissenting traditions—Austrian and Institutional economics—is to be welcomed, especially if, as seen likely, there are prospects of fruitful collaboration and even convergence between them. This symposium is therefore a useful starting point for more systematic and detailed research into the AE/IE relationship, and the following comments are designed to highlight matters that would repay investigation in an effort to extend rather than simply to repeat arguments put by the other symposiasts.

Warren Samuels' useful ground-clearing paper is essentially taxonomic and his emphasis on the heterogeneity of the views and individuals associated with each 'school' (if, indeed, that is an appropriate term) offers an immediate entry point. He perhaps wisely sidesteps the difficult task for differentiating between the essential and the inessential elements within each school; yet this task cannot be postponed indefinitely. It is not enough to catalogue features: we need either measures of central tendency or a clear identification of the filiation of ideas within each camp before crucial similarities and differences can be assessed. This is no easy task, and it may be advisable to approach the matter historically, identifying the key individuals and leading doctrines in each case before attempting to determine which are integral to each movement. For example, on the Austrian side it seems clear that Menger was not only the founder, but also the key figure in the first generation. Then how far do Wieser's views belong in the same general category? (Böhm-Bawerk is no doubt a much less difficult individual to 'place'.)

In what may loosely be termed the middle generation, what are the characteristically Austrian features that unite such leading disparate figures as Hayek, Machlup, Mises, Morgenstern and Schumpeter? The last named, it is often held, cannot properly be viewed as a member of the 'school' given, for example, his eclectic methodological views and the variety of work he produced, though business cycles has been a unifying topic of study in all five cases, presumably (in part) because of their native country's experiences. Mises and Hayek are obviously key figures, the former because of his exceptionally strong views and his enormous influence on the American revival of interest in Austrian economics after World War II. His pedagogical influence via his seminars was crucial; yet his vigorously expressed methodological a priorism has been repudiated by many who admired other aspects of his work, and has even been regarded as a source of embarrassment. Of Hayek, none will deny his intellectual eminence or the remarkable impact he made at the LSE during the 1930s; but of course his later economic work, especially after his impenetrable *Pure Theory of Capital*, has proved to be a dead end, and the Austrianism of his later methodological views is now the subject of direct and profound disagreement among the experts. According to some he has revealed disconcerting Popperian sympathies, and even if he has not undergone major shifts of methodological allegiance, as has been claimed, he is certainly no Misesian. Nor can Machlup's or Morgenstern's Austrian lineage be viewed as pure, although both have made significant contributions to methodology and economic theory, and both share many of the familiar Austrian ideological views.

It is, however, with the recent (mainly) American Neo-Austrian revivalists that the greatest problems of classification arise. Directly or indirectly influenced by Mises as most of them have been, they nevertheless disagree sharply both with the master and among themselves. As noted by other symposiasts, Menger is the forefather who commands the greater respect, but was he in any sense typical? And what are the similarities and differences between Menger and Mises? However defined, they are certainly substantial. Some of the new Austrians can be unequivocally characterised as "true believers," especially Rothbard; but others deviate so strongly from earlier views that one feels that either they should be excluded from the "school" or that the membership is so heterogeneous as to cast doubt on the descriptive value of that term. Whereas Rothbard, for example, is clearly an outsider as far as mainstream neo-classical economics is concerned, Kirzner, whatever his designation, is widely recognized as a perceptive and important contributor of suggestive new ideas. Perhaps the later generation of neo-Austrians is too varied and independent minded to be usefully classified as such, and the characterisation is further blurred by the inclusion (by some commentators) of older generation figures such as Lachmann (undeniably Austrian), Shackle (possibly, but less assuredly) and Hicks (perhaps least convincing). And when we get into the difficult issue of the relationships between Austrian economics and subjectivism, the possibility of identifying a unifying central tradition and its branches becomes remote.

It has seemed appropriate to cite the Austrian case first because the elements of unity and continuity among writers usually included under this rubric—with respect to their philosophy, methodology, theory, policy, and ideology—have usually been taken for granted by economists who have not seriously studied their works. Even now I do not wish to deny that such unity and continuity may exist, but merely to emphasize that on closer inspection the case appears much weaker and more difficult to establish than appeared at first sight.

By contrast, with the institutionalists there have long been fewer doubts about their right to be viewed as a "school." Their common characteristics have often been depicted as negative—i.e., a matter of polemical orientation, or point of view, rather than matters of constructive aims or doctrine. Peter Boettke's reservations aside, Veblen did not have any literal disciples, though many were influenced by him; whereas Ayres, in some ways undoubtedly a disciple, developed idiosyncratic views and, while exercising a deep influence on undergraduates, generally failed to inspire postgraduates or younger faculty to take up and develop his ideas into a research programme (using that term in a non-technical sense). They tended to repeat Ayres's views parrot fashion, or to apply them to some specific topic in a more-or-less mechanical fashion. Of the other members of the original institutionalist triumvirate, Mitchell founded a great research institution and an approach to the study of central economic issues, but he did not found a doctrinal school. Nor, indeed, did Commons, despite his great personal influence on his Wisconsin "Friday Nighters" and others who came under his spell. A great practitioner who taught many other successful practitioners, no doubt he was; but not the founder of a theoretical tradition.

In this, as contrasted with the Austrian case, there is a considerable and useful secondary literature on the relations between the ideas of Veblen, Mitchell, Commons and Ayres and other later economists with declared institutionalist learnings. But as with the Neo Austrians the difficulties mount rapidly as we enter the post 1945 world. Allan Gruchy utterly failed to identify and characterise members of the so called "neo-institutionalist" persuasion (school is hardly the proper word here). Common ideas and interests there certainly are, as Warren Samuels (1977, 1978) showed in two survey articles in the Journal of Economic Issues. The problem here is rather to identify the unifying beliefs and practices, and to deal with the problem that many "applied" economists accept (perhaps only in moments of weakness) the institutional label, without any very clear or intentional commitment to membership of a school.

Perhaps one simple conclusion from this meandering discourse is that the term "school" has relatively little value—too little concreteness and far too much flexibility—to be of much use to the analyst or historian of the discipline.

NOTES

1.   For example, Milton Friedman (in Breit and Spencer 1986, p. 90) has argued, on a number of occasions that, "If scientific issues are separated from policy and value issues, there is widespread agreement among economists whatever their political views." More than fifty years ago Joseph Schumpeter (quoted in Schneider 1975, p. 40) argued, "there is no room for schools in our discipline. As a matter of fact we do find a great convergence of the really leading and capable brain workers in our discipline." Controversy between schools is a waste of energy, he continued, for, "There

is no use fighting something which life will sooner or later eliminate anyway. Unlike business and politics, just what matters in science is not monetary success. All we can say is that if in science something wins through it will have proved its right to exist, and if the thing is not worth anything it will surely wither.''

In recent years there have been a number of systematic efforts to assess the degree of consensus among economists. Broadly speaking it appears to be significantly greater on micro than on macro economic issues.

2. For example, Cole, Cameron and Edwards 1983 and Dow 1985. These texts incorporate divisions among economists into the pedagogical process. There are of course a number of one-line dissident texts, for example, by Marxists, Radicals, Post Keynesians, and Institutionalists.

REFERENCES

Breit, William, and Roger W. Spencer, eds., (1986) *Lives of the Laureates.* Cambridge: MIT Press.

Cole, Ken, John Cameron, and Chris Edwards, (1983) *Why Economists Disagree: The Political Economy of Eonomists.* London: Longmans.

Dow, Sheila, (1985) *Macroeconomic Thought: A Methodological Approach.* New York: Basil Blackwell.

Earl, Peter, ed. (1988) *Psychological Economies.* Norwell, MA: Kluwer Academic Publishers.

Frey, Bruno, (1978) *Modern Political Economy.* Oxford: Martin Robertson.

————— , (1983) *Democratic Economic Policy. A Theoretical Introduction.* Oxford: Martin Robertson.

Heller, Walter W., (1975) "What's Right With Economics," *American Economic Review*, March, *65*, 1–26.

Hogarth, Robin, and Melvin Reder, eds. (1987) *Rational Choice: The Contrast Between Economies and Psychology.* Chicago: University of Chicago Press.

MacDougall, Donald., (1974) "In Praise of Economics," *Economic Journal*, December, *84*, 773–786.

Samuels, Warren J., (1977) "Technology vis-à-vis institutions in the JEI: A Suggested Interpretation," *Journal of Economic Issues*, December, *11*, 871–895.

————— , (1978) "Information Systems, Preferences, and the Economy in the JEI," *Journal of Economic Issues*, March, *12*, 23–41.

Schneider, Erich, (1975) *Joseph A. Schumpeter: Life and Work of a Great Social Scientist.* Translated by W. E. Kuhn. Lincoln: Bureau of Business Research, University of Nebraska.

ISMATICALLY SPEAKING:

ARE AUSTRIANS INSTITUTIONALISTS?

Kenneth Dennis

Etymologically speaking, the *Oxford English Dictionary* informs us that a very long time ago the noun suffix '-ism' grew out of the verb suffix '-ize' (as in 'baptism' from 'baptize'). Only more recently did the suffix give rise to the quasi-substantive 'ism' used to mean 'a form of doctrine, theory or practice.' Also gracing the pages of the venerable *O.E.D.* are such exotic cognates as 'ismal,' 'ismate,' 'ismatize,' 'ismatic' and even 'ismdom' (Volume V, 504–05). Backed by such an authority, I shall refer hereafter to 'ismatic thinking' as that which tends to construe everything in terms of one system or another.

However ancient in origin some of the isms may be, the latter seem to have taken hold as prominent features of learned debate (especially in the social sciences) only during the nineteenth century, and not always first in their English form, viz. Comte's 'positivisme,' Louis Blanc's 'capitalisme,' the French revolutionaries' 'socialisme,' and so

Research in the History of Economic Thought and Methodology,
Volume 6, pages 107-114
Copyright © 1989 by JAI Press Inc.
All rights of reproduction in any form reserved.
ISBN: 0-89232-928-9

on. Quite often starting out life as official or semi-official names for what are (or are supposed to be) well-defined systems of thought or practice, the isms sometimes take a long time to emerge. 'Mercantilism' awaited the twentieth century before displacing Adam Smith's 'mercantile system,' and Karl Marx himself never once used 'capitalism' (Braudel 1982, 237 who maintains that it was Werner Sombart's *Der moderne Kapitalismus* of 1902 that finally gave currency to that much overworked ism).

Whatever their origins, these isms, insofar as they ever once do achieve some prominence as permanent fixtures in some intellectual setting, very quickly lose any cognitive precision and intellectual utility they might have initially possessed. By serving as larger-than-life symbols, banners, rallying cries, epithets or (worse still) intellectual crutches propping up ill-formed and half-baked thought patterns, the isms soon acquire emotive connotations that perform merely ceremonial functions. At their very worst, isms come to mean all things to all people, with subtly differing shades of meaning for each of us, yet all the while masquerading as precise and highfalutin technical terms gratuitously bestowing upon their users all the trappings of scholarly accomplishment.

Needless to say, really committed ismatizers will dispute the foregoing assessment, and of course a case can be made in favor of their retention. Given the welter of opinion, we cannot avoid simplifying generalizations about the myriad similarities that bind and differences that divide individual thinkers into coherent and competing schools. There just is no other way for us to gain perspective, to sensibly identify and discuss major and minor currents of thought, and introducing isms into this process is merely to abbreviate, that is, to eliminate lengthy and tiresome repetition by labelling closely related groups of ideas into distinct bundles.

But even so, the problem is that these artificial isms never do possess a clear and unanimously agreed upon meaning in the first place, but are instead subjected to continuous re-definition and re-deployment, thus degenerating into fuzzy verbal missiles hurled back and forth with little effect. Clarity and precision in the formulating of ideas give way to the mushiness of ismatic writing, a form of intellectual laziness in which the mere appearance of learnedness substitutes for the genuine article.

Only in the skilled hands of those who are forewarned of the dangers and limitations of ismatic analysis can the latter achieve the desired result of illumination. Thus it is that in Warren J. Samuels' ''Austrian and Institutional Economics: Some Common Elements'' the qualifications stand every bit as important as the generalizations about the two schools in question, and this is exactly as it should be. Readers are not misled into a false sense of precision about what the Austrian and institutionalist schools of thought comprise, and yet both genuine and revealing perspectives are provided. What Samuels terms the ''heterogeneity problem'' is firmly implanted in the reader's mind before the many and various similarities and differences are carefully delineated. When I first read Samuels' article (in June 1983), I found that it either confirmed my own preconceptions or else pointed quite plausibly and judiciously to similarities and differences that I had hitherto not considered.

By contrast, Pete Boettke's ''Evolution and Economics: Austrians as Institutionalists'' (which I first read in April 1986) came as quite a surprise. It seemed to be calling for nothing less than a major rewriting of one significant portion of the history of economic thought. To be sure, for several decades the Anglo-American tradition in the history of economic thought labored under some misconceptions as to what Austrian economics was really all about, e.g. casually treating Carl Menger as little more than a member of the marginal utility triad of the 1870s, an error that more recent scholarship has largely corrected. But Boettke's case carries this correcting process so far in the other direction as to create a new misconception.

Before elaborating upon this concern, I should perhaps first indicate my own affiliations with the two schools of thought under review. Even though my earliest inclinations were clearly institutionalist in nature (Galbraith's *The Affluent Society* being my first exposure to economics, long before any formal study, with Galbraith remaining a major influence on me in subsequent years), my growing interest in the subject of competition (fuelled by a thorough disliking of the theory of perfect competition) eventually led me to study of Joseph Schumpeter's work. My M.A. thesis (1970) was entitled ''Schumpeter on Competition: A Radical Conservative's Critique and Revision of Neoclassical Analysis,'' and Schumpeter's influence was still very apparent (though not dominant) in my doctoral dissertation (Dennis 1977), though I would very hastily deny being a ''Schumpeterian'' if that appellation were in any way to be construed as putting me into the ''Austrian'' camp.[1]

The point is that while I have always been (whether consciously or not) an institutionalist,[2] I have nevertheless found some aspects of ''Austrian'' thought (and not Schumpeter's alone) either stimulating or useful in my own researches, but I have remained essentially sceptical about the very idea that there are precisely definable entities to be labelled as the "Austrian" and "institutionalist" schools of thought. In large measure, these and similar labels merely reflect the exigencies of modern-day scholasticism in marking out convenient chapter heads for discussing what are really very diverse individual contributors to economics.

Having registered this scepticism about hypostatizing "Austrian" and "institutionalist" essences, I shall nevertheless revert to a limited recognition of that hypostasis by addressing one of Boettke's principal contentions. Boettke argues that the Austrian school "has in actuality consistently applied an evolutionary perspective in their analysis" which, though traceable back to Menger, has "reached its most advanced level of articulation in the work of F. A. Hayek" (Boettke 1989). Leaving aside the alleged origins of "evolutionary" thinking in the Austrian tradition, I shall focus fairly exclusively upon the work of Hayek, undoubtedly the most celebrated of modern-day Austrian economists.

In arguing his case, Boettke takes note that Samuels himself writes at one point that the Austrian tradition (like the institutionalist) envisions "the economic world as an emergent, evolving process" (Samuels 1989; Boettke 1989). But this is the only instance in Samuels' article where 'evolving' is linked to 'Austrian,' and Samuels never does apply the adjective 'evolutionary' to Austrian thought. Furthermore, many of the contrasts Samuels does draw between Austrian and institutionalist modes point in the direction of my reasoning for doubting Boettke's case.

Modern Austrian thinking, epitomized best in the work of Hayek, places heavy emphasis upon individual rational decision-making in which the element of uncertainty is a dominant consideration, uncertainty springing as much from our individual limitations in collecting, digesting, recalling and properly interpreting masses of information as from the continuous changes occurring in the environment in which such decision-making takes place. Mere *change*, however, ought not to be equated with *evolutionary change*. Evolution is an unfolding process whereby the element of *novelty* manifests itself in a tendency away from initially *simple* towards increasingly *complex* patterns. Human progress consists chiefly in meeting or successfully coping with challenges in the form of *fundamentally new problems*. Such problem-solving behavior we call evolutionary adaptation. Thus, historian William H. McNeill (to cite just one example among many) speaks of historical progress as a tendency towards "civilized complexity" (McNeill 1971, 77).

But not all changes are evolutionary. *Devolution* is a pattern of disintegration from the complex to the simple, a regress from sophisticated to crude form, not to be confused with a mere reversal of the steps of evolutionary change. (When civilizations descend into decline, they do not revert to earlier stages of development—except perhaps in some superficial ways—any more than individual organisms approach death by returning to a state of infancy.) Some changes are neither evolutionary nor devolutionary but little more than variations on some basic pattern: repetition in some slightly disguised form.

The question is: Can we describe modern-day Austrians, or F. A. Hayek in particular, accurately as proponents of an "evolutionary" approach to economics? True enough, Hayek does make much ado about evolution (especially in Hayek 1982), but even if it could be said truly that he embraces evolutionary principles, he does so in a manner quite fundamentally different from institutionalists. He certainly acknowledges the tendency towards complexity as an essential feature of man's civilizing progress (Hayek 1982, I:50), as indeed would anyone who accepts Adam Smith's doctrine of the division of labor, but the crucial point is that Hayek does not see in this process towards complexity the emergence of any essentially or *fundamentally novel truth* about the nature of reality, any profound changes in the nature of problems facing us. At most, progress consists in the refinement of those *eternal* truths that Adam Smith and a few others have already revealed to us, however imperfectly, so that for Hayek successful evolutionary adaptation requires only the effective application of eternal, not emergent, truths to increasingly complex variations on basic patterns.

The key to truth and progress for Hayek lies in unravelling all of the (no doubt magical) implications of the word 'spontaneity,' a modern-day substitute for Adam Smith's 'invisible hand' imagery for 'the Great Society.' Problems can be solved only after we have established the distinction between 'spontaneous' and 'deliberate' or 'planned' order. Hayek writes:

> It is because it was not dependent on organization but grew up as a spontaneous order that the structure of modern society has attained that degree of complexity which it possesses and which far exceeds any that could have been achieved by deliberate organization. In fact, of course, the rules which made the growth of this complex order possible were initially not designed in expectation of that result; but those people who happened to adopt suitable rules developed a complex civilization which often spread to others. To maintain that we must deliber-

ately plan modern society because it has become so complex is therefore paradoxical, and the result of a complete misunderstanding of these circumstances.
The fact is, rather, that we can preserve an order of such complexity not by the
method of directing the members, but only indirectly by enforcing and improving the rules conducive to the formation of a spontaneous order (Hayek 1982, I:
50–51).

Hayek's penchant for locating universal truth is not merely one of
doctrine; it is symptomatic of Austrian methodology at large. Samuels
quite properly (i.e. with suitable qualification) distinguishes Austrians
for their 'a priori deductivism'' and ''dogmatism'' from institutionalists for their ''pragmatism'' and ''eclecticism'' (Samuels 1989).
Whereas institutionalists stress the differentiating role of context in
their study of human experience, Austrians seem to be seeking unifying principles to reduce all human experience to some universally
valid pattern. Hayek wrote several decades ago in a methodological
treatise:

> . . . There is nothing paradoxical in the claim that all mind must run in terms of
> certain universal categories of thought, because where we speak of mind this
> means that we can successfully interpret what we observe by arranging it in
> these categories. . . . Particular propositions of social theory may have no ap-
> plication at certain times, because the combination of elements to which they
> refer to [sic] do not occur. But they remain nevertheless true. There can be no
> different theories for different ages (Hayek 1964, 78–79).

It is worth noting here that both Hayek and Ludwig von Mises have
tried (in what are faint echoes of the distant thunderclaps of the famous
Methodenstreit of the 1880s) to distinguish the 'theoretical' from the
'historical' as that between what is universally and eternally true and
what is of passing and spatially limited applicability (Hayek 1964;
Mises 1957). To institutionalists schooled on evolutionary principles,
such a distinction will appear to be founded on a category confusion, a
failure to appreciate the differing time-frames of the various aspects of
cosmic reality in their evolutionary contexts. The emergence, for example, of increasingly complex atomic and molecular structures over
eons of time is no more eternal or universal or context-free than is, say,
the emergence of increasingly complex patterns of human interaction
over very much shorter periods of time. Rather than linking 'historical'
to 'context-bound' and 'theoretical' to 'context-free,' institutionalists
(I venture to say) are more likely to view theories of any kind (no matter what their level of generality or space-time bounds might be) as
nothing more than conjectures and to treat all theories as context-

bound, that is, subject to limitations imposed by the evolutionary nature of all reality.

This, then, is my reason for doubting Boettke's case for making out Austrians as institutionalists. By allowing myself to slip into an ismatic idiom, I have no doubt over-drawn (for rhetorical purposes) the not so sharp distinction between eternal and emergent truth, an injustice to both schools of thought and to their many individually differentiated contributors. The irony is that both schools could accuse one another of parochialism. Institutionalists (Austrians might argue) often fail to rise above the accidental peculiarities of their own time and place to see human experience in its broadest perspectives, confusing temporary aberrations (such as state interventionism!) for essentially new phases in the evolutionary process. (This, of course, ignores the work of those institutionalists who stress comparative or cross-cultural analysis.) Austrians (institutionalists might argue) unwittingly project their own parochial concerns and attachments (such as to the boundless wonders of "the market-place"!) upon the rest of humanity, confusing a passing epoch in human history for eternal revelation.

Some will see in this tension between the relativist and the reductivist enterprises an irreconcilable opposition, while others (like myself) will see in it nothing more than the two sides of the same coin. All inquiry must ultimately identify both the similarities and the differences by which distinct things are related to one another, and in that sense the reductivist and the relativist approaches represent a difference of emphasis, not of objective. I concur with both Samuels and Boettke that members of the two schools have much to learn from each other.

NOTES

1.   I mention this because in the recent edition of their *History of Economic Theory and Method*, authors Robert Ekelund and Robert Hébert decided (and gratifyingly so) to cite my history on competition, but they did so in a chapter entitled "Competition Expanded: Neo-Austrian Developments" (Ekelund and Hébert 1983, p. 497–539), presumably because they include Schumpeter (along with Mises) as a second-generation Austrian economist. Though the authors do not explicitly identify my history as Neo-Austrian, the scholastic habit of classifying individuals into recognized schools does create hazards at times. As for Schumpeter, I would have thought he was unique, in a class by himself, yet revealing numerous influences besides those of Austrian origin. Indeed, even within the first generation of the so-called "Austrian School," I have never found much binding unity, any more than with the subsequent generations of Austrians or with the originating triumvirate of the institutionalist tradi-

tion. As a case in point, it has always seemed to me that Wieser's hefty *Grundriss der Sozialökonomik* of 1914 has more in common with Schmoller's even heftier *Grundriss der Allgemeinen Volkswirtschaftslehre* of 1900–1914 than with the seminal Austrian literature of the 1880s.

2. I say this with all the hesitant ambivalence of someone who wishes to remain a fiercely independent thinker yet, all the while, enjoying the considerable comforts of belonging to a group of like-minded people!

REFERENCES

Boettke, Pete., (1989) "Evolution and Economics: Austrians as Institutionalists." *Research in the History of Economic Thought and Methodology*, Vol. 6 Greenwich, CT: JAI Press Inc.

Braudel, Fernand., (1982) *The Wheels of Commerce*. Volume II of *Civilization & Capitalism: 15th-18th Century*. Translated by Siân Reynolds. New York: Harper and Row.

Dennis, Ken., (1977) *'Competition' in the History of Economic Thought*. New York: Arno Press.

Ekelund, Robert B., Jr. and Robert F. Hébert., (1983) *A History of Economic Theory and Method* (1975). 2d edition. New York: McGraw-Hill.

Hayek, F. A., (1964) *The Counter-Revolution of Science: Studies in the Abuses of Reason* (1955). Paperback edition. New York: Free Press of Glencoe.

Hayek, F. A., (1982) *Law, Legislation and Liberty* (1973, 1976 and 1979). Revised edition. London: Routledge and Kegan Paul, Vol. I, p. 50.

McNeill, William H., (1971) *A World History* (1967). 2d edition. New York: Oxford University Press.

Mises, Ludwig von., (1957) *Theory and History: An Interpretation of Social and Economic Evolution*. New Haven: Yale University Press.

Samuels, Warren J., (1989) "Austrian and Institutional Economics: Some Common Elements." *Research in the History of Economic Thought and Methodology*, Vol. 6 Greenwich, CT: JAI Press Inc.

AUSTRIANS VS. INSTITUTIONALISTS:
WHO ARE THE REAL DISSENTERS?

William M. Dugger

AUSTRIANS ARE PRETENDERS

Taking their cue from the paranoid style of rightwing U.S. politics, Austrians take pleasure in and profit from their posturing as the persecuted dissenters of economics. Their posturing profits them by protecting them from intellectual attack—poor fellows, everyone treats them so badly, why not give them a break? Austrians pretend to be a viciously persecuted minority, when in fact they are not. But this gives them a kind of unsung hero complex, as they come to believe that their own pretended heroic stance is truly heroic. Austrians are critics of mainstream economics only so far as they criticize the mainstream for not being mainstream enough. They are economic fundamentalists, not economic dissenters. Lester Thurow (1983) recently pointed out that

Research in the History of Economic Thought and Methodology,
Volume 6, pages 115-123
Copyright © 1989 by JAI Press Inc.
All rights of reproduction in any form reserved.
ISBN: 0-89232-928-9

supply side economists are fundamentalists, but the Austrians are even more so. Austrians do love to posture. As do other reactionaries, they love to feel that the misguided, evil world is against them. They love to feel like they are lone voices crying out in the wilderness. Peter Boettke tries to justify the Austrian's reactionary paranoia by claiming that Austrians are actually Institutionalists. And, of course, Institutionalists really have been economic dissenters. The Institutionalists really have been lone voices crying out in the wilderness.

In spite of the commonalities Warren J. Samuels explores, Austrians are not Institutionalists. They do not swim against the stream by proposing national economic planning to replace alleged market automaticity, as do the Institutionalists. Numerous Institutionalists swim against the pro-market stream to propose democratic economic planning (Cochran 1955; Dugger 1984a; Gruchy 1939, 1972, 1984; Stanfield 1979). But no Austrians do so. Instead, they write self-righteous tracts for the pro-market mainstream, harshly condemning those who deviate from mainstream faith in the dynamism of the entrepreneurial drive and in the social beneficence of the unfettered market. Austrians direct particularly venomous attacks at those who propose national economic planning, such as the Institutionalists (Hayek 1944; Mises 1947). As Institutionalist J. Ron Stanfield sees it, planning is an Institutionalist imperative (Stanfield 1979, 72–105). Institutionalists being such avowed proponents of national economic planning, it is hard to take Boettke's claim seriously that Austrians are Institutionalists. Austrians are not Institutionalists because they do not advocate economic planning like Institutionalists do.

Austrians are not Institutionalists because they do not criticize the growth of entrenched corporate power, like the Institutionalists do (Samuels 1979). Instead, Austrians decry the lack of freedom of their so-called praxeological entrepreneurs. ("Praxeology" is a word invented by the Austrians. It is the study of hypothetical human action.) Austrians are not Institutionalists because they do not go against the corporate establishment to propose reforms that strengthen government regulation of private power, like the Institutionalists do (Solo 1982). Instead, Austrians defame the personal integrity and good character of those who do dare to criticize corporate power and of those who do dare to propose political ways to reduce it. Ludwig von Mises referred to the authors of reform proposals in the following way:

Their authors are driven by the dictatorial complex. They want to deal with their fellow men in the way an engineer deals with the materials out of which he builds houses, bridges, and machines. They want to substitute "social engineer-ing" for the actions of their fellow citizens and their own unique all-comprehensive plan for the plans of all other people. They see themselves in the role of the dictator—the *duce*, the *Fuhrer*, the production tsar—in whose hands all other specimens of mankind are merely pawns (Mises 1962, 40–41).

Mises was not alone in his hatred of economic planners—of Institutionalists. Friedrich A. von Hayek's snide innuendo that his "socialist colleagues" support socialism because it will benefit them personally is typical of the mean-spirited nature of Austrian thought. Hayek stated, "In fact, I am always told by my socialist colleagues that as an economist I should occupy a much more important position in the kind of society to which I am opposed—provided, of course, that I could bring myself to accept their views." (Hayek 1944, xxi) In statements such as these, Austrians imply that while they are acting out of the highest sense of personal duty and altruism, their "socialist" opponents are acting out of a desire for personal gain. Ironic indeed: that which the Austrians applaud in their praxeological entrepreneurs (pursuit of self-interest) is self-righteously denied in themselves but bitterly condemned in their academic critics. The Austrians have im-proved upon the old double standard: they have invented the triple standard! Austrians are not Institutionalists. They are the bullies of what is essentially a conservative discipline.

The proof of a pudding is in the eating. The puddings (policies) of the Austrians and Institutionalists are completely different. Using in-strumentalism, the philosophical base to which most Institutionalists subscribe, (Tool 1981) one must reject the claim that Austrians are Institutionalists. They cannot be, because their policies are opposed to Institutionalist policies. Nevertheless, Austrians love to claim kinship with some of the real bad boys of academic economics (Veblen, in par-ticular) because it allows them an air of bravado. But the bravado is false. It takes no courage whatsoever to stand for entrepreneurial free-dom in the United States. But it takes considerable intellectual forti-tude to stand for the underdog: Where were the Austrians when Veblen tried to support the Industrial Workers of the World and when Com-mons tried to support labor's right to collective bargaining? Were they helping Commons's students and followers design a social security system for the United States? Were they helping design a new system of workman's compensation? They were not even helping Paul Douglas struggle against the public utility magnates. Austrians cannot claim to be Institutionalists, because they have never stood with Institutionalists when it mattered—when progressive policies were being constructed, in spite of orthodox resistance to policy experimentation. The fact of the matter is, Austrians are dissenters only in a very limited sense. Only in the sense that they demand a theoretical fundamentalism, a much stricter orthodoxy than most orthodox economists really practice, can Austrians claim to be dissenters. They are not policy dissenters, and policy is what really counts to Institutionalists. So they fail the crucial instrumental test.

The Austrians fail another important test. Institutionalism is inherently egalitarian. To be an Institutionalist means to be for the "underdog." The Austrian school, however, is inherently elitist. To be an Austrian means to be for the "great man." Both normatively and positively, the Institutionalists are for the poor and the workers; while, both normatively and positively, the Austrians are for the rich and the entrepreneurs. The difference is fundamental and cannot be glossed over by less important similarities. The Institutionalist egalitarian perspective has been developed by nearly every major Institutionalist thinker. Helping the underdog is instrumental. It is both right and efficient, according to Institutionalism, for egalitarianism furthers the life process. It includes more people in the work force. It keeps effective demand growing apace with industrial output. It spreads knowledge and improves health. It increases participation. Robin Hood was right (Dugger 1984b). David Hamilton stated the Institutionalist view quite clearly:

> Our rising "welfare costs" in recent years, rather than being reason for alarm, are evidence that we had been going in the right direction. The problems that agitate us most are bookkeeping problems. These are most certainly surmountable. But before we can successfully solve even the nit-picking problems we must transform our conception of income maintenance programs. We need to view them as essential to a healthy and thriving economy. Until there is such a transformation, we can expect only a hard life for those who have been passed over by our economy (Hamilton 1984, 157).

The Austrians argue that egalitarianism is wrong and inefficient. Aiding the poor and the working class hurts everyone because it taxes the rich and the entrepreneurs or because it restricts their liberty to invest, to hire and to fire at will, and to innovate. Hence, Robin Hood was wrong, according to the Austrian view. Contrast the following statements of von Mises with Hamilton's egalitarianism:

> In the market economy the better people are forced by the instrumentality of the profit-and-loss system to serve the concerns of everybody, including the hosts of inferior people (Mises 1962, 112).

> The inferiority of the multitude manifests itself most convincingly in the fact
> that they loathe the capitalistic system and stigmatize the profits that their own
> behavior creates as unfair (Mises 1962, 113).

> These dull beneficiaries of the capitalistic system indulge in the delusion that it
> is their own performance of routine jobs that creates all these marvels [a horn of
> plenty provided the masses by the entrepreneurs] (Mises 1962, 113).

From the classical elitism of European thinkers like Robert Michels, Gaetano Mosca, and Vilfredo Pareto, the Austrian economists inherited a strong distrust of the common man and an admiration for the great man. They also adopted a hard-boiled, cynical approach to their study (Mills 1960, 192–291). From the nineteenth century populism and radicalism of American thinkers like Edward Bellamy, Henry Demarest Lloyd, and Henry George, the Institutionalists inherited just the reverse: a strong distrust for the great man, an admiration for the common man, and an optimistic, progressive approach to their study. (A discussion of U.S. populism is in Pollack, 1966.) The two schools of thought could not be farther apart on the egalitarian issue. The Institutionalists argue that more income and participation for the common man would serve the higher good but is strongly resisted by the vested interests in the economy. The Austrians argue that redistribution of income and of participation to the "inferior" workers and to the "inferior" poor would be detrimental to the higher good and is a ruse used by power-seeking politicians and allied intellectuals.

I. HISTORY AND INSTITUTIONS IN ECONOMICS

Austrians have not grounded their work in "a Veblenian appreciation of institutional and historical factors in economics," as Boettke claims in this volume. The claim is without foundation in fact. Were an Austrian actually to ground her work in "a Veblenian appreciation of institutional and historical factors in economics," other Austrians would disown her. The Austrians have no use for historical treatises (the German Historical School can vouch for that) and no use for institutional explanations of human action. Austrian analysis, praxeology, is the aprioristic "science" of economics. Austrian analysis is neither institutional nor historical. It is hypothetical, the a priori "explanation" of human action deduced from subjective, individual utility and disutility.

Austrians do not even believe that institutions, as such, exist. Only individual subjectivity exists in Austrian praxeology. Institutional ex-

planations are dismissed by von Mises, for example, as "anthropo-
morphic." (Mises 1962, 82–83) Institutions play no causal role in
Austrian explanations of human action because the Austrians rely on
methodological individualism, not methodological collectivism. Human action has its origins exclusively in the "free will" of the human
actor, not in historical traditions nor in institutionalized habits of
thought. Deviation from the Austrian methodological position is
equivalent in the Austrian mind to belief in ghosts and things that go
bump in the night. Mises states, "The rejection of methodological individualism implies the assumption that the behavior of men is directed
by some mysterious forces that defy any analysis and description."
(Mises 1962, 82) Thorstein Veblen, the founder of Institutionalism,
tried to explain human action in terms of institutional factors. An institution, according to Veblen, was a habit of thought. And, in recent
times—say the last two or three centuries—one prevalent habit of
thought has been that molded by the incidence of the machine process.
Those involved in industrial employments have been particularly sus-
ceptible to it. On the other hand, those involved in pecuniary
employments—business especially—have habits of thought molded
into a pecuniary animus. The industrially-employed picked up a desire
to be serviceable. The pecuniarily-employed picked up a desire to be
rich. This making of goods versus making of money, in oversimplified
form, is Veblen's famous dichotomy (Veblen 1919a). Seymour
Melman and many other institutionalists continue to apply the dichotomy to contemporary problems (Melman 1983). It forms one of the
central features of Institutional thought. Austrian Murray N. Rothbard
dismisses Veblen's dichotomy in a footnote as a "spurious distinction." (Rothbard 1970, 904) Rothbard's treatment of institutional factors is typical of Austrian thought in general—they are dismissed. So,
Boettke's claim that Austrians base their analysis on Veblen's institutional factors is false.

According to leading Austrian Ludwig von Mises, economics is not
history; nor is it grounded in history. History is not the proper subject
of inquiry for Austrian praxeology. "The economist does not base his
theories upon historical research, but upon theoretical thinking like
that of the logician or the mathematician." (Mises 1962, 73) In fact,
Mises refers to economic history as a "research fable." (Mises 1962,
73) And, the Mises position on such matters is quite definitive in Austrian circles. So, Boettke's claim of a historical foundation for Austrian economics is also false. Austrians are profoundly anti-historical
in their methodology. After all, they sharpened their teeth attacking the

German Historical School. While Veblen also criticized the German Historical School, he had a profound appreciation for what they were trying to do (Veblen 1919b). Their work is to Institutional economics what Linnaeus's work is to evolutionary biology. Many Institutionalists followed in the footsteps of the German Historical School. The Austrians hold historismus in contempt while the Institutionalists, following Wesley Clair Mitchell's lead, try to build on it (Mitchell 1950).

Both the Institutionalists and the Austrians reject the rational expectations hypothesis approach to economics. But the Austrians have made no attempt to forge an evolutionary economics, as Boettke claims. Their economics attempts to explain human action in terms of subjective forces—spiritual essences, if you will, such as the entrepreneurial spirit. Institutionalists attempt to explain human action in terms of objective forces—material processes, if you will, such as the spread of the industrial revolution. The two approaches go off in totally different directions, though they both start with a critical view of a part of the mainstream. In Institutional theory, the variables used to explain human action are institutional and historical change. In Austrian theory, the explanatory variables are individual utility and disutility. Institutionalists urge their mainstream brethren to sally forth into history, law, political science, and social psychology in a search for causal relations. Austrians urge their mainstream brethren to stay strictly within the bounds of "praxeology"—the hypothetical analysis of subjective, individual utility and disutility. (Further discussion of the scope of economics is in Dugger 1979a, 1979b.) So the two treatments of the other social sciences are antithetical. The Institutionalist treatment is inclusive, recognizing none of the discipline boundaries imposed by arbitrary academic departmentalization. The Austrian treatment is exclusive, drawing tight boundaries around its "praxeology," the only proper treatment of economics. It is true that both are critical of parts of the mainstream. Nevertheless, when doing her own fishing, the Institutionalist is in constant danger of casting her net too broadly and coming up with more fish than she can handle; while the Austrian is in constant danger of casting her net too narrowly and coming up with only hypothetical fish.

II. THE REAL THING

Institutionalists are the real thing. They are dissenters from mainstream economics. Austrians are poseurs. Institutionalists deny that markets are automatically beneficent and suggest that democratic economic planning could significantly improve over existing exchange arrangements. Institutionalists also argue that both equity and efficiency require that the workers, the unemployed, the impoverished, the minorities, and the exploited be given more power and more income. Their position amounts to nothing less than economic heresy. Neoclassical trickle-down apologies and Keynesian hydraulics is not for them. The Austrians are poseurs because, although they too criticize aspects of the Keynesian-neoclassical synthesis, their criticism never cuts to the core faith in the automaticity and beneficence of the market as the central economic institution. Dissent from that core faith is not for them. Instead, the Austrians share the mainstream faith in the market. The Institutionalists do not. That is the definition of "belief" and of "heresy." The Austrians fit the former, the Institutionalists the latter. Austrians swim with the mainstream. Institutionalists swim against it.

REFERENCES

Cochran, Kendall P., (1955) *The Concept of Economic Planning in Institutional Economics, Dissertation*, Ohio State University.

Dugger, William M., (1979a) "The Long Run and Its Significance to Social Economy," *Review of Social Economy*, October, 37, 199–210.

————, (1979b) "Methodological Differences Between Institutional and Neoclassical Economics," *Journal of Economic Issues*, December, 13, 899–909.

————, (1984a) *An Alternative to Economic Retrenchment*, Princeton: Petrocelli Books.

————, (1984b) "The Nature of Capital Accumulation and Technological Progress in the Modern Economy," *Journal of Economic Issues*, September, 18, 799–823.

Gruchy, Allan G., (1939) "The Concept of National Planning in Institutional Economics," *Southern Economic Journal*, October, 6, 121–44.

————, (1972) *Contemporary Economic Thought*, Clifton, NJ: Augustus M. Kelley.

————, (1984) "Uncertainty, Indicative Planning, and Industrial Policy," in Marc R. Tool, ed., *An Institutionalist Guide to Economics and Public Policy*, Armonk, NY: M. E. Sharpe.

————, *The Reconstruction of Economics*, New York: Greenwood Press, 1987.

Hamilton, David, (1984) "The Myth Is Not the Reality: Income Maintenance and Welfare," in Marc R. Tool, ed., *An Institutionalist Guide to Economics and Public Policy*, Armonk, NY: M. E. Sharpe.

Hayek, Friedrich A., (1944) *The Road to Serfdom*, Chicago: University of Chicago Press.

————, (1962) *The Ultimate Foundation of Economic Science*, Kansas City: Sheed Andrews and McMeel.

Melman, Seymour, (1983) *Profits Without Production*, New York: Alfred A. Knopf.

Mills, C. Wright, ed., (1960) *Images of Man*, New York: George Braziller.

Mises, Ludwig von, (1947) *Planned Chaos*, Irvington-on-Hudson, NY: Foundation for Economic Education.

Mitchell, Wesley C., (1950) *The Backward Art of Spending Money and Other Essays*, New York: Augustus M. Kelley.

Pollack, Norman, (1966) *The Populist Response to Industrial America*, New York: W. W. Norton.

Rothbard, Murray N., (1970) *Man, Economy, and State*, Los Angeles: Nash Publishing.

Samuels, Warren J., ed., (1979) *The Economy as a System of Power*, New Brunswick, NJ: Transaction Books.

Solo, Robert A., (1982) *The Positive State*, Cincinnati: South-Western Publishing.

Stanfield, J. Ron, (1979) *Economic Thought and Social Change*, Carbondale, Illinois: Southern Illinois University Press.

Thurow, Lester C., (1983) *Dangerous Currents: The State of Economics*, New York: Random House.

Tool, Marc R., (1981) "The Compulsive Shift to Institutional Analysis," *Journal of Economic Issues*, September, 15, 569–92.

————, (1986) *Essays in Social Value Theory*, Armonk, NY: M. E. Sharpe.

Veblen, Thorstein, (1919a) "Industrial and Pecuniary Employments," in *The Place of Science in Modern Civilization and Other Essays*, New York: B. W. Huebsch.

————, (1919b) "Gustav Schmoller's Economics," in *The Place of Science in Modern Civilization and Other Essays*, New York: B. W. Huebsch.

COMMENT ON THE COMPARING
OF THE AUSTRIAN AND
INSTITUTIONALIST SCHOOLS
OF ECONOMIC THOUGHT

R. A. Gonce

The "typical" position of the Austrian school and of the
Institutionalist school are identifiable, W. J. Samuels proposes. He
compares the two and finds many differences, but also many "common elements." Although the two schools are usually believed to be
antithetical, P. Boettke observes, his own comparison of the "modern" Austrian school (and he features F. A. von Hayek, but also cites
L. E. von Mises, and mentions often C. Menger) and the Institutionalists (and he features T. B. Veblen, but also refers to J. R. Commons)
leads him to the finding that the two share an "evolutionary perspective," an appreciation of historical and institutional factors, and a
somewhat similar conception of individualism.

Research in the History of Economic Thought and Methodology,
Volume 6, pages 125-132
Copyright © 1989 by JAI Press Inc.
All rights of reproduction in any form reserved.
ISBN: 0-89232-928-9

Two reasons for dissent exist. First, the essential attributes defining the class "Austrians" are relatively few. And those defining the "Institutionalists" are fewer still (see Knight, x; Bronfenbrenner, 19). Each class quickly breaks down into many subclasses, their differentiae being the result of the originative genius of such men as Menger, Mises, and Hayek (see Hutchison, 203–232), as well as Veblen and Commons. As Samuels does and Boettke does not state, each class breaks down into subgroups and branches. It follows that if the classes rather than the subclasses are seized upon, and if the two classes are compared, the comparison will be perilous. For variation in the particular man or men selected and emphasized as a member or as members of each class will yield variation in the findings of the comparison of the two classes.

Second, while Samuels and Boettke find common elements, many of these are titles of broad categories of ideas, not specific doctrines. For example, both classes concern themselves with human action, institutions, law, freedom, social order, evolution, and so on. But while their ideas fall below such titles, this does not establish significant commonality. For when the Austrians and the Institutionalists develop their own specific doctrines falling below these titles, or get down to "specifics," as Samuels admirably acknowledges, differences appear.

To illustrate these two reasons, let the selection be varied so as to emphasize Mises vis à vis Commons, and let their specific doctrines be compared. The result will be findings at variance with those of Samuels and Boettke.

The foundation for economic theory is sociology, according to Commons (1899–1900, 3, 10; 1934, 120, 121) and also Mises, who renames sociology "praxeology" (1933, viii). The sociology of each involves specific doctrines falling below a series of titles.

a.   Human nature, Mises contends, is marked by libertarianism, self-interest that creates a "natural conflict of interests" (1963, 673), rationality, and inequality. To Commons, man is an evolving creature at present affected by a cultural determinism that "institutionalizes" him (1934, 73, 74, 155, 156, 697–699); self-interest that creates conflicts; passion, stupidity, and inequality.

b.   Society originates, Mises reasons, due to one of the "natural laws of social life" (1951, 329), namely the law of the harmony of individuals' rightly-understood, long-run self-interests (1933, 42; 1951, 329; 1963, 674). This law is the "starting point of all sociology" (1933, 42; 1951, 64, 290). Rational individuals recognize this natural law when they calculate the benefits of a society involving private ownership over property, greater productivity due to division of labor, and competitive exchange. Rational self-interest impels them to forsake autonomy for society. Society is a scene of individuals, all groups such as social classes and institutions having no "perseity" (1962, 79). Harmony prevails. Commons attacks natural law (1899–1900, 57; 1934, 41, 50, 92, 135–139, 162, 681) and harmony of interest theoreticians (1934, 6, 108, 109). He maintains that man and society originated together. Society is a scene of conflicting interests among men who organize themselves into classes to attain collective power to control others, only to find themselves embroiled in class conflict.

c. As for social order, Mises explains it by arguing that awareness of the natural law of harmony of interests inspires rational individuals to abandon conflict and enmity for peaceful social cooperation (1951, 294, 295; 1962, 104, 105; 1963, 274–276, 667, 673). Within the social order productive power and purchasing power exist, but power over other individuals does not. Men enjoy "sociological" or "natural" ownership over property, signifying a physical custody and control over things that is "independent of social relations between men" (1951, 37), a definition Mises later overturns by allowing that private ownership excludes others and by distinguishing between "direct" and "indirect" or "social" ownership over factors of production (1951, 39–42). With power excluded it follows that coercion, defined as physical force or threats of it based on power, is nonexistent. Thus prevails freedom, defined to be the opposite of coercion. This freedom, constrained only by natural conditions, is "praxeological freedom," the most perfect freedom attainable by man (1963, 279–287). Enjoying this freedom, human action proceeds. Individuals engage in competition, but (thanks to man's awareness of the natural law of the harmony of interests) it is not antisocial, "pitiless biological competition" (1962, 88, 105), but "praxeological competition" (1963, 116, 117, 273–276). To Commons, however, social order is the outcome of institutions, broadly defined to include habit, moral beliefs, customs, and especially deliberately formed organizations all of which enforce artificial laws. These laws produce conflict resolution, not harmony of interests. These laws specify not control over things, but instead person-to-person relations with respect to things. These relations are used to specify the exact meaning of private ownership and freedom. And freedom Commons defines to be liberty, (an absence of duty) plus power (1924, 111, 118–120, 364). His definition is at odds with

Mises's, and it is one attacked by Hayek (1960, 17). Those with this freedom compete and exercise powers of coercion within limits set by laws enforced by institutions.

   d.   The state, Mises believes, is made necessary by defective individuals who cannot grasp or obey the praxeological laws (1963, 148, 149). Knowledge of Stalin's Russia and Hitler's Germany, not of English or American political and legal history, helped to form Mises's conception of the state. It is monstrous power. It is "by necessity the opposite of liberty" (1963, 285). To Commons, a student of English and American legal history, the American state is a necessary, corrupt, but corrigible institution. Enormous power it has, but due to its English lineage and its own unique constitution, it can apply force to individuals only in a reasonable way.

   e.   Juristic law Mises distinguishes from praxeological law (1963, 280, 761, 762). The former signifies coercion, the opposite of liberty. To Commons juristic law signifies sets of jural correlatives and limits that create and allocate liberty and freedom under law.[1]

   f.   As for capitalism and its legal foundation, if the state confines itself to the role of a "night watchman" state (1927, 37, 38) enforcing solely juristic laws sanctioning the natural conditions of the social order, such as natural ownership and praxeological freedom, then "pure" capitalism (renamed the "unhampered" free market economy) will occur, Mises believes, adding that it is a system that has "never been fully and purely tried" (1963, 264). To Commons, capitalism means the American case instance of it that rests on its actual legal foundations enforced by the actual state.

   g.   The evolution into being of capitalism only slightly interests Mises. He explains it by invoking the law of greater productivity due to the division of labor as one of the "great basic principles of cosmic becoming and evolutionary change" (1963, 145), and the force of ideology (1963, 500, 501, 620). Has then the historical caused the natural to evolve into being? Or has the natural tended to realize itself in history? The latter is more coherent with Mises's thought. To Commons, the evolution of capitalism is a crucial topic, and to explain it he relies largely on the notions of class conflict and "artificial selection" (1934, 657).

   In sum, the theories of sociology of Mises and Commons are different. One relies on natural, the other on positive law. One is slightly concerned with evolution, the other is preoccupied with it. On his version of sociology Mises constructs his economics, renaming it "catallactics," and on his Commons his "institutional" economics.

h.   As one part of his method Mises uses equilibrium analysis as a
first step on the way toward an understanding of the "market process"
(1951, 163; 1963, 248).[2] Commons, preoccupied with evolution, repu-
diates equilibrium analysis and doubts the value of the notion of ceteris
paribus (1934, 388; 1950, 138).

i.   Economic theory, Mises argues, proves that the consequences
of the economic laws of pure capitalism will fulfill the natural law of
harmony of interests, the interests pertaining to those individuals qua
consumers with purchasing power, or, in short, to the "consumer sovereignty." As he phrases it, the "whole functioning and operation" of
the market society is the "consummation" of the principle that "the
selfish concerns of all individuals" will be best served in the long run
(1963, 845). As one part of his proof of this Mises broadly describes
how entrepreneurs form and reform plans, giving rise to an evolving
sequence of actions. In his culminating treatises Commons attempts to
construct an "institutional" economics, making his controversial assertion that it is to "round out" or supplement rather than to deny or
supplant orthodox economics (1934, 5, 6). But if evolution keeps all in
perpetual flux, can any theory be developed? Only "general principles
and methods of investigation" can be, he replies (1934, 612). His general principles he entitles custom, sovereignty, scarcity, efficiency,
and futurity. Below these titles he opaquely presents specific doctrines
to serve as a propaedeutic for the construction of economic laws and
theories relative to time and place. Among these general principles he
tends to emphasize sovereignty, meaning not consumer sovereignty,
but collective power held by the state and legally empowered private
institutions that enforce evolving juristic laws and "working rules."
This sovereignty he identifies as the source of the artificial scarcity
imposed by man on natural scarcity (1924, 386), and the secure expectations and legal instrumentalities making up much of the meaning of
"futurity." On occasion he presses sovereignty's role to an extreme,
saying, for instance, that "all the phenomena of political economy"
are "the present outcome of rights of property and powers of government . . ." (1924, 378).[3]

This makes Commons vulnerable to Mises's charge that all
institutionalists deny the reality of economic law (1951, 531).[4] However, two factors condition Commons's vulnerability to the charge.
First, he does not deny the existence of short-lived economic laws relative to the "institutional set-up" at a given time and place. Second,
although his belief in evolution makes implausible the existence of
economic laws having spatiotemporal generality, counterpoising evi-

dence nonetheless exists. In his writings before 1924 he affirms R. T. Ely's economic law of the twenty-first competitor, the economic law that competition spells unsafe working conditions and long hours and low wage rates for labor, and the economic law that competition tends to lead to monopoly. And finally, he does contend that his "institutional" economics contains general principles that are "general," and that they are intended to supplement and not deny orthodox economics (and, presumably, its economic laws).

    j.   Public policy deeply concerns both men. Both regard themselves as saviors of capitalism. Mises grounds his position in his economic laws. By origin natural and by deduced consequences beneficial, they foretell that nonintervention by a night watchman state will yield insuperable welfare, while intervention in the long run will end in horrors. Commons bases his position on "perpetual investigation and experiment" (1934, 107). He advocates interventionism (see Bronfenbrenner, 23). He urges political policies to reform the state, such as the formation of diverse administrative commissions amounting to a "fourth" branch of government as an initial preparatory step to facilitate the democratic enactment of economic policies usually catering to the labor interest. Such policies will resolve conflicts and bring betterment, he believes; they will destroy harmony and bring horrors in the long run, Mises believes.

    All told, if Mises is selected to represent the Austrians as a class, and Commons the Institutionalists as a class, and if their specific doctrines are compared, then findings at variance with those of Samuels and Boettke emerge. Although the findings confirm the differences Samuels finds, they disconfirm the common elements he finds. The findings vary greatly from those of Boettke. They reveal that the two share no common viewpoint toward evolution, for they differ as to what evolves, and how evolution is to be explained. They indicate moreover that the two do not understand and appreciate historical and institutional factors in the same way, and that the two do not share a somewhat common conception of individualism and human action. They suggest that in general the two are antithetical to one another.

    These findings, however, are merely relative to the selection of Mises and Commons. The selection and emphasis of other men to represent the respective classes, and the comparison of the two classes would yield still other findings.

    The essential attributes defining the class "Austrians" are relatively few, and those defining "Institutionalists" fewer still. Each class quickly gives way to numerous subclasses. If this is indeed true, then efforts to identify and denominate these subclasses may be a useful next step on the way toward a further advancement of the effort Boettke and Samuels have so commendably carried on to compare the Austrians and the Institutionalists.

NOTES

1. Commons would endorse Pound (p. 1): "Liberty under law," referring to the case of the United States of America and its English legal heritage, "implies a systematic and orderly application" of the force of society, or the state, "so that it is uniform, equal, and predictable, and proceeds from reason and upon understood grounds rather than from caprice or impulse or without full and fair hearing of all affected and understanding of the facts on which official action is taken."
2. See the discussion in Cowan and Fink.
3. Commons's "writings and important practical activities centered on the causality of economic magnitudes, primarily values or prices, by processes other than market competition (or monopoly), i.e., by collective action, particularly by the courts in fixing 'fair value' and by labor unions in wage bargaining" (Knight, p. x).
4. Mises suggests an issue. Böhm-Bawerk frames it as *"Macht oder ökonomisches Gesetz"*

REFERENCES

Bronfenbrenner, Martin, (1985) "Early American Leaders—Institutional and Critical Traditions," *American Economic Review*, Vol 75, December, pp. 13–27.

Commons, John R., (1965) *A Sociological View of Sovereignty* (1899–1900). N.Y.: Kelley.

———, (1959) *Legal Foundations of Capitalism* (1924), Madison, Wis.: Univ. of Wis. Press.

———, (1961) *Institutional Economics* (1934), 2 vols. Madison, Wis.: Univ. of Wis. Press.

———, (1970) *The Economics of Collective Action* (1950). Madison, Wis.: Univ. Of Wis. Press.

Cowan, Tyler, and Fink, Richard, (1985) "Inconsistent Equilibrium Constructs: the Evenly Rotating Economy of Mises and Rothbard," *American Economic Review*, Vol. 75, September, pp. 866–869.

Hutchison, Terence W., (1981) *The Politics and Philosophy of Economics: Marxians, Keynesians and Austrians*. New York and London: New York Univ. Press.

Knight, Frank H., (1958) "Foreword," Harris, Abram L., *Economics and Social Reform*. N.Y.: Harper, pp. vii–xii.

Pound, Roscoe, (1957) *The Development of Constitutional Guarantees of Liberty*. New Haven, Conn.: Yale Univ. Press.

von Böhm-Bawerk, Eugen R., (1962) "Macht oder ökonomisches Gesetz" (1914). Trans. by John R. Mez as "Control or Economic Law" (1931). von Böhm-Bawerk, Eugen R., *Shorter Classics of Eugen von Böhm-Bawerk*. Vol. I. South Holland, Ill.: Libertarian Press, pp. 139–199.

von Hayek, Friedrich A., (1960) *The Constitution of Liberty.* Chicago, Ill.: Univ. of Chicago Press.

von Mises, Ludwig E., (1978) *Liberalism* (1927). 2nd ed. Trans. by Ralph Raico. Edited by Arthur Goddard. Kansas City, Mo.: Sheed Andrews and McMeel.

————— , (1960) *Epistemological Problems of Economics* (1933). Trans. by George Reisman. Princeton, N.J.: Van Nostrand.

————— , (1951) *Socialism.* New ed. Trans. by J. Kahane. New Haven, Conn.: Yale Univ. Press.

————— , (1962) *The Ultimate Foundation of Economic Science.* Princeton, N.J.: Van Nostrand.

————— , (1963) *Human Action.* 3rd rev. ed. Chicago, Ill.: Regnery.

COMPARING AUSTRIAN AND INSTITUTIONAL ECONOMICS

Wendell Gordon

The Austrian economists have not been unaware of institutionalism. According to Ludwig von Mises: "The Historical School in Europe and the Institutionalist School in America are the harbingers of the ruinous economic policy that has brought the world to its present condition and will undoubtedly destroy modern culture if it continues to prevail" (1960 [1933], xvii): And: "The writings . . . of the American Institutionalists confused, rather than advanced, our knowledge of . . . the fundamental logical problems of economics" (1960 [1933], x). To return the compliment, this institutionalist alleges that a good deal of what Austrian economics is all about is an effort by those with culture, status, wealth, and perquisites to protect themselves from (the) hoi polloi. "The uncouth hordes of common men are not fit to recognize duly the merits of those who eclipse their own wretchedness" (Mises 1962, 112–113). Mises laments: "Thus, boxing champions and au-

Research in the History of Economic Thought and Methodology,
Volume 6, pages 133-141
Copyright © 1989 by JAI Press Inc.
All rights of reproduction in any form reserved.
ISBN: 0-89232-928-9

thors of detective stories enjoy a higher prestige and earn more money than philosophers and poets'' (1962, 112).

Austrian economists have been sensitive to the charge that they are engaging in special pleading. Hayek wrote in the preface to *The Road to Serfdom*: ''I am as certain as anyone can be that the beliefs set out in it [this book] are not determined by my personal interests. I can discover no reason why the kind of society which seems to me desirable should offer greater advantages to me than to the great majority of the people of my country'' (1956 Phoenix Books ed. [1944], xxi).

The Austrians find that both do-gooders and not-so-do-gooders are all perversely fostering totalitarianism and tyranny. Hayek has written: ''As a result, many who think themselves infinitely superior to the aberrations of naziism, and sincerely hate all its manifestations, work at the same time for ideals whose realization would lead straight to the abhorred tyranny'' (1956 [1944], 4). The Austrians are prone to lump institutionalism along with fascism, naziism, socialism, Marxism, communism, planning, collectivism, and government intervention (interventionism) of any sort in the economy, as playing similar roles in propelling the world toward totalitarian serfdom (Hayek 1956 [1944], 3, 4, 5, 167–180; Mises 1966 [1949], 769). However, if, also, using Chile as an example, one observes that fostering the market system also leads to totalitarian tyranny, one might become pessimistic as to whether the world can avoid the fate of totalitarianism, regardless of what it does.

One may compare Austrian economics with institutionalism in terms of their methodologies.

Endorsement of pragmatism, instrumentalism, the scientific method, inductive logic, statistical testing, and the usefulness of ''knowledge gained by experience'' would seem to be features of institutionalism. However, such endorsement does not involve a condemnation of the use of deductive argument in circumstances where that type of logic would seem to be useful.

For its part, however, Austrian economics, at least as epitomized by Mises, does condemn the use, in the social sciences, of propositions based on experience. The situation may be conceded to be different in the natural sciences, but that is another story. In the social sciences, they frequently allege that the only valid arguments involve a priori or deductive reasoning and all that matters in economics can be derived by deduction from a limited number of assumptions. For example, Mises wrote: ''. . . economics . . . theorems are not open to any verification or falsification on the ground of experience. . . . The ultimate yardstick of an economic theorem's correctness or incorrectness is solely reason unaided by experience'' (1966 [1949], 862). The implications of this procedure can go pretty far. Mises speaks of ''the irrefutable proof provided by economics that trade-union policy can never permanently raise wages for all workers'' (1960 [1933], 59). (It should be mentioned that Hayek seems not to take as strong a position in this regard as does Mises. In fact several important differences in the views of Hayek and Mises make it difficult to visualize a fully coherent Austrian system.)

It is interesting to check how a priori logic works to explain what seems to be going on. For example, Mises identifies the marginal productivity theory of wages as a correct catallactic theorem (1966 [1949], 772, 775–779). In his frame of reference the expression ''correct catallactic theorem'' means that the correctness of the marginal productivity theory of wages has been proven by deductive logic. But, in fact, no such proof exists for the real world on half-way reasonable, realistic assumptions as to what is going on. The proof would need to demonstrate both the possibility of paying labor its marginal product and that this actually happens. For marginal productivity theory to be defensible as a principle, it must be that all the factors of production earn their marginal product and that when this happens the product is exactly exhausted, otherwise there is either not enough to pay all their marginal products or there is surplus for those with the leverage to ''cut themselves in.'' Incidentally this might exactly be the role of the labor unions, to function as the leverage ''cutting labor in'' on the surplus. This possibility raises a question concerning the Austrian contention ''that trade-union policy can never permanently raise wages for all workers.''

Paying all of the factors of production their marginal products (whether or not this actually happens) would be possible if constant returns to scale characterize production or if all firms actually operate at the lowest point on their long-run average cost curves. I am subject to correction on this issue, but I believe that nowhere does Mises even claim that constant returns to scale characterize production or that firms operate at the lowest point on those cost curves. In fact Mises goes to considerable effort to avoid being shackled by the pure competition assumption of innumerable buyers and sellers. In addition I am reasonably sure that nowhere in the writing of Mises is there even an effort to demonstrate that workers actually receive their marginal products.

An area where there is similarity between Austrian and institutional views involves emphasis on the importance of ongoing process (as distinct from centering attention, as does neoclassical economics, on static equilibrium and the maximization or optimization of something conceived to be desirable during a given time period when all the conditions are pre-set). Ideas, attitudes, and institutionalized behavior norms or values are the product of an ongoing process. "An individual is at any instant of his life the product of all the experiences to which his ancestors were exposed plus those to which he himself has so far been exposed" (Mises 1957, 159). "It is a task of history, for example, to trace back the origin of India's caste system to the values which prompted the conduct of the generations who developed, perfected, and preserved it. It is its further task to discover what the consequences of this system were and how these effects influence the value judgments of later generations" (Mises 1957, 21).

With regard to the issue as to whether the behavior norms generated in this process represent values that should be considered to be eternal verities, Mises gives a very clear answer in the negative: " 'Thou shalt not kill' is certainly not part of natural law. . . . There is, however no such thing as a perennial standard of what is just and what is unjust. Nature is alien to the idea of right and wrong. . . . There is neither right nor wrong outside the social nexus" (1966 [1949], 720–721). This writer believes that on this issue institutionalism is in agreement with the Austrians but realizes that all institutionalists may not be.

Beyond this area of agreement the differences multiply. Institutionalism develops an argument that identifies evolving technology as a major influence in determining what these behavior norms will become. On this point, Mises merely says: "In searching for the origin of new ideas history cannot go beyond establishing that they were produced by a man's thinking" (1957, 160).

Even more important is the difference in the view as to the implications of the institutionalized behavior norms that prevail at the moment. The Austrians believe that the currently prevailing attitudes represent some sort of superior, or for the moment at least not to be questioned, judgment. The Austrians venerate the customary rules which are in existence, whereas the institutionalists do not.

For the Austrians, these attitudes about values assume a sort of infallibility role. According to Mises: ". . . judgments of value are ultimate choices on the part of the individual who utters them" (1957, 342). And: "For the sciences of human action the ultimate given is the judgment of value of the actors and the ideas that engender these judgments of value" (1957, 306). Or: "There is no yardstick that a scientific investigation can apply to human action other than that of the ultimate goals the acting individual wants to realize in embarking upon a definite action. The ultimate goals themselves are beyond and above any criticism" (1966 [1949], 651). (This argument, then, may be alleged to answer the charge of inconsistency made three paragraphs earlier.)

A principal object of veneration on the part of the Austrians is the institution which might be called the market system: a system characterized by laissez-faire, and being free of planning, or government regulation, or government ownership. Hayek says: "In other words: man has certainly more often learnt to do the right thing without comprehending why it was the right thing, and he still is often served better by custom than understanding" (1979, 157). "This exchange society and the guidance of the co-ordination of a far-ranging division of labour by variable market prices was made possible by the spreading of certain gradually evolved moral beliefs which, after they had spread, most men of the Western world learned to accept" (1979, 164). But the argument, stated in this form, may leave one wondering as to just what is the criterion for identifying "the right thing."

Be that as it may, the Austrians, then, assume the merit of the values prevailing at the moment and proceed to apply them in an exercise involving a priori or deductive logic to arrive at propositions which are then alleged to be definitively proven. "All the theorems of catallactics [the theory of the market economy] are rigidly and without any exception valid for all the phenomena of the market economy, provided the particular conditions which they presuppose are present" (Mises 1966 [1949], 646).

In contrast with the Austrian veneration for currently prevailing behavior norms (or rather, if the truth be told, the behavior norms they would like to have be currently prevailing), the institutionalist position would seem to be that the prevailing norms, having come into being in the past and therefore probably being more appropriate for dealing with the problems of the period when they came into existence than with the changed problems of the present, should be considered as continually subject to thoughtful and constructive change, "constructive" in terms of what an evolving society chooses to believe is constructive.

But the Austrian advocacy of freedom and liberty (read laissez [l'entrepreneur] faire) is a position that has another problem. What is the basis for arguing for moving away from a situation in being that involves a mixture of private enterprise and government regulation—if you venerate the status quo. This would seem to be the system in being that represents the accumulated wisdom of society and should therefore, according to one aspect of the Austrian argument, be perpetuated? What is the basis for arguing for movement to a system, in this case laissez faire, that has never been tried? The Austrians want to have it both ways, to impose some value judgments and to venerate the status quo at the same time. It may be noted that the Austrians do not endorse liberty and freedom on the grounds that their desirability is an eternal verity or a natural law (Mises 1966 [1949], 720–721; 1957, 22; Hayek 1960, 29, 54), despite their apparent endorsement of an a priori, deductive logic methodology.

Despite the Austrian fervent and repeated endorsement of something they merely call "economics," it turns out that in fact they do not endorse pure-competition-type price theory in the standard form in which price theory is taught in American universities (Mises 1966 [1949], 243). The denunciation of Milton Friedman in Murray Rothbard's writing is close to vitriolic (1978 [1973], 27, 260–261). It is a bit difficult to find in the Austrian writing a synthesis as to what they actually do stand for. They endorse competition, but it seems to be a rather impure sort of competition that does not claim to establish equilibrium or maximize the general welfare in any mathematically demonstrable sense. This rough and ready competition, free of government interference, is argued to be desirable because: "Those fighting for free enterprise and free competition do not defend the interests of those rich today. They want a free hand left to unknown men who will be the entrepreneurs of tomorrow and whose ingenuity will make the life of coming generations more agreeable" (Mises 1966 [1949], 82–83). One might believe that the proponents of such views would want everyone to start with equal opportunity. But not so. . . . (Rothbard 1978 [1973], 41).

Some of the more specific concepts that one gleans here and there as being endorsed by the Austrians may be noted. "For example, we deduce from our theory that when the price of a commodity rises, its production will be increased. However. . . ." (Mises 1960 [1933], 163). In the international trade area, the theory of comparative cost and its implications for free trade are endorsed. The division of labor is eulogized (Mises 1966 [1949], 145). Carl Menger's conception of diminishing marginal utility is endorsed with its implications for a subjective approach to valuation as distinct from the emphasis on a labor (or cost side) theory of value, such as had characterized classical and Marxist economics. According to Menger "value is subjective": "Hence not only the *nature* but also the *measure* of value is subjective'' (1963 [1883], 146). "In the value of goods, therefore, we always encounter merely the significance we assign to the satisfaction of our needs—that is, to our lives and well being'' (Menger 1963 [1883], 121–122). In elaboration of this approach there is the concept of diminishing marginal utility: ''. . . the satisfaction of any one specific need has up to a certain degree of completeness, relatively the highest importance, and that further satisfaction has a progressively smaller importance, until eventually a stage is reached at which a more complete satisfaction of that particular need is a matter of indifference'' (Menger 1963 [1883], 125).

Above all, "the market solution'' (laissez [l'entrepreneur] faire) is endorsed and government intervention in the working of the economy is condemned. This is what Hayek's book, *Road to Serfdom*, is all about. And Mises wrote: "And finally, the science of economics proves with cold, irrefutable logic that the ideals of those who condemn making a living on the market are quite vain, that the socialist organization of society is unrealizable and contrary to the ends at which it aims, and that therefore the market economy is the only feasible system of social cooperation'' (1960 [1933], 196).

The institutionalist view contrasts with the Austrian view as to the definitiveness of the currently-held value judgment. (This statement of the institutionalism view is expressed with some misgiving. I cannot guarantee that it is generally held in institutionalists. Be that as it may, my allegation is the following.) The currently-held institutionalized behavior norms or value judgments are the view of society at the moment as to valuations. And there exists no higher authority. This is true despite the fact that those behavior norms came into being at some earlier time and there exists the presumption that they are a bit obsolescent, since conditions have changed from the time when they came into being and the probabilities are that they were more appropriate to the circumstances that brought them into being than to the changed circumstances of the present. The safeguard is the view that these currently-held valuations are not sacrosanct. And much of institutional economics is devoted to understanding the process by which these valuations get changed.

Be that as it may. Here we are and here they are. For the moment, currently-held value judgments are the basis of the rules which society is respecting and enforcing. And deviationists deviate at their peril and become either heroes or outcasts. However the basic situation is that the thoughtful and concerned citizen, instead of accepting the merit and definitiveness of prevailing norms, as the Austrians do, can be expected to observe how well they seem to be working and whether the results seem to be satisfactory or could be improved upon. Experience, thus, indicates the desirability of changing valuations or of changing the procedures for implementing valuations.

The Austrians with their praxeology and catallactics have debarred themselves from thinking in these terms. "The value judgments that are made in human action are ultimate data" (Mises 1960 [1933], 16) and their implications are established by a priori or deductive logic. Learning by experience is ruled out: ". . . a proposition of an aprioristic nature can never be refuted by experience" (Mises 1960 [1933], 28–29). "However, economics also stops here. It does not go further back. It does not inquire into what lies behind the decision of acting men, why they act precisely in the way they do and not otherwise. . . . Economics is distinguished from psychology by the fact that it considers action alone and that the psychic events that have led to an action are without importance for it" (Mises 1960 [1933], 208). "Action is, by definition, always rational" (Mises 1960 [1933], 35). (So much for "rational expectations.") (On the other hand, other Austrians, Hayek for example, are not so categorical as is Mises on these matters. So, neither the Austrian nor the institutionalist positions may be quite as categorical as is implied here.)

What is the meaning of the freedom the Austrians are talking about? Freedom from what? Slavery, a nagging wife, a brutal husband, taxes, responsibility, garbage? The Austrians keep saying they are not self-serving or merely protective of the interests of the affluent. Apparently their consciences hurt them a little, but not enough. Laissez (l'entrepreneur) faire, and devil take the hindmost or the unfortunate, or leave them dependent on the whims of voluntary charity.

It is possible that the freedom advocated by the Austrians is not a general concept at all. The issue should be stated the other way round. The advocate of restraining rules, or of intervention affecting the behavior of others, appropriately, should offer reasons. The issue than becomes one in terms of a social judgment as to the reasonableness or the desirability of the restriction.

Platitudes about "free to choose," and the desirability of freedom or liberty, in the abstract, contribute very little to the resolution of problems. On the other hand, controls for the sake of controls scarcely make much sense either, but neither does shaking one's fist at the law of gravity (if it is a law).

REFERENCES

Hayek, Friedrich, (1960) *Constitution of Liberty*, Chicago: University of Chicago Press.

_____, (1979) *The Political Order of a Free People*, Chicago: University of Chicago Press.

_____, (1956) *Road to Serfdom*, Chicago: Phoenix Book (University of Chicago Press, [1944].

Menger, Carl, (1963) *Problems of Economics and Sociology*, Urbana: University of Illinois Press, [1883].

Mises, Ludwig von, (1960) *Epistemological Problems of Economics*, New York: Van Nostrand, [1933].

_____, (1966) *Human Action*, 3rd rev. ed., Chicago: Henry Regnery, [1949].

_____, (1957) *Theory and History*, New Haven: Yale University Press.

_____, (1978) *Ultimate Foundation of Economic Science*, Kansas: Sheed, Andrews & McMeel, [1962].

Rothbard, Murray N. (1978) *For a New Liberty: The Libertarian Manifesto*, rev. ed., New York: Collier Books (Macmillan), [1973].

COMMENT ON W. SAMUELS, "AUSTRIAN AND INSTITUTIONAL ECONOMICS: SOME COMMON ELEMENTS" AND P. BOETTKE, "EVOLUTION AND ECONOMICS: AUSTRIANS AS INSTITUTIONALISTS"

William S. Kern

As Peter Boettke points out in his paper, Austrian and Institutional economics are usually viewed as the antithesis of one another. Yet authors Samuels and Boettke have managed to pierce through this veil of received opinion to point out that the two schools of thought have in fact a large number of commonalities, as well as their perhaps better known differences.

Research in the History of Economic Thought and Methodology,
Volume 6, pages 143-149
Copyright © 1989 by JAI Press Inc.
All rights of reproduction in any form reserved.
ISBN: 0-89232-928-9

The two papers are complementary to one another and represent a productive division of labor. Samuels' paper surveys a much wider range of commonalities and explores the differences in approach. What I find particularly insightful in his comparison is his attention both to doctrinal matters and the sociological aspects such as the perception of being outsiders vis à vis neoclassicism and the tendency toward formation of subgroups with differing methodological and normative approaches. One suspects that these sociological characteristics are common not only for Austrians and Institutionalists but Marxists also, as well as any other group outside the mainstream.

The Boettke paper is comparatively more narrow in focus. It explains the extent to which Austrian economics is similar to Institutionalism; thus it is more "unidirectional" in its comparisons. It focuses upon two of the most important similarities between the schools: the focus on process and the role of institutions and does so in more detail than Samuels' paper.

My comments are directed mainly toward clarification of aspects of the position of each of these schools on certain issues as presented by authors Samuels and Boettke. In addition to the clarification of Institutionalist and Austrian views I also seek to discuss much more the question of differences between the schools; my view being that paradoxically the most important differences stem from the areas in which they are most alike!

In his characterization of Austrian views of the choice process Samuels claims "that Austrian economists tends to focus on choice within opportunity sets and institutional economists on the formation of opportunity sets and preferences" (8). This puts Austrian economics much more in the camp of neoclassicals with their (neoclassicals) focus on "Robbinsian maximizers" who function within a framework of known preferences and known constraints. Recent work by a number of Austrians, especially Kirzner, has attempted to make a clear distinction between the "Robbinsian" view and theirs.[1] The focus of Austrians upon radical subjectivism and uncertainty is certainly at odds with a view of choice within known opportunity sets. While choice must, in the Austrian view, be influenced by constraints, recent work has focused much more upon the exploratory and discovery—like nature of choice and opportunities.

A second view that emerges from Samuels' survey of Austrian thought is that while Austrians have denigrated the state they have not viewed the state "as a basic choice process inextricably intertwined with the operation of markets" (9). It is certainly true that Austrians have tended to denigrate the state. Perhaps earlier Austrian analysis did little more than that, though Mises' analysis of bureaucracy was an attempt at a positive theory of the state. Certainly it is not true of the recent work of Hayek who has carefully integrated the role of the state and law into the framework of a market economy. There are other signs as well that Austrians have accepted the work of the Public Choice school as compatible with their methodological stance.[2] This supplies the Austrians with the positive theory of the state they may have lacked heretofore. Thus I find that there is more element of commonality in this regard than does Samuels. It should be clear, however, that this commonality is rather limited. The vision of the state, both in the normative and the positive, is decidedly different. What is clear is that both schools of thought have long considered the role of the state to be crucial to their research programs as compared to neoclassicism.[3]

Boettke's paper explores the similarities in approach between the Austrian and Institutionalist views on process and institutions. To be sure there is a certain commonality of views on these issues, but to my mind the important differences in approach to these two issues are the crucial ones leading to the antithetical relationship between the two schools. As Samuels notes, "if one approaches their respective work without trying to emphasize normative or ideological differences . . . one finds much substantive agreement" (19). But to neglect the normative and ideological elements is to neglect an awfully important component of the thought of both schools.

Samuels notes in his paper that each school has "tended strongly to identify itself vis-à-vis neoclassical economics" (3). Clarence Ayres, in searching for the "first principles" of institutionalist thought, noted that his own attempts toward that end "began with a repudiation of the 'classical' tradition" (1962, xi). Furthermore he noted that while a definitive definition of Institutionalist principles was difficult, he nonetheless asserted that "if there is anything that all institutionalists have in common it is dissatisfaction with 'orthodox' price theory (xi). Similarly, modern Austrians have also indicated that the primary impetus in their work has been their dissatisfaction with the orthodox presentation of economic analysis (Kirzner 1973, 3). The sources of dissatisfaction of both schools with orthodoxy are similar but also widely at odds with one another.

The primary Austrian criticisms of neoclassicism are that it fails to include in it's analysis certain key features of market activity and economic choice. Kirzner has emphasized neoclassicism's neglect of the

role of the entrepreneur. O'Dricscoll and Rizzo focus upon the importance of subjectivism and the much neglected concept of time. Hayek
has criticized the neoclassical assumptions about knowledge and its
importance for understanding the process of competition. But what is
also clear is that Austrians have little quarrel with orthodoxy's conception of the economy as "market organized." That is, Austrians agree
with neoclassicals that understanding of the economy derives from an
understanding of markets and individual choice. They disagree in their
descriptions and characterizations of each of those entities. This is
much in contrast to the view of the Institutionalists.

Institutionalists are not only critical of the static, equilibrium-bound
conception of markets as portrayed by neoclassicism, but also choose
to dissent from the traditional, i.e., market oriented, conception of the
economic process. According to Ayres, his initial concerns about the
theory of value and capital ultimately led him to the conclusion "that
the economy itself which has all the time been the subject of our discipline has been completely misconceived" (1962, xiv). What is misconceived according to Institutionalists is that it is industrial technology which is "the real substance of the modern economy"—which
does not deny the existence of markets and prices but which does question their importance.

What this signies to this commentator is that in spite of their differences Neoclassicals and Austrians are much closer to one another than
are Austrians and Institutionalists, in spite of the similarities among the
latter cited by Samuels and Boettke. Indeed what is hoped for from the
exposition of Austrian ideas is a "better" theory of price determination and allocation of resources through markets by the incorporation
of Austrian insights. Thus there is no real quarrel about the end to be
achieved. On the other hand Institutionalists have rejected the view
that any sort of reconciliation of their views and those of the mainstream is possible. According to Ayres,

> the prevailing opinion seems to be that wheras the classical and institutionalist
> schools were once thought to be diametrically opposed, economists now 'recog-
> nize' the differences to be only one of emphasis. ... Needless to say, Veblen
> would have repudiated this interpretation. His attack on John Bates Clark, for
> example, affords no ground whatever for the presumption that the only differ-
> ence between Clark's way of thinking and his own was one of emphasis (1962,
> 12).

Thus it would seem that the similarities between Institutionalists and
Austrians are epiphenomenonal in the sense that the similarities derive

from a common reaction to the static, processless, equilibrium focused approach of neoclassicism rather than a sharing of a fundamental conception about the economy. I think this is brought out by a further comparison of the Austrian and Institutionalist views on process and institutions.

Boettke points out, and rightly so, that the area of greatest commonality between Austrians and Institutionalists is their views on the evolutionary nature of social institutions. He claims that there is a methodological common ground between Austrians and the work of Veblen that provides a basis for the Austrian criticism of neoclassicism. I share Boettke's view that the Austrian and Institutionalist views on the nature of social institutions are process and evolution oriented. However, I also think that there are signicant disagreements between the two on these issues.

The primary difference, it seems to me, is a normative one. Austrians regard the evolutionary process of institutional change in Darwinian terms. The Darwinian aspect of the development of social institutions is best represented by Hayek's view that;

> the institutions did develop in a particular way because the co-ordination of the actions of the parts which they secured proved more effective than the alternative institutions with which they had competed and which they had displaced. The theory of evolution of traditions and habits which made the formation of spontaneous orders possible stands therefore in a close relation to the theory of evolution ... (1967, 101).

Thus Austrians regard these emergent institutions, such as the market system, as *superior* to those forms of social organization which had preceeded them because they enhance the degree of plan coordination possible.

A second Austrian theme concerns the extent to which conscious action may improve upon social institutions which ''are the result of human action but not of human design.'' The Austrian position is that owing to fundamental limitations upon our knowledge, existing institutions such as the law and the market are orders ''which we cannot improve upon but only disturb by attempting to change by deliberate arrangement any one part of it'' (Hayek 1967, 92). What change is possible must be done by improving the framework of the existing institutional matrix of the market system and the inhereted legal tradition rather than replacing them.

In contrast, Institutionalists, while viewing institutions from a similar evolutionary perspective, have a much different view. The first of these differences surrounds the question of whether the market system is the result of an unconscious evolutionary process or of human design. This question was addressed by Polanyi who attempted to demonstrate that the development of the market system was the result of a deliberate attempt at its creation, while reaction to it and attempts at its moderation were not.

> The road to the free market was opened and kept open by an enormous increase in continuous, centrally organized and controlled interventionism. . . . While laissez-faire economy was the product of deliberate state action, subsequent restrictions on laissez-faire started in a spontaneous way. Laissez-faire was planned; Planning was not (Polanyi 1944, 141).

Polanyi himself noted the extent to which this interpretation contrasted with the explanation of the events of the nineteenth century as provided by Mises and others (ibid).

Though both Institutionalists and Austrians share a view that human social institutions change and grow in an evolutionary process, Institutionalists do not share the Austrian view that the existing set of social institutions, particularly the private, free enterprise system of economic organization, represent progressive forms in the interest of future economic progress. One of the central tenets of institutionalist theory is that established social institutions inhibit, if not absolutely prevent change. In particular, Institutionalists regard the commitment to the free market form of economic organization as a definite impediment to economic progress and traditional economic theory used to support it as mythology. The continuing existence of both the market system and the economic analysis that supports it constitute, in Veblenian terms, "the triumph of imbecile institutions over life and culture." Because Austrian economics exhalts existing institutions and cautions against their replacement, it must thus be regarded as ceremonialism "and as such it is an impediment to economic progress as ceremonial propensities have always been" (Ayres 1962, 202).

In summation, it would seem that the large gap which separates Institutionalist and Austrian economists is unlikely to be bridged. Fundamental differences in each school's conception of the economic process and the role of social institutions in that process are unlikely to be resolved by the recognition that both schools share a common approach and interest in similar questions. It is true that each may be able to benefit from a greater awareness of the work of the other but their ideological differences make it seem doubtful that they can ever become very strong "intellectual allies in their fight against the ahistorical economics of the mainstream."

NOTES

1. Kirzner's paper "Robbins' Nature and Significance 50 Years Later" presented to the 1982 meetings of the History of Economics Society is an excellent example.
2. See for example Ch. 7 of D. Reekie's *Markets, Entrepreneurs and Liberty: An Austrian View of Capitalism.*
3. "Austrian economist, to a much greater extent than the neoclassical school, have given prominence to their view of the nature of the state and its relationship to the individual" (Shand 1984, p. 178).

REFERENCES

Ayres, Clarence., (1962) *The Theory of Economic Progress*, New York: Schocken Books.
————, (1966) "The Nature and Significance of Institutionalism," *Antioch Review*, Spring.
Hayek, F. A., (1967) *Studies in Philosophy, Politics, and Economics*, Chicago: The University of Chicago Press.
————, (1973) *Law, Legislation and Liberty*, Chicago: The University of Chicago Press, Vol. I, "Rules and Order."
Kirzner, I., (1973) *Competition and Entrepreneurship*, Chicago: University of Chicago Press.
————, (1985) *Discovery and the Capitalist Process*, Chicago: University of Chicago Press.
O'Driscoll, G. and Rizzo, M., (1985) *The Economics of Time and Ignorance*, New York: Basil Blackwell.
Polanyi, K. (1944) *The Great Transformation*, Boston: Beacon Press.
Reekie, D., (1984) *Markets, Entrepreneurs, and Liberty*, New York: St. Martin's Press.
Shand, A., (1984) *The Capitalist Alternative: An Introduction to Neo-Austrian Economics*, New York: N.Y.U. Press.
Veblen, T., (1919) *The Place of Science in Modern Civilization*, New York: Viking Press.
————, (1914) *The Instinct of Workmanship*, New York.

COMMENT ON BOETTKE AND SAMUELS:
AUSTRIAN AND INSTITUTIONAL ECONOMICS

Edythe S. Miller

The papers by Professors Boettke and Samuels, while differing in approach and emphasis, share a common theme. The purpose of each is to identify affinities between Austrian and Institutional economics, schools of thought generally held to be poles apart by members of the economics profession, and by none more so than by those of the schools themselves. The subject matter of the papers thus is both original and provocative, and if for no other reasons, almost certainly will be controversial. On this ground alone, the authors are to be congratulated.

Unfortunately, however, the effort, even if interesting, essentially fails of achievement. It fails because the wider theoretical frameworks

Research in the History of Economic Thought and Methodology,
Volume 6, pages 151-158
Copyright © 1989 by JAI Press Inc.
All rights of reproduction in any form reserved.
ISBN: 0-89232-928-9

of the systems of thought are so at variance, so dissimilar their views of reality, so at cross purposes their world views that in almost every instance the perceived similarities translate into differences. Inevitably, the visions and frames of reference that hold together the theories inform and color as well their mode of analysis, their selection and interpretation of facts and their public policy conclusions.

The antithetical nature of Austrian and Institutional economics can, perhaps, be seen in starkest relief if they are viewed in terms of certain frame characteristics. Accordingly, the schools will be considered on the basis, respectively, of their methodologies, and of their theories of human nature, of development and of value.

Methodologically, Austrian economics is aprioristic and individualistic. The Austrian method, it has been observed, is "simply put, to spin out by verbal deductive reasoning, the logical implications of a few fundamental axioms" (Dolan, 7). That is, the nature of the economic problem is seen as the discovery and description of general laws that are present in any economic system.

Within modern Austrian economics, there is some dispute as to the role experience plays in axiom derivation. But for even that branch that holds that axioms, at bottom, are derived from experience, it is a strange, almost a mystical form of empiricism that controls. Thus, "the axioms of praxeology are radically empirical . . . They rest . . . on universal *inner* experience, as well as on external experience . . . that is, the evidence is *reflective* rather than purely physical; and . . . they are therefore a priori to . . . events . . ." (Rothbard 25, emphasis in original).

But even so qualified an empiricism is not uniformly accepted. Austrians also specify ". . . the absurdity of subjecting valid deductions from true axioms to superfluous empirical tests" (Dolan 1976, 14). Most Institutional economists would find Austrian apriorism clearly within a tradition that conforms, as described by Thorstein Veblen, to ". . . the metaphysics of normality and controlling principles" (Veblen 1898, 70).

An additional central feature of Austrian economics is that of methodological individualism. Here the central precept is that aggregate social phenomena are reducible to and find their significance in individual acts and interrelations; that individual action must be the "basic building block of economic theory" (Dolan 1976, 5). All cultural and social conditions are strictly construed as the summation of the acts of humans separately seeking their own ends.

The contention that behavior can be understood only in individual terms leads to the denial that there are collective bodies with attributes different from those of individuals (Bell and Kristol 1981, x) or that can be distinguished and examined as economic or social phenomena. Thus, exception is taken to a focus on such collective entities as government or culture; the use of aggregates such as GNP is foresworn; even the term "macroeconomics" is rejected (Dolan 1976, 11). It follows that collective action is viewed by Austrians as mischievous or pernicious.

Institutional economics, in contrast, is unreservedly empiricist and collectivist. It sees economic knowledge, not as a reflection of an underlying and antecedent reality, but rather as centered in experience, created in the here and now by individuals interacting with others and with their environments, with each being changed in the process. It abjures such concepts as the "normal" or the "natural" in reference either to human characteristics or to social and economic organization.

Institutional economics views individuals as part of a social milieu that both shapes and is shaped by its human participants. Where Austrians abstract from most historical and institutional factors and focus attention on one institution, that of the market, broad institutional analysis is at the very heart of Institutional economics. Keynesian economics easily is incorporated into the Institutional paradigm; for the Austrian, it is anathema.

The theories of human nature that inform Austrian and Institutional thought also exhibit stark differences. The primary axiom of Austrian theory is that of purposeful human action. It is contended that because action is purposeful, it follows that it is rational (Caldwell 1984, 366). Economic science, then, is viewed as the science of choice; consumers are moved to action by a desire for utility maximization within a given income constraint. The system is driven by consumer sovereignty. Although Austrian economics claims to find no constants in human action (Dolan 1976, 14), it would seem that its *homo economicus* engaged in optimizing behavior is an abiding and controlling constant, indeed. Austrian economics further contends that "the fact that praxeological economic theory rests on the universal fact of individual values and choices means . . . that economic theory does 'not need to investigate the origin of choices' " (Rothbard 1976, 31).[1]

That Austrian economics views humans as purposive rather than passive beings is one of the factors that gives rise to the claim of comparability with Institutional economics. The human purposiveness that each theory perceives is vastly different, however. In Austrian thought it is bounded by rationality, by maximizing motives, by the irksomeness of labor.

Institutional economics, in contrast, perceives human action as guided both by rational and irrational tendencies. It sees individual action impelled in various ways; by customs, convention, moral suasion and coercion—all facts of group life—in addition and opposition to self interest. It views preferences frequently as acquired, with emulation, producer manipulation and social conditioning generally perceived as forces helping to shape tastes. The collective is posited as conditioning and supporting individual actions and relations in diverse and important respects. The origin of choice and the advantages— indeed, the very existence—of consumer sovereignty are challenged. A consistent thread running throughout the Institutional literature is the theme that all expenditure decisions and all productive efforts are not equally legitimate (See, for example, Veblen 1899, passim; Galbraith 1958, passim).

The Austrian and Institutional theories of development are similarly divergent. The Austrian theory is centered on the market as the arena of change and the entrepreneur as its agent. The market is perceived as a continuous process, with no state of rest, no equilibrium (Lachmann 1976, 59). The Austrians reject, as do the Institutionalists, both the static equilibrium models and the "scientism" of orthodoxy. Also, both schools observe a world of uncertainty and imperfect knowledge as the setting for the human drama. But at this juncture the similarity, if indeed it can be so characterized, quickly fades. The human dramas the schools see unfolding vary substantially.

Austrian economics contends that it is the market process that imposes order in a world of incomplete information and uncertainty about the future. The entrepreneur, sensitive to opportunities to buy cheap and sell dear (Kirzner 1976, 119–20) coordinates and disseminates the scattered knowledge that exists over the many parts of the economic system and otherwise assumes the burden of uncertainty in a world of divergent expectations. In return, he secures the opportunity for future reward. If any potential for change over time in the human factor is recognized, it is merely a change in barter and exchange skills and market niche filling capacities; in persons' pecuniary, as opposed to their industrial capabilities, to borrow Veblen's terms (Veblen 1901, passim). Economic progress consists in an increase in the range and improvement in the quality of goods. The market is perceived as an unbiased, even an equitable mechanism.

Economic progress is attributed by Institutionalists, not to entrepreneurial decision making within a free market, but to technological advance. They interpret technology broadly as "the state of the industrial arts"; that is, they see it as including both the existing level of equipment and technique and of human technical knowledge. Technology is viewed as part of the common stock of a culture; that is, as a fact of collective life. Since the physical properties of materials do not vary over time, progress can be understood only in terms of changes in human understanding of the ways in which they can be used (Veblen 1898, 71–4, 1914, 103). The entrepreneur is not perceived as the hero of the human drama; he even may be anti-hero. Institutional economics recognizes both the exploitative and creative tendencies of individuals, as typified by the Veblenian distinction between ceremonial and instrumental behavior.

Institutionalists envision change as a function of the creative imagination. Individual curiosity and the instinct of workmanship energize advances in scientific understanding and technique. Humans, in turn, are changed in the process. From the perspective of Institutionalism, the concept of economic progress in Austrian thought involves economic change in the absence of economic development.

Finally, the theories of value espoused by each school exhibit sharp disparities. While I agree with Samuels that both schools are activist in the sense that each argues for the adoption of a particular set of policies,[2] the position of each in regard to the normative-positive debate is instructive. Austrians uniformly see themselves as positivist and the discipline as value-free. Institutionalists, in contrast, exhibit a substantial ambiguity in regard to the question. While some purport to see the discipline fundamentally as descriptive, a sizeable proportion view it as value laden, in countless ways, and its function as that of problem solving.

When it comes to the set of policy prescriptions advanced by each school, differences could not be more sharply drawn. Austrian economics sees the free market as imposing "spontaneous order" (Vanberg 1986, 76). In keeping with this perspective, it opposes central planning and government intervention generally. Public planning is viewed, first of all, as inefficient, as contended in the well known debate in the economic literature of the twenties and thirties on economic calculation under socialism. But in any event, and regardless of the perceived outcome of that debate, it is seen as resulting in a curtailment of liberty (Hayek 1944, passim). Unplanned order is equated with individual freedom.

The policy prescriptions follow. Austrian economics argues for a strict policy of laissez-faire within a free market. It favors open entry, condemns regulation of business, does not quarrel with vast scale or the ability of business to set price, and feels that an anti-trust policy that does not recognize these principles "threatens the viability of American industry" (Kirzner 1981, 117). Austrian thought is a celebration of unrestrained market capitalism.

Institutional economics, in contrast, is frankly interventionist and experimental. Although there is some disagreement among its adherents as to the appropriate extent of public planning, the school generally favors a pragmatic and eclectic approach to questions of market form, seeing no specific structure as inherently "normal" or "natural."

Nor does institutionalism perceive the market as a creative force in bringing about a desirable unplanned order. They see it instead as as often controlled as controlling; controlled by entities in possession of market power whose decisions therefore may result, not in economic progress, but in economic inefficiency and exploit. Institutionalists thus view the market, not as a neutral or equitable mechanism, but as a potentially biased one. They urge that business be subject to social control in a public interest so as to avoid its operation for purposes of the aggrandizement and protection of powerful private interests.

Institutionalism thus looks to questions of equity, as well as efficiency. In contrast, the Austrian preferred policy of laissez-faire extends to equity considerations. Thus, it is contended: "There is no distributional process apart from the . . . processes of the market. . . . [S]ince this process benefits all participants . . . and increases social utility, . . . the 'distributional' results of the free market also increases social utility" (Lachmann 1984, 311).[3]

Institutionalists see production as a cooperative act, rendering individual contribution incalculable, indeterminate and, at bottom, meaningless even as an abstraction. Since, the contribution of each worker to the product rests upon and blends into that of his or her co-workers, and ultimately is dependent upon the level and availability of the communally held stock of technology, the market does not necessarily appropriately reward. Rather, market distribution is largely a matter of relative power and bargaining strength.

In sum, the papers do not seem to me to have hit their mark. In all honesty, I must confess to some confusion as to what exactly that mark is. If the attempt is to reconcile the theories, it clearly has not been successful. The differences between the schools are not of nuance, but of essence. So substantially do the systems of thought differ—in perspective, in focus, in their very boundaries—that any effort at reconciliation would have small chance of success.

If, instead, the purpose is the less ambitious one of drawing forth similarities in the service of a different goal, say in an effort to illustrate through a demonstration of compatibility of parts that the theories are not as antagonistic as is generally believed, it seems to me that effort as well has failed. The parts of a system, viewed in isolation, will no more yield an understanding of the whole than will the individual musical chords embedded in a symphony, taken out of their context, reveal its often subtle, complex and total sound. To the contrary, the parts can be understood and, in fact, take their very meaning from their rootedness and connectedness within the larger context.

If, on the other hand, the intent simply and somewhat aimlessly was to make some comparisons for their own sake—well then, who am I to disparage idle curiosity?

NOTES

The author is retired. Her most recent association was with the Colorado Public Utilities Commission, where she served as commissioner from 1975 to 1987.

1. Rothbard identifies the internal quotation only, and without citation, as having been taken from "Dorfman's summary of Davenport's thought" (loc. cit.).

2. However, I would take it the further step and contend that in that sense, and it is an appropriate and valid sense, all schools, explicitly or implicitly, are activist.

3. The comment is quoted with approval by Lachmann from Murray N. Rothbard, "Toward a Reconstruction of Utility and Welfare Economics."

REFERENCES

Bell, Daniel and Kristol, Irving, eds. (1981) *The Crisis in Economic Theory*, New York: Basic Books, Inc.

Caldwell, Bruce J., (1984) "Praxeology and its Critics: An Appraisal," *History of Political Economy*, Fall, 16, 363–79.

Dolan, Edwin G., (1976) "Austrian Economics as Extraordinary Science" in Dolan, Edwin G., ed., *The Foundations of Modern Austrian Economics*, Kansas City: Sheed and Ward, Inc., 3–15.

Galbraith, John Kenneth, (1958) *The Affluent Society*, Boston: Houghton Mifflin Company.

Hayek, Friedrich A., (1944) *The Road to Serfdom*, Chicago: The University of Chicago Press.

Kirzner, Israel M., (1976) "Equilibrium versus Market Process: in Dolan," Edwin G., ed., *The Foundations of Modern Austrian Economics*, Kansas City: Sheed and Ward, Inc., 115–125.

————, (1981) "The 'Austrian' Perspective" in Bell, Daniel and Kristol, Irving, eds., *The Crisis in Economic Theory*, New York: Basic Books, Inc., 111–122.

Lachmann, Ludwig M., (1976) "From Mises to Schackle: An Essay" *Journal of Economic Literature*, March, 14, 54–62.

————, (1984) "Methodological Individualism and the Market Economy" in Hausman, Daniel M., ed., *The Philosophy of Economics*, Cambridge: Cambridge University Press, 303–311.

Rothbard, Murray N., (1976) "Praxeology: The Methodology of Austrian Economics" in Dolan, Edwin G., ed., *The Foundations of Modern Austrian Economics*, Kansas City: Sheed and Ward, Inc., 19–39.

Vanberg, Viktor, (1986) "Spontaneous Market Order and Social Rules: A Critical Examination of F. A. Hayek's Theory of Cultural Evolution" *Economics and Philosophy*, April, 2, 75–100.

Veblen, Thorstein, (1961) "Why is Economics Not an Evolutionary Science?" (1898) in *The Place of Science in Modern Civilization*, New York: Russell and Russell, 56–81.

————, (1953) *The Theory of the Leisure Class*, (1899), New York: The New American Library.

————, (1961) "Industrial and Pecuniary Employments" (1901), in *The Place of Science in Modern Civilization*, New York: Russell and Russell, 279–323.

————, (1964) *The Instinct of Workmanship* (1914), New York: W. W. Norton and Company.

SOME ISSUES IN THE COMPARISON OF AUSTRIAN AND INSTITUTIONAL ECONOMICS

Malcolm Rutherford

I. INTRODUCTION

Although certain areas of similarity and difference between Austrian and Institutional Economics have been discussed before (von Mises 1949; Streissler and Weber 1973; Seckler 1975; Dugger 1983a; Perlman 1985; Gunning 1986), the issues involved in the comparison of Austrian and Institutionalist economics have gained importance because of the recent and not inconsiderable involvement of Austrian thinking, particularly as derived from Menger (1883) and Hayek (1967; 1973; 1979), in what has become known as the 'new institutional economics' (Langlois 1986).[1]

As yet, little has been done on the comparison of the Institutionalism of Veblen, Commons, Mitchell and Ayres with that of the new institu-

Research in the History of Economic Thought and Methodology,
Volume 6, pages 159-172
Copyright © 1989 by JAI Press Inc.
All rights of reproduction in any form reserved.
ISBN: 0-89232-928-9

tional economics,[2] but the brief comments of many of those involved
with the latter clearly indicate a desire to differentiate sharply their
own work from what they see as the failures and shortcomings of the
former (Langlois 1986; Coase 1984).[3] In particular, the output of the
Institutionalists is seen as lacking in theory, utilizing a faulty holistic
method, and failing to properly address the more interesting issues.
Veblen is presented as having adopted a behavioristic psychology
which "rid economics of any sort of human intelligence or purpose,"
and Commons is dismissed for concentrating only on institutions as
deliberately designed (Langlois 1986; Schotter 1981; Seckler 1975).
These points are contrasted with the theoretical purpose, methodological individualism, and concentration on institutions as the undesigned
and unintended results of individual action which, it is argued, are
characteristic of the new institutional economics, most specifically in
its Austrian manifestations. Of course, one can also find criticisms of
Austrian approaches written from an Institutionalist perspective; criticisms which most often relate to what are seen as the Austrian's radical
versions of individualism and subjectivism, questionable psychological assumptions, and extreme normative position with respect to spontaneous market orders (Veblen 1898; Bush 1981a and 1981b; Alter
1982; Dugger 1983a). It is particularly noteworthy that neither side
necessarily rejects the methodological terms used by the other to describe their own position. For example, Institutionalists have often
affirmed their acceptance of behaviorism and holism (Gruchy 1947;
Wilber and Harrison 1978; Dugger 1979), while Austrians have just as
often stressed their commitment to subjectivism and individualism
(Shand 1980; O'Driscoll and Rizzo 1985).

   In contrast to the above, the papers by Boettke (1989) and Samuels
(1989) in this symposium concentrate on the similarities between Institutional and Austrian Economics; on the facts that both Institutionalists
and Austrians have a concern with process, change and evolution; that
both stress the importance of institutions; and that both reject neoclassical equilibrium theorizing and the standard neoclassical treatment
of knowledge. These similarities obviously do exist, but the more interesting question relates not to their mere existence but to their
significance. That is: Do these similarities represent only superficial resemblances between fundamentally different research programs, or do
they indicate that Austrians and Institutionalists have more of their basic ideas in common that either group seems to like to admit? In order
to try to provide an answer to this question, three of the issues raised in
the literature will be discussed further: (i) whether it is correct to di-

chotomize the methodological approaches to social science into individualist versus holist; (ii) how institutions and institutional change are conceptualized in the Austrian and Institutionalist literatures; and (iii) the basis of the normative stance taken by each group.

II. INDIVIDUALISM VERSUS HOLISM?

Both Boettke and Samuels argue that the difference between the professed methodological individualism of the Austrians and the professed methodological holism of Institutionalists is much less extreme than might at first be thought. Unfortunately, neither author refers to papers by Joseph Agassi (1960; 1975) and Robert Nozick (1977) which serve to throw much light on this issue.

A great lack of clarity surrounds the debate over methodological individualism and holism. Methodological individualism is most usually associated with the reductive (or pychologistic) claim that "all true theories of social science are reducible to theories of individual human action, plus boundary conditions specifying the conditions under which persons act" (Nozick 1977, p. 353). Put another way this means that the only allowable exogenous variables in a social science theory are to be natural and psychological givens (Boland 1982). All social or collective phenomena such as institutions are to be endogenized and explained in terms of individual human action. The emphasis is therefore on how individual action gives rise to institutions and institutional change. In contrast, holism is associated with a stress on the social influences that bear on individual action. The individual is seen as socialized, as having internalized the norms and values of the society he inhabits. The emphasis of the holist is on how social 'forces' (institutions, social conventions, etc.) condition individual behavior. This may even be taken to the point where such social forces appear almost as autonomous entities with distinct functions, purposes or wills of their own. Whether or not the argument is taken to this extreme, the holist would certainly deny the reductivist claim that all social phenomena can be explained in terms of theories of individual behavior alone.

The major distinction between reductive methodological individualism and holism, then, is to be found in the primacy given to the individual in the former as opposed to the primacy given to the social or institutional in the latter. The reductive nature of the usual methodological individualist program in fact forces the theorist to postulate some basic, biologically or psychologically given, human nature to provide the preferences, values and goals that individuals possess. Such preferences cannot themselves be seen as the result of socialization to pre-existing norms and conventions without violating the reductive requirement. Thus, as Hodgson argues: "The key element in classic statements of methodological individualism is a refusal to examine the institutional or other forces which are involved in the moulding of individual preferences and purposes" (Hodgson 1986, 211). Even if some recognition of social influence is made, the reductive program requires that the theorist postulate some (clearly mythical) pre-institutional state, some definite starting point from which subsequent human cultural and institutional development can be derived (Agassi 1960, 255). Holism, on the other hand, exactly stresses the significance of 'society' or institutions in the formation of the individual's aims, values and preferences and tends to concentrate on man as a social product rather than on society as a product of the actions of individual men.

Of course, as Agassi and Nozick have argued, it is more than possible to argue *both* that only individual actions create and alter institutions *and* that institutions shape the goals and aims of individual actors. One does not have to decide which came first, individuals or institutions, or which has ultimacy or primacy, one can simply accept that institutions and individuals have evolved together in continual interaction. This would be to reject both the possibility of a complete reduction of social phenomena to individual actions alone and explanations running in terms of supra-individual or holistic functions or purposes. This methodological middle ground has been dubbed "institutional individualism" by Agassi (1975), and perhaps also suggests a middle ground between the "oversocialized" concept of man common in sociology and the "undersocialized" concept of man evident in conventional economics (Granovetter 1985, 483–484). Institutional individualism brings together the reasonable aspects in the individualist and holist programs and is, in fact, a methodology that has often been adopted, although only implicitly, by social theorists (Agassi 1975, 154–155). Institutional individualism, then, raises the possibility that the methodological differences between Institutionalists and Austrians are more matters of emphasis than of principle.

As far as Austrians are concerned many writers do avoid a reductive individualism. Mises probably comes closest to adopting reductivism due to his insistence that "the ultimate judgments of value and the ulti-

mate ends of human action are given for any kind of scientific inquiry''
(1949, 21). Mises does discuss the fact that most individuals take over
their values and goals from the society that surrounds them, but goes
on to argue that the common man ''chooses to adopt traditional patterns or patterns adopted by other people because he is convinced that
this procedure is best fitted to achieve his own welfare. And he is ready
to change his ideology and consequently his mode of action whenever
he becomes convinced that this would better serve his interests'' (46).
The other pole within the Austrian tradition is to be found in the social
economics of Friedrich von Wieser (1927). Wieser strongly criticises
both organic analogies and 'naive' individualism. Organic metaphors
are at fault for ignoring the fact that it is individuals who are ''the sole
possessors of all consciousness and of all will'' (154), while 'naive'
individualism is in error for ignoring the power of institutions over individuals and for treating individuals as ''entirely independent.'' Thus:
''one must hold himself aloof from the excesses of the individualistic
exposition, but the explanation must still run in terms of the individual'' (154). A similar viewpoint can be found in the work of Menger
and Hayek. It has been claimed that Menger worked with ''an assumption about consumer tastes akin to that used by U.S. institutionalists
(Endres 1986, 898), while Hayek has made it more than clear that the
individual's psychology is not to be thought of as exogenous to his cultural and institutional context. Thus, Hayek argues that 'mind' has
''developed in constant interaction with the institutions which determine the structure of society'' (1973, 17) and that ''culture and reason
develop concurrently'' (1979, 155); an argument that might easily
have been made by Wesley Mitchell in his discussion of the effect of
pecuniary institutions on rationality (Mitchell 1910 and 1937,
169–176).

Among institutionalists, a significant part of Veblen's work and virtually all of Commons' consists of an analysis of individual decision
makers operating (rationally) within a given cultural and institutional
context, and of the intended and unintended consequences of their decisions (Rutherford 1983 and 1984).[4] Even Commons' references to
the 'common will' imply only the outcome of legal and political processes of reconciling the conflicting wills of many individuals. Of
course, it is true that institutionalists have the unfortunate habit of
slipping into arguments concerning social forces (institutions versus
technology) without always properly or persuasively analyzing how
such social forces arise out of individual action or how they impact on

the situations faced by individuals, but the fact remains that at least a significant part of work of Institutionalists and Austrians is *not* as methodologically incompatible as is usually thought.

III. INSTITUTIONS AND INSTITUTIONAL CHANGE

The Austrians research program with respect to institutions is built around the question posed by Menger: "How can it be that institutions which serve the common welfare and are extremely significant for its development come into being without a *common will* directed toward establishing them" (1985, 146). Both the emphasis on institutions as the unintended products of individual action and the connection drawn between institutions and the common welfare are significant. Menger himself distinguished his program from the investigation of "pragmatic" institutions (those that are the result of design) which has often been seen as the main focus of Commons' work (Seckler 1975, 127–131; Schotter 1981, 3–4), while the emphasis on the welfare enhancing effect of institutions might perhaps distinguish Menger's program from that inspired by Veblen, with its tendency to concentrate on the socially *dysfunctional* aspects of many social norms and institutions. Nevertheless, these differences do not mean that the Austrian program is completely incompatible with Institutionalist thinking, and areas of complementarity (or potential complementarity) undoubtedly exist.

The most extensive effort to develop the Mengerian program has been made by F. A. Hayek, although Hayek's success in this endeavor is open to question. In fact, it is precisely in the difficulties that Hayek has faced that the possible complementarities between Austrian and Institutionalist thinking become most obvious. In Hayek's argument, socially beneficial or efficient rules or institutions evolve as a result of a process of "group selection." That is, as "the result of a process of winnowing or sifting, directed by the differential advantages gained by groups from practices adopted for some unknown and perhaps purely accidental reasons" (1979, 155). The process of "group selection" is utilized by Hayek presumably because of the difficulty of arguing, in true 'invisible hand' terms, that rules operating in the social advantage will result simply from individuals' pursuit of their own advantage. Of course, such results may occur under certain circumstances, but although the individualistic invisible hand notion of cultural evolution is of considerable interest and not without content, "the range of its explanatory applicability and the normative inferences it allows for are clearly limited" both because many rules are in fact "implemented and enforced by some organized apparatus," including many of the rules necessary for the market order, and "because, for systematic reasons, certain kinds of rules cannot be expected to emerge from and to be enforced by a spontaneous process, except under certain restrictive conditions" (Vanberg 1986, 97).[5] Unfortunately, Hayek's notion of "group selection" fails to provide a solution to this problem as it is vague and lacking in any clear specification of any mechanism that would ensure the selection of efficient or socially beneficial institutions (Vanberg 1986), a point that has also been noted by other Austrians (O'Driscoll and Rizzo 1985, 40).

These weaknesses in Hayek's argument bring out several important points. First, that an understanding of the processes of institutional development would seem to require a close analysis of *both* invisible hand processes and processes involving collective decision making[6]; second, that it cannot be presumed on vague Darwinian grounds that only efficient institutions will survive over the longer term; and third, that this implies the need for a careful analysis of the functional and dysfunctional aspects of existing institutions. It might be added that for an adequate economic theory of institutional *change* to be developed the sources of that change must be made endogenous (Boland 1979). In other words, innovation, the development of knowledge or of the economic system itself can be seen as altering the circumstances and interests of individuals, creating new problems or conflicts and resulting in unintended and intended institutional modifications. To this program both Austrians and Institutionalists can contribute.

The possibly complementary nature of Austrian and Institutionalist approaches can be examined further by briefly outlining the major Institutionalist programs. As noted above, Commons is often seen as concentrating on institutions as deliberately designed. Even if this were entirely true the considerations outlined above would provide a role for the analysis of deliberative processes of the Commons type, but in fact Commons' analysis is both more complete and more complex. Commons' basic approach has something in common with the Austrian program as Commons, too, is concerned with how it is that institutions arise which can create a viable or 'workable' overall social and economic order out of conflicting individual interests. Many of the rules or institutions that govern individual behavior Commons sees as arising spontaneously in the form of custom and common practice, but his major concern is with the processes involved where the invisible hand fails; that is in the processes involved in resolving the conflicts that inevitably arise between individuals and groups over the practices and rules to be followed. Where such conflicts arise processes of selection and enforcement are required, hence Commons' concentration on legislatures and courts, both of which are seen as somewhat imperfect methods of selecting and enforcing rules and practices in order to maintain the workability of the system in the face of conflict (see Rutherford 1983). In this, a Darwinian type of group selection process may be seen as operating over the very long term, in the sense that if legislative and judicial processes of generating mutuality fail badly enough the society will fall into disorder and, in effect, cease to exist. It should be noted that in Commons' work the selection processes only operate to generate viability or workability, a criterion very much looser than economic efficiency alone. Considerable inefficiencies may be contained within a workable overall order.

The Veblenian program has an altogether different focus as Veblen, like the Austrians, wishes to analyze institutional change in terms of unintended consequences and not in terms of deliberate collective decision making. For Veblen, however, there is no presumption that evolutionary processes will lead to efficient institutions. Indeed, the bulk of Veblen's analysis concerns the adverse effects of institutional norms on such things as technological insight, innovation and productively efficient organization. There is really nothing in Veblen's system which necessarily works to select out 'imbecile institutions.'[7] The institutional system does evolve but it does so through the unintended effects of technological innovation on the situations and goals of decision makers.[8] The stress on the unintended effects of innovation provides an obvious link with Austrian thinking, but Austrians would find difficulty with Veblen's concentration on *technology* as the object of innovation and hence the only major endogenous source of change,[9] and his often highly unsatisfactory analysis of the link between technological change and the beliefs, goals and actions of decision makers. Furthermore, his tendency to ignore the explicit analysis of political and judicial processes is an omission that is particularly severe in the case of complex societies with advanced division of labour and within which new technology will not impact on all groups or alter their ideas and goals in similar ways (see Rutherford 1984). Nevertheless, Veblen's work does serve both to locate the unintended and endogenous sources of institutional change in innovative activity and to point up the differential effect of different institutional systems on the level of innovative activity that does take place.

IV. SCIENCE AND SOCIAL REFORM

At first sight it might be thought that nothing could be clearer than the different positions of Austrians and Institutionalists with respect to deliberative institutional reform; Austrians tending to argue the virtues of the spontaneous market order and Institutionalists its weaknesses and shortcomings. At one level this difference is very real and based on fundamentally different views on the potential of scientific knowledge for the guidance of social and economic reform. In the bulk of the Institutionalist literature scientific investigation and the growth of knowledge in the social sciences is seen as capable of leading to an ability to rationally appraise existing institutions and suggested alternatives. There are a variety of versions of this view, from Commons' idea of the 'fourth branch' to investigate existing rules and practices and experimentally institute new rules in an attempt to avoid conflict (Commons 1939; 1951), through Mitchell's arguments for planning and for government sponsored research agencies to study social and economic problems and construct welfare indices (Mitchell 1939, 42–136), to Ayres' extraordinarily optimistic view of science as capable of leading to the location of 'true' values and of creating a consensus around those values (Ayres 1961; see also Rutherford 1981). Despite this variety, virtually all of the positions found in the Institutionalist literature would appear to run afoul of the usual Austrian arguments concerning the subjective nature of knowledge, the complex and ill-understood nature of systems of social order, and the benefits of spontaneous forms of organization. In other words the Institutionalists often appear to have adopted exactly that 'rationalist' doctrine, that through science man can rid himself of all the nonsensical 'ceremonialism' inherited from earlier and more ignorant times, that the Austrians have been so concerned to reject (Hayek 1978, 3–22). On the other hand the simple dichotomization of Austrians and Institutionalists into anti-rationalists and rationalists may overstate their divisions.

The first point to note here is that the Austrian argument in favor of spontaneous orders does rely either on the existence of invisible hand or other non-deliberative processes which serve to generate efficient rules. If, as argued above it is the case that such processes have more limited force than many Austrians suppose, then the problem of the existence of dysfunctional institutions cannot be evaded and the thorny issue of how to judge alternative institutional arrangements has to be faced. Second, and on a more practical level, many Austrians and Institutionalists might be classified as cautious reformers. The papers by Boettke and Samuels both make this point but it is worth the repetition to stress that (i) among institutionalists only Veblen felt the need for *radical* institutional adjustment, even Ayres, despite his views on science and the strength of his rhetoric concerning the failures of the market system (see particularly Ayres 1962), put forward only fairly modest reform proposals; and (ii) that many Austrians, including Menger and Hayek, have shown awareness of the possible failure of spontaneous processes, the need for careful scientific investigation of even 'organic' institutions and of government intervention to correct such failures as are found. The difficulties that both Austrians and Institutionalists face, then, are very much the same. They lie much more in the definition of the criteria by which to judge institutional success and failure than in the acceptance or rejection of 'rationalism.'

V. CONCLUSION

For the above it follows that the observed similarities between Austrian and Institutional Economics represent more than merely accidental or superficial resemblances. The research programs pursued by Austrians and Institutionalists do have more in common, methodologically and theoretically than is usually supposed. This is not to say that their research programs are *identical*, only that much of the best work in each can be reconstructed as examples of the method of institutional individualism and that in methodological, theoretical and philosophical matters there is a degree of agreement or at least of actual or potential *complementarity* that has often been obscured by the use of dichotomies (individualism versus holism; organic institutions versus pragmatic institutions; anti-rationalism versus rationalism) which are quite possibly false and which have effectively served to mask opportunities for fruitful communication and mutual gain. It might be concluded that the traditional relationship of suspicion between Institutionalists and Austrians is an example of a spontaneous evolution which has singularly failed to enhance the efficiency or viability of either group.

ACKNOWLEDGMENT

An earlier version of this paper was presented at the History of Economics Society meetings in June 1987. Many helpful comments were received.

NOTES

1.   The term 'new institutional economics' seems to have been first used by Williamson (1975) to refer to his own and related work. Langlois (1986) extends the term to cover a variety of neoclassical and Austrian inspired efforts to deal with institutions. See also the editorial preface to the symposium on "The New Institutional Economics" by Furubotn and Richter (1984).

2.   Some comparison of Institutionalism with the work of Williamson and North is contained in Dugger (1983b) and Rutherford (1983), while Hutchison (1984) compares the New Institutional Economics with the "old" institutionalism of the German Historical School.

3.   Exceptions are Williamson (1975 and 1985) who pays tribute to J. R. Commons' work on transactions, and Douglass North who at least admits that something might be learned from Institutionalists. North, however, would see any such contribution as fitting into an overall neoclassical framework (North 1978).

4.   Hodgson (p. 214) has accused the present author of an "over-enthusiastic" attempt to "discover vestiges of 'methodological individualism' in the works of Thorstein Veblen." It should be noted that the definition of methodological individualism used in my earlier papers followed Popper. Popper's definition corresponds to Agassi's "institutional individualism" in that it involves no acceptance of the reductive or psychologistic program. It is to be admitted that most definitions of methodological individualism do imply the reductive program. This more common definition is adopted in this paper.

5.   For recent game-theoretic investigations of invisible hand processes of institutional growth see Lewis (1967), Ullmann-Margalit (1977), and Schotter (1981). For analyses of the limitations of such an approach see Mirowski (1981 and 1986) and Field (1984) as well as Vanberg (1986).

6.   In connection with Menger's original work on 'organic' institutions, Hutchison argues that the notion of spontaneous institutions requires a degree of unselfconsciousness rarely encountered in modern societies: "Once this awareness . . . has come into existence . . . about any kind of social phenomena, decisions will be subject to deliberate, conscious or 'planned' intervention" (1973, 25–26).

7.   It is perhaps ironic that Veblen did not develop a Darwinian type of argument such as Hayek. Veblen, after all, made great polemical use of Darwin's name and frequently argued that biology was the paradigm to be followed by social science.

8.   Wesley Mitchell adopted a very similar view to Veblen's. Austrians could agree with Mitchell's description of the institutions of the money economy as a system "no man willed" and which is beyond the control of any individual and possibly "of even society as a whole." See Mitchell (1910, 208–209) and Rutherford (1987).

9.   In some places Veblen identifies technology with instrumental knowledge. This identification is made clearer in the work of Ayres, but this also has the result of se-

verely reducing the content of the 'institutions/technology dichotomy' utilized by
Veblen and Ayres (see Ayres 1962).

REFERENCES

Agassi, Joseph, (1960) Methodological Individualism. *British Journal of Sociology*,
11: 244–270.
————, (1975) Institutional Individualism. *British Journal of Sociology*, 26:
144–155.
Alter, Max, (1982) Carl Menger and Homo Oeconomicus: Some Thoughts on Austrian Theory and Methodology. *Journal of Economic Issues*, 16 (March):
149–160.
Ayres, C. E., (1961) *Toward a Reasonable Society*. Austin: University of Texas
Press.
————, (1962) *The Theory of Economic Progress*. 2nd Ed. New York: Schocken.
Boettke, Pete, (1989) Evolution and Economics: Austrians as Institutionalists. *Research in the History of Economic Thought and Methodology*.
Boland, Lawrence A., (1979) Knowledge and the Role of Institutions in Economic
Theory. *Journal of Economic Issues*, 13 (December): 957–972.
————, (1982) *The Foundations of Economic Method*. London: George Allen and
Unwin.
Bush, Paul, (1981a) Radical Individualism vs. Institutionalism I: The Division of
Institutionalists into 'Humanists' and 'Behaviorists'. *American Journal of Eco-
nomics and Sociology*, 40 (April): 139–147.
————, (1981b) Radical Individualism vs. Institutionalism II: Philosophical Dual-
ism as Apologetic Construct Based on Obsolete Psychological Preconceptions.
American Journal of Economics and Sociology, 40 (July): 287–298.
Coase, Ronald H., (1984) The New Institutional Economics. *Zeitschrift fur die
gesamte Staatswissenschaft*, 140 (March): 229–231.
Commons, John R., (1939) Twentieth Century Economics. *Journal of Social Philosophy*, 5 (October): 29–41.
————, (1951) *The Economics of Collective Action*. New York: Macmillan.
Dugger, William, (1979) Methodological Differences Between Institutional and Neoclassical Economics. *Journal of Economic Issues*, 13 (December): 899–909.
————, (1983a) Two Twists in Economic Methodology: Positivism and Subjectiv-
ism. *American Journal of Economics and Sociology*, 42 (January): 75–91.
————, (1983b) The Transaction Cost Analysis of Oliver E. Williamson: A New
Synthesis? *Journal of Economic Issues* 17 (March): 95–114.
Endres, A. M., (1984) Institutional Elements in Carl Menger's Theory of Demand: A
Comment. *Journal of Economic Issues*, 18 (September): 897–903.
Field, Alexander James, (1984) Microeconomics, Norms and Rationality. *Economic
Development and Cultural Change*, 32 (July): 683–711.
Furubotn, Eirik G., and Richter, Rudolf, (1984) The New Institutional Economics:
Editorial Preface. *Zeitschrift fur die gesamte Staatswissenschaft*, 140 (March):
1–6.
Granovetter, Mark, (1985) Economic Action and Social Structure: The Problem of
Embeddedness. *American Journal of Sociology*, 91 (November): 481–510.

Gruchy, Allan G., (1947) *Modern Economic Thought, The American Contribution.* New York: Prentice-Hall.

Gunning, J. Patrick, (1986) The Methodology of Austrian Economics and Its Relevance to Institutionalism. *American Journal of Economics and Sociology,* 45 (January): 79–91.

Hayek, F. A, (1967) *Studies in Philosophy, Politics and Economics.* London: Routledge and Kegan Paul.

————, (1973) *Law, Legislation and Liberty, Volume I: Rules and Order.* London: Routledge and Kegan Paul.

————, (1978) *New Studies in Philosophy, Politics, Economics and the History of Ideas.* London: Routledge and Kegan Paul.

————, (1979) *Law, Legislation and Liberty, Volume 3: The Political Order of a Free People.* London: Routledge and Kegan Paul.

Hodgson, Geoff, (1986) Behind Methodological Individualism. *Cambridge Journal of Economics,* 10 (September): 211–224.

Hutchison, T. W., (1973) Some Themes from *Investigations Into Method.* In J. R. Hicks and W. Weber, eds., *Carl Menger and the Austrian School of Economics.* Oxford: Oxford University Press.

————, (1984) Institutionalist Economics Old and New. *Zeitschrift fur die gesamte Staatswissenschaft,* 140 (March): 20–29.

Langlois, Richard N., (1986) The New Institutional Economics: An Introductory Essay. In Richard N. Langlois, ed., *Economics as a Process: Essays in the new Institutional Economics.* Cambridge: Cambridge University Press.

Lewis, David K., (1969) *Convention: A Philosophical Study.* Cambridge, Mass.: Harvard University Press.

Menger, Carl, (1985)(1883) *Investigations into the Method of the Social Sciences with Special Reference to Economics.* New York: New York University Press.

Mitchell, Wesley C., (1910) The Rationality of Economic Activity, II. *Journal of Political Economy,* 18 (March): 197–216.

————, (1950)(1937) *The Backward Art of Spending Money.* New York: Augustus M. Kelley.

Mirowski, Philip, (1981) Is There a Mathematical Neoinstitutional Economics? *Journal of Economic Issues,* 15 (September): 593–613.

————, (1986) Institutions as a Solution Concept in a Game Theory Context. In Philip Mirowski, ed., *The Reconstruction of Economic Theory.* Hingham, Mass: Kluwer-Nijhoff.

Mises, Ludwig von, (1949) *Human Action.* New Haven: Yale University Press.

North, Douglass C., (1978) Structure and Performance: The Task of Economic History. *Journal of Economic Literature,* 16 (September): 963–978.

Nozick, Robert, (1977) On Austrian Methodology. *Synthese,* 36: 353–392.

O'Driscoll, Gerald, P., and Rizzo, Mario J., (1985) *The Economics of Time and Ignorance.* Oxford: Basil Blackwell.

Perlman, Mark, (1986) Subjectivism and American Institutionalism. In Israel M. Kirzner, ed., *Subjectivism, Intelligibility and Economic Understanding.* London: Macmillan.

Rutherford, Malcolm, (1981) Clarence Ayres and the Instrumental Theory of Value. *Journal of Economic Issues,* 15 (September): 657–673.

————, (1983) J. R. Commons's Institutional Economics. *Journal of Economic Issues,* 17 (September): 721–744.

172   MALCOLM RUTHERFORD

————, (1984) Thorstein Veblen and the Processes of Institutional Change. *History of Political Economy*, 16 (Fall): 331–348.

————, (1987) Wesley Mitchell: Institutions and Quantitative Methods. *Eastern Economic Journal*, 13 (March): 63–73.

Samuels, Warren J., (1989) Austrian and Institutional Economics: Some Common Elements. *Research in the History of Economic Thought and Methodology*.

Schotter, Andrew, (1981) *The Economic Theory of Social Institutions*. Cambridge: Cambridge University Press.

Seckler, David, (1975) *Thorstein Veblen and the Institutionalists*. Boulder, Colorado: Colorado Associated University Press.

Shand, Alax H., (1980) *Subjectivist Economics: The New Austrian School*. Exeter: Short Run Press.

Streissler, E. and Weber, W., (1973) The Menger Tradition. In J. R. Hicks and W. Weber, eds., *Carl Menger and the Austrian School of Economics*. Oxford: Oxford University Press.

Ullmann-Margalit, Edna, (1977) *The Emergence of Norms*. Oxford: Oxford University Press.

Vanberg, Viktor, (1986) Spontaneous Market Order and Social Rules: A Critical Examination of F. A. Hayek's Theory of Cultural Evolution. *Economics and Philosophy*, 2 (April): 75–100.

Veblen, Thorstein, (1919)(1898) Why is Economics Not an Evolutionary Science? In *The Place of Science in Modern Civilization*. New York: W. B. Huebsch.

Wieser, Friedrich von, (1967)(1927) *Social Economics*. New York: Augustus M. Kelley.

Wilber, Charles and Harrison, Robert. The Methodological Basis of Institutional Economics: Pattern Model, Storytelling and Holism. *Journal of Economic Issues*, 12 (March): 61–89.

Williamson, Oliver E., (1975) *Markets and Hierarchies*. New York: Free Press.

————, (1985) *The Economic Institutions of Capitalism*. New York: Free Press.

OF PARADIGMS AND DISCIPLINE

J. R. Stanfield

In light of the widely perceived limitations of the neoclassical synthesis (Eichner, Stanfield) one must applaud any efforts to find an alternative or supplemental paradigm. This is especially so in the cases of Warren Samuels and Pete Boettke, two very well read, eclectic intellects. Although one must also applaud open-mindedness and reject dogma, there may be a problem at the other extreme as well, namely, lack of paradigm discipline. I return to the issue of paradigm indiscipline below, following direct discussion of the papers by Samuels and Boettke.

On the whole, with one major exception, I find the papers by Samuels and Boettke to be very unconvincing. The similarities they review seem to be either forced, dubious, or readily explicable by social-intellectual history in ways that have little to do with the positive content of the two schools of thought in question.

The major exception, i.e., the most convincing discussion that I encountered in either of the two papers, is Samuels's discussion of the fundamental differences that exist between the two schools. For exam-

Research in the History of Economic Thought and Methodology,
Volume 6, pages 173-179
Copyright © 1989 by JAI Press Inc.
All rights of reproduction in any form reserved.
ISBN: 0-89232-928-9

ple, he notes that the central problem of economics is perceived differently by the two schools, that both have very strong and conflicting attitudes toward the nature of capitalism, that they differ markedly on their views of the state, that they have markedly different theories of value, and that they have different methodological approaches. These differences not only make evident Samuels's understanding of both schools of thought but also convincingly indicate that the differences between the two schools are far more important than the similarities discussed elsewhere in the two papers.

As I said, many of the similarities would seem to have more to do with social-intellectual history than with anything involved in the positive content of the two schools of thought. For example, Samuels observes that both schools consider themselves to be outsiders with respect to Neoclassicism, that both define themselves vis-à-vis Neoclassicism, and that much effort is spent in articulation of an identity and in preoccupation with matters of the method and philosophy of economics. This would seem to be explicable by the dissenting status of each school of thought and by the immature scientific community and lack of strong paradigm discipline in each school. Much the same applies to Samuels's discussion of the heterogeneity of the two schools. It may well be that dissenting schools of thought tend to lack discipline because they lack critical mass and communication forums. One might think that Marxism is an exception here. After all, radical political economy in the United States is characterized by a relatively high degree of paradigm discipline. This is clearly indicated by the recent contribution of Attewell. This may be an exception to my point above but one should note that Marxism globally is quite wide-spread and that this global Marxism may well exercise considerable discipline on the radical economics paradigm.

I also think that some of the authors's arguments are rather dubious. For example, Samuels indicates that both schools stress the entrepreneur. It seems impossible that Institutionalism would lay stress on the entrepreneur given the predominance of the Ayresian theory of innovation. This theory downplays the importance of select individuals within economic history and innovation and the theory of select individuals would appear to be a necessary ingredient if one is to be said to emphasize the entrepreneur.

Another example is the insistence by both Samuels and Boettke that only subjective individual preferences count in the theory of human action. Samuels goes so far as to argue that both schools of thought operate with a similar kind of subjectivism. This would seem to be inconsistent with the Institutionalist social value theory. This theory maintains that there is a social value which is not identical to the sum of individual value functions. Boettke's argument that meaning can be attached to human action only at the individual level is similarly inconsistent with this social value theory. Indeed meaning is a cultural product and therefore in the Institutionalist theory it can only be understood via an institutional analysis of cultures as concrete patterns of human interaction. (Stanfield 1986, 54–65) The neglect by both authors of the importance of social value theory probably has much to do with their refusal to face the significance within Institutionalist thought of the issue of character formation, an issue to which I return below. The issue of character formation is relevant here because it is precisely in the formation of individual characters that social value most clearly exists. In other words, once you have individuals with defined utility functions, then it might well be that social value is simply the sum of individual values. However, a social value certainly exists in the kinds of individual characters that society develops.

This brings up the issue of the place of economy in society, since certain kinds of economic institutions affect society and the characters that society generates. Boettke argues that both schools of thought agree that the central question of economic analysis is the way in which the economy is instituted in society and the implications of alternative institutional arrangements. However, even if the Austrians shared the Institutionalist insistence on subordinating narrowly defined economic efficiency to wider social values, they would undoubtedly have very different views of the wider values. The Institutionalists have several values in mind, roughly those elaborated by Ayres whereas the Austrians would seem to treat freedom above all else and indeed undertake a rather absolutist definition of freedom itself (Stanfield 1986, 139–150). For the Austrians, freedom would appear to be primarily the freedom of the middle class from the state with very little else involved.

Boettke's discussion of the Austrian emphasis on economic change and process is also dubious. Hayek's discussion of economic problems arising in consequence of change does not alter the fact that the economic problems Hayek envisages are those of the allocation of scarce resources to given ends. This static problem is continually revised by change but that does not make change itself the focal point of analysis and central content of the economic problem as it is in Institutional economics. For Institutionalists, of course, institutional adjustment is *the* economic problem, not simply a background condition that continuously requires new calculations with respect to the economic problem of responding efficiently to changing relative prices.

Samuels's argument that both schools "share the policy activism of the so-called social engineer" is also quite dubious. It is difficult to compare Hayek, with his trenchant criticism of scientism and his distaste for consciously shaping social change versus leaving the matter to society's organic process (Hayek 1944, 17–21; Kern, Chs. 2, 3), to the Institutionalist call for conscious social reform and increasing collective action in control of individual action.

In addition to similarities which are either dubious or which would seem to have little to do with the positive content of the two schools, there are also important differences between the two schools which are finessed by Samuels and Boettke. None of these is more important than that of the process of individual preference formation. Samuels here agrees that the Austrians are not interested in exploring the origins of preferences but argues that this has also been neglected by the Institutionalists who have not made the topic part of "a serious and extensive research program." Boettke on the other hand argues that the Austrians accept acculturation in the formation of individual preferences. Samuels neglects the fact that this issue has always been a major element of Institutionalism. Simply the example of John Kenneth Galbraith is sufficient. Boettke seems not to realize that it is one thing to accept acculturation in the formation of individual preferences and quite another to make the matter a significant factor in the paradigm. Its inclusion leads to a critical theory of institutions and the power that institutions allocate among people and groups. In the Institutionalist theory this is indeed a major preoccupation. One can also see that an absolute cultural relativist can accept the fact of acculturated preferences but not use this fact in any way as a critique of institutions and power. The issue then becomes whether there are any transcendent values to form a basis for a critique of the way preferences are currently being formed. Institutionalists do indeed offer such a transcendent theory of value, i.e., instrumentalism (Ayres). The Austrians in contrast would seem to offer no transcendent value except that of bourgeois freedom.

Hayek is a good example of the treatment of character formation by the Austrians. In his discussion (Hayek 1965) of Galbraith's *The Affluent Society*, he treats as a relatively insignificant truism the fact that individual preferences are socially formed. Hayek utterly ignores the main point of Galbraith's dependence effect, soon to be the revised sequence: the acculturation of individual preferences to serve the inter-

ests of the powerful. In *The Road to Serfdom*, Hayek mentions changing character in the early pages but does nothing with it in the subsequent discussion. Indeed, his change in character is no change at all
but merely a response, given (rent-seeking) characters, to changing
relative prices. As with the neoclassical and public choice discussions
of rent-seeking, no attempt is made by Hayek to explain the formation
of the rent-seeking individual character or its connection to the market
mentality. This is in sharp contrast to Veblen's theory that predatory
instincts have been culturally selected over several thousand years, a
discussion which explains the formation of the rent-seeking personality.

Finally, neither Samuels's paper nor Boettke's provide very much in
the way of rationale for discussing the similarity or forging the synthesis between Institutionalism and the Austrians. Samuels provides very
little in the way of justification for the importance of the project and
what he does provide comes at the very end of his paper. He says only
that it is interesting to note the similarities for those idly curious about
economic thought and that the similarities may be informative with regard to the processes of the development of the history of economics.
One cannot debate the interest of the idly curious but one can point out
that Samuels gives no idea as to how this comparison may be informative with regard to the processes of development of the history of economics. Boettke's rationale is essentially that it is good to be well read
and that the two schools may find an ally in each other. I have no debate with being well read, but I do not think it includes educing forced
similarities between vitally different schools of thought. I find the possible alliance between Institutionalism and the Austrians not only dubious but somewhat disconcerting. Boettke should be curious as to why
the two have not allied before. The reason is, I suspect, that there is
much that keeps them apart. The purpose of a paradigm is to effect
practice and in Institutionalism this effect is meant to be a movement
toward a planned society, whereas in Austrian thought, this effect is
meant to be a movement to a society than is even less planned than the
present one.[1] I find the idea that the reactionary Austrians and the social democratic Institutionalists would somehow ally with one another
to throw out neoclassism to be ludicrously farfetched.

The most interesting inference to be drawn from Samuels's and
Boettke's papers may have to do with the issue of paradigm discipline.
That these papers could be written, extolling the similarities of
Institutionalist and Austrian economics, despite the profound differ-
ences between the two paradigms, probably speaks to the lack of con-

sensus within the two communities of scholars. Without a degree of paradigm discipline, individual practitioners are all over the park, each one resurrecting this or that piece of seminal literature to provide scholarly authority to this or that axe to be ground. Scholarship tends to lack focus and published works do not interact and build upon one another in the time-honored fashion of the scientific, artistic enterprise. In short, there is no Kuhnian normal science with its advantages of discipline, focus, and direction.[2]

One need not resort to the dominant paradigm of the neoclassical synthesis to establish a counter example. As mentioned above, U. S. radical or Marxist economics has demonstrated a very clear conception of itself. Attewell's review is indicative. His chapters place radical economic thought in historical context and then review the radical literature on economic stratification and poverty, the labor process and the firm, crisis theory, and imperialism and dependency. With the addition of one topical area that Attewell neglects, the criticism of wants, I think these topics largely exhaust the thrusts of the articles published in the *Review of Radical Political Economics*. Radical economics is therefore rather well-defined and focused. The literature in the *Review of Radical Political Economics* is also interactive and my *impression* is that its authors build upon its previously published articles to a much larger extent than the authors who have published in the *Journal of Economic Issues* during its lifespan.

My conclusion is that paradigm indiscipline is the reason Samuels and Boettke found so many examples of similarities between two fundamentally different paradigms. If so, one would expect the similarities, where valid, to be in relatively peripheral areas that are not central to the core interests and *differentia specificae* of the two paradigms. I have argued above that this is, indeed, the case. Then, too, the sloppiness of definition that accompanies paradigm indiscipline can be said to have left room for the *apparent* similarities drawn by Samuels and Boettke, the validity of which I contested above.

NOTES

1.   I use planning in the ordinary sense of national economic planning and not in Hayek's sense (Hayek, 1944, pp. 34–35).

2.   I should add that arrested development within a paradigm can occur for reasons that are the very opposite of indisicipline: dogmatic discipline. Where a paradigm is well-insulated from anomalous happenstance and competing perspectives, ossification can generate arrested or distorted development.

REFERENCES

Attewell, Paul, (1984) *Radical Political Economy Since the Sixties*. New Brunswick, NJ: Rutgers University Press.

Ayres, C. E., (1961) *Toward a Reasonable Society*. Austin: University of Texas Press.

Boettke, Pete, (1989) "Evolution and Economics: Austrians and Institutionalists," **this volume**.

Eichner, Alfred S., (1983) "Why Economics is Not Yet a Science," in Eichner, ed., *Why Economics is Not Yet a Science*. White Plains, NY: M. E. Sharpe.

Hayek, Friedrich A., (1944) *The Road to Serfdom*. Chicago: University of Chicago Press.

————, (1965) "The *Non Sequitur* of the 'Dependence Effect'," reprinted from the *Southern Economic Journal* in Edmund S. Phelps, ed., *Private Wants and Public Needs*. NY: Norton, 37–42.

Kern, William S., (1982) *"The Implications of Limited Knowledge: The Economics and Social Philosophy of Friedrich A. Hayek,"* doctoral dissertation, Colorado State University.

Samuels, Warren J., "Austrian and Institutional Economics: Some Common Elements," **this volume**.

Stanfield, J. R., (1979) *Economic Thought and Social Change*. Carbondale, IL: Southern Illinois University Press.

————, (1986) *The Economic Thought of Karl Polanyi: Lives and Livelihood*. NY: St. Martin's and London: MacMillan.

AUSTRIAN INSTITUTIONALISM:
A REPLY

Peter J. Boettke

I. INTRODUCTION

My paper intended to stimulate a discussion among members of the respective schools. In order to get at the essence of the truth claims that writers within these apparently antagonistic traditions were making, it seemed necessary that they confront one another in a reasonable manner. I originally intended to stress the similarities between Austrians and Institutionalists, so that lines of communication would open. Once these lines opened, then the differences could be discussed. I believed then, as I still do, that if both schools of thought are indeed asking similar questions concerning the nature of institutions in society, then the ensuing conversations would be, and has shown to be, most interesting. In contrast to Miller (1989), therefore, I view both the attempts

Research in the History of Economic Thought and Methodology,
Volume 6, pages 181-202
Copyright © **1989 by JAI Press Inc.**
All rights of reproduction in any form reserved.
ISBN: 0-89232-928-9

by Warren Samuels and myself as a successful first step in bridging the gap between two very interesting and powerful approaches to economic analysis.

While Samuels's (1989) paper could be described as an Institutionalist perspective on Austrian economics, my paper was from the opposite direction, an Austrian look at Institutional economics. Samuels, however, added the caveat that his paper at the very most was "one institutionalist's view of the elements common to, in general relation to the differences between, Austrian and institutional economics." I left such a caveat out of my paper, perhaps leaving the impression that I was 'uncommitted' or 'eclectic,' but I will state now that my original paper and the comments to follow are those of one Austrian economist. Points I made and will make are different from those that other Austrians would make and, in fact, might be considered heresy by some. The points I wish to make, however, concerning the relationship of theory and history, the importance of institutional detail in economic analysis, the critique of equilibrium economics, and the political economy of Austrian institutionalism all fall within a coherent paradigm that was first developed by Menger, Boehm-Bawerk and Wieser and later refined by Mises and Hayek.[1] This uniquely Austrian perspective to economic analysis continues to be developed by thinkers such as Kirzner, Lachmann, Rothbard, and more recently O'Driscoll, Rizzo, Garrison, White, Lavoie, Ebeling and High. Austrian economics in not a monolith, but it is a well-defined paradigm.

I shall argue, therefore, in contrast to Stanfield (1989), and in agreement with Caldwell (1989), that the points of agreement between Austrians and Institutionalists do not so much result from paradigm indiscipline, but from the attempt to tackle similar problems from different sides of the issues. In particular, I think Caldwell was perceptive in recognizing the key role that the calculation debate had on the Austrians realizing and developing their unique perspective on market phenomena. I would also suggest that the Hayek-Keynes debate is very similar and, in fact, produced the same result as the calculation argument for the same reasons.[2] The reasons, however, that the Austrians were perceived by the profession to have lost both debates are reasons that Institutional economists should not be happy with. The arguments used to defeat the Austrian positions, both theoretical and practical, were arguments that deny that an Institutional economics is either useful or intellectually legitimate.[3] My challenge to Institutional economists, therefore, will be for them to answer the theoretical and practical problems that Austrian economists have posed against government planning of the economy with arguments that do not undermine their own paradigm.

As I pointed out in my paper (1989, fn. 8) the calculation debate poses an interesting problem for Institutional economists. I have not seen a direct response by an Institutionalist to the Mises-Hayek position that socialist planning (in its Marxian sense) is impossible. Perhaps the impression may be that Mises and Hayek lost the debate over rational socialist economic calculation to the market socialists, but to do so would be to side with neoclassicism against institutionalism. Lange argues that Mises' argument must be rejected precisely because Mises allowed institutional and historical factors to play a vital role in his theory (c.f., Lange 1970[1939], 62).

None of the commentors chose to respond to this question concerning the Institutional perspective on planning and the Mises-Hayek position; those who were concerned with the policy divergence between Austrians and Institutionalists merely asserted that planning is the Institutionalist policy prescription. I am asking them to provide a reason why Mises and Hayek are wrong and defend statements like "But since institutionalists lack the orthodox economists's faith in the market, support for economic planning is inherent to institutional economics" (Dugger 1987, 88). Because this seems to be the crux of the disagreement between the two schools, perhaps a response to the Mises-Hayek argument is warranted from anyone who is solely preoccupied with policy discussion. And because these ideological differences seem to be a major stumbling block to greater awareness and appreciation of the work of one another, perhaps we can improve the current conversation in two ways: (1) put aside discussion of policy implications and discuss the differing conceptions of the nature of economic science, and, once we understand the respective paradigms a little better, (2) confront the political economy questions head-on and see where it takes us. I shall attempt within the space allotted to me to briefly discuss the Austrian view of the nature of economic science and issues concerning the radical political economy of Austrian institutionalism.

II. PHILOSOPHICAL BACKDROP OF THE AUSTRIAN PARADIGM

The seeds of Austrian economics were planted in the soil of fin-de-siecle Vienna. The Viennese soil was fertilized by the philosophical writings of Wilhelm Dilthey, Franz Brentano, and Edmund Husserl.

Just as it is necessary to understand American institutionalism as possessing philosophical roots in American pragmatism (c.f., Mirowski 1987), the nature of Austrian economics must be understood in terms of the continental thought within which it developed. Through the interaction of classical political economy and continental philosophy the unique characteristics of Austrian economics emerged.[4]

Recognition of these philosophical underpinnings is essential if one wishes to understand what Austrians are up to, for their economics is more than the hope for "a 'better' theory of price determination and allocation of resources through markets by the incorporation of Austrian insights" (Kern 1989). Austrian economics is a distinct paradigm to and, in fact, in conflict with, mainstream economics. One can not simply add another dimension to a neoclassical argument and call that an Austrian point. Rather, Austrian economics redefines the whole problem and questions the understanding that other theorists have of the problem in the first place. The Austrian research program laid out by Menger, Boehm-Bawerk and Wieser, and more fully developed by Mises and Hayek, is radically different from mainstream economics at the level of the basic questions that are asked and considered important. Austrian economics can best be understood as a philosophical revolt against mainstream economics centering on the nature of scientific inquiry, in general, and the human sciences, in particular.

III. CONCEPTION AND UNDERSTANDING IN AUSTRIAN INSTITUTIONALISM

The relationship between theory and history has been a topic of discussion among Austrian economists since the founding of the school in the 1870s. This topic, however, is one of the least understood by outside ûbservers of the school. Menger's use of the term 'exact laws,' Mises's statements of the Kantian a priori categories of the mind or either Mises's or Rothbard's insistence of the apodictic certainty of Austrian economics are partly responsible for the misunderstanding.[5] But Austrian economics *never* denied the essential role of historical analysis in scientific progress. The primary purpose of theory is to *aid* the act of historical interpretation.[6] Menger's contributions to the methodenstreit was to defend the place of theoretical discussion in political economy discourse. He sought to demonstrate the necessity of a theoretical framework for historical interpretation (c.f., Menger 1985[1883]). As Boehm-Bawerk stated, "The historical school have

[sic] discarded abstract deduction, but they cannot write three pages on economic questions, even in the historical style, without general theory, and one can construct no general theory without the use of abstract deduction. *"For facts are not so accommodating as to present themselves to the eye of the investigator ranked in a scale ascending from the most special facts to ultimate general facts"* (1890, 260, emphasis added).

The point that the particulars must be organized through the filter of a general theoretical framework is a now widely recognized philosophical position (c.f., Polanyi 1962[1958]; Bernstein 1983). In addition, the recognition of the historicity of all knowledge has emerged out of the continental tradition and is consistent with an Austrian understanding of the nature of the human sciences (Gadamer 1985[1960]; Lavoie 1985c).[7] Using theory to read history and allowing history to inform theoretical direction is essential to the advancement of the human sciences, in general, and economics, in particular. Mises's contribution to our understanding of social phenomena rests on these principles. Theory and history constitute two halves of the Misesian system; insufficient attention paid to one or the absence of either produces unsatisfactory results (c.f., Mises 1981b[1933], 68–145; 1966[1949], 30–71; 1985b[1957]).

There is a distinction between theory and history, but not a dichotomy: Conception (theory) is necessary for organizing the 'facts' and providing the framework for understanding (history). But it is also true that the theorist is embedded within a certain historicity. The theorist can not escape his 'prejudices.' Nor would it be desirable for him to do so. These prejudices, as Gadamer has insightfully shown, enable the theorist to interpret what would otherwise be a chaotic bombardment of meaningless data (1985[1960], 245–74). The tacking back and forth between the general and the particular constitutes, within the setting of scholarly commitment to truth, honesty and critical discourse, the nature of the scientific process.

IV.   INSTITUTIONAL ANALYSIS AND AUSTRIAN ECONOMICS

Human science is deductive science that begins with reflections upon the essence of human action. "The starting point of praxeology," Mises states, "is not a choice of axioms and decision about methods of procedure, but reflection upon the essence of action" (1966[1949],

39). In contrast to neo-classical economics, which begins with the unrealistic assumption of maximizing behavior subject to given constraints, Austrian economics[8] understands man as an active, creative force in economic analysis. Man is the center of attention in Austrian analysis. Reflection upon human action reveals what to the Austrian are the hard-core principles of economics. The general principle that human action is goal oriented implies that the motive for action is a current unsatisfactory state of affairs, that in striving to remove the felt uneasiness individuals must make plans and try to implement them for the removal of the current uneasy state. This understanding of purposive human action serves as an indespensible aid to understanding social phenomena.[9]

While these principles are necessary for sound social reasoning, they are not sufficient. Attention must be paid to the social and institutional environment in which man finds himself (the cultural norms, the scientific perceptions of his civilization, etc.) in order to yield a useful understanding of both the intended and unintended outcomes of human action. Austrian methodological principles, therefore, call for a social analysis similar to that advocated by 'interpretive' social thinkers, such as Clifford Geertz (1979). Stress is on the meaning that the agents themselves place on their actions, this is what is meant by Austrian radical subjectivism. The task of the social scientist, however, does not stop at 'merely' understanding the meanings individuals attach to their actions, but traces out the unintended consequences of these actions. Economic theory helps in understanding the purpose and consequences of activities under investigation, it does not exhaust the analysis, but provides the framework from which the theorists can "fuse horizons" with the subject.[10]

Austrian economics, while deriving its basic principles through philosophical reflection upon the essence of human action, nevertheless recognizes the crucial role of the cultural and institutional environment. Internal appeals to the logical consistency and beauty of the system, while making some claim in theory-choice, are not the major reason one adopts an Austrian approach. Austrian economics attempts to render the world intelligible in terms of purposive human actors. As such, it appeals externally to its ability to aid in reading the historical record. Given the goal of making the human condition, both historically and at present, more intelligible, the Austrian economists cannot ignore complex issues of cultural traditions, legal rules, scientific technology, and other social products that help produce the complex web of social experiences we call 'society.'

An example of Austrian concern with institutional analysis that has largely been misunderstood among critics is the Austrian theory of the trade cycle. The attempt to apply basic choice theoretic principles like marginal utility to understanding monetary phenomena was the crux of Mises's 1912 contribution in *The Theory of Money and Credit* (1980[1912]). The Austrian theory of the trade cycle was first developed in that work and then later refined by Hayek in *Monetary Theory and the Trade Cycle* and *Prices and Production*. Mises and Hayek both felt that the crucial problem that any theory of the trade cycle must illuminate and help us understand is the 'cluster of errors' that occurs during a bust. For a theory to be 'successful,' it must render the preponderance of mismatched plans during the bust intelligible in terms of both the meanings businessmen place on their actions and the unintended consequences of those actions. The institutional environment of modern capitalism, in particular the financial and banking industries, played an extremely important role in the Mises-Hayek understanding of booms and busts. For example, the fact that in the 1800s and early 1900s 'new' money usually chanelled its way into the economy by way of industrial loans helps us in understanding the cluster of business errors without recourse to the assumption that all businessmen are stupid or that the speculative bubble just bursts. Rather, the Mises-Hayek theory suggests that business error occurs because intervention in the loanable funds market (manipulation of the interest rate) produces 'false' signals which businessmen act upon. Since most loans, at that time, were lent to business concerns, the artificially lower rate signalled businessmen to borrow money and invest in production processes that otherwise would not have appeared profitable. The corresponding malinvestments reveal themselves when markets adjust to convey the underlying preferences of consumers and producers.

The theory of the trade cycle, thus, should be understood as one instance of the more general theory of the inflation process. This understanding of the inflation process, which derives its basic insights from Richard Cantillon and David Hume, recognizes that 'new' money works its way through an economic system by incremental changes in relative prices and questions any monetary theory that asserts the neutrality of money. Money, to Austrians, is a social phenomena (a product of human action, not of human design) and is non-neutral by its very nature (changes in the supply of money can have real effects on the economy). Monetary theory, therefore, has to be intimately familiar with the institutional and legal environment in which money operates within an social system. The claim by Mises and Hayek was never that their theory of the trade cycle as explicated in 1912, 1933, or 1949, was universally valid, just that the general principles they followed, such as rendering the cluster of errors intelligible or recognizing the non-neutrality of money, were requirements for an adequate understanding of business cycles. With changes in the institutional assumptions, such as the shift from the dominance of industrial loans to loans to consumer or changes in banking regulations, the theory needs to be revised and re-worked. Each generation must apply the theory again taking into account the new institutional environment in order to render cyclical business fluctuations understandable and hopefully offer positive suggestions for reform in the attempt to prevent future malcoordination.

V.   BEYOND STATIC THEORIZING

Stanfield argues that my discussion of the Austrian emphasis on change and market processes is dubious. He argues that "Hayek's discussion of economic problems arising in consequence of change does not alter the fact that the economic problems Hayek envisages are those of the allocation [of] scarce resources to given ends." "This static problem," Stanfield continues, "continually revised by change but that does not make change itself the focal point of analysis and central content of the economic problem as it is in Institutional economics" (1989). While I find this an interesting point, I disagree that Austrians postulate essentially a static problem that continuously changes and attempted to document this in my original paper.

The role of equilibrium in economics is a point of contention among Austrians themselves.[11] I believe, though, that the confusion over the role of equilibrium in economics among Austrian economists results from two connected misunderstandings on the part of Austrians themselves: (1) a failure to fully recognize the uniqueness of Austrian economics; and (2) a failure to appreciate fully the meaning attributed in mainstream literature to general competitive equilibrium. These two misunderstandings result in 'neo-classical Austrianism'—the attempt to fit neatly into the neo-classical paradigm rather than attempt to break out of the existing neo-classical orthodoxy. This leaves those vaguely familiar with Austrian economics wondering what they are up to—is it just that mainstream economics describes the conditions of the end-state and Austrian economics explains the process by which we get to equilibrium? I think not. The work of Mises and Hayek points beyond itself to an approach to economics that perhaps they did not or have not fully comprehended. In addition, the research of Kirzner (1973; 1979; 1985), Lachmann (1978[1956]; 1977; 1986), and Rothbard (1970 [1962]; 1977[1970]) has added valuable insights into the nature of market phenomena that is both consistent with the older Austrian understanding of market adjustment and points to a future research program which might move beyond the confines of static theorizing.

Gordon (1989) has raised an interesting objection to the static theorizing he perceives in the Austrian understanding of marginal productivity theory. Despite the fact that he chose to spend the majority of his time making remarks about the Austrian's so-called 'elitism' and pulling quotes out of context, his challenge to Austrian economists to reformulate the marginal productivity theory of distribution to be consistent with their emphasis on market processes and non-equilibrium economics I find most interesting. I agree with Gordon that no proof of the exhaustion theorem "exists for the real world on half-way reasonable, realistic assumptions as to what is going on." The exhaustion theorem might have simply been a quick and easy response by neoclassical economists to the Marxian exploitation theorem—substituting an equilibrium condition, arrived at through rigorous mathematical derivation, for real-world analysis of capitalist processes.

Gordon is also correct in pointing out that, to the extent this proof relies upon the assumption of perfectly competitive markets, Austrians must question the usefulness of the analysis. But let me suggest a possible reformulation of capitalist processes of production and distribution that does not rely on equilibrium conditions or assumptions of perfect competition and is consistent with the methodological propositions I laid out above.[12]

Within the constant flux of economic activity profit seeking entrepreneurs must make judgments on two counts.[13] They have to look at the perceived marginal product of a factor, and since price, in this understanding of market activity, is a variable (not a parameter as in equilibrium theory) they have to make judgments about the expected market price of the final product. Technically, this means that entrepreneurs have to make judgments or estimates of the marginal revenue product of factors of production. Since the entrepreneur is a profit seeker he will not pay a factor more than his estimate of the marginal revenue product—in fact, he will want to, if he can, pay the factor less. The competitive flux, however, puts the lower limit on what he can pay—the entrepreneur must pay the factor enough to be able to bid it away from alternative uses. A payment scale, ranging from the higher limit, where the factor is paid exactly what the perceived marginal revenue product of its services are, and the lower limit, where the factor is just paid enough to bid it away from alternative uses, is established. The whole process of these judgments interacting with others judgments makes up the market process. By viewing the market as the interaction of human minds we can begin to reformulate our understanding of market phenomena in a manner that is both more realistic and interpretively useful than standard price theoretic models.[14]

VI. THE RADICAL POLITICAL ECONOMY OF AUSTRIAN INSTITUTIONALISM

Hopefully my preceding comments have clarified my interpretation of the Austrian tradition. My personal caveat must be reiterated even stronger in regard to issues of political economy. My policy position in no way reflects 'the' Austrian policy position—political economy requires more than just economic understanding. Policy and political philosophy is a mixture of ethical concerns, an understanding of political processes, and economic knowledge.

Issues in political and economic organization are complex issues, involving our deepest passions and making us risk our image of what the world could be against the image held by others. Political discourse, though, can be reasonable and truth seeking. It is with this goal in mind that I shall briefly venture into this area.[15]

One could not defend the political economy of Mises, Hayek or Rothbard within the space of one paper, let alone a section of an article.[16] My purpose, therefore, is merely to present counter evidence to the idea ''that a good deal of what Austrian economics is all about is an effort by those with culture, status, wealth and perquisites to protect themselves from [the] hoi polloi'' (Gordon 1989). Or claims that Austrians are ''mean-spirited'' and take ''their cue from the paranoid style of rightwing U. S. politics'' (Dugger 1989).

Austrian economists have not always been defenders of laissez-faire, nor is it a prerequisite for the acceptance of Austrian insights on the nature and significance of economics to support the free-market or the principles of classical liberalism or radical libertarianism (c.f., Boehm 1985). Given the epistemological critique of planning, as presented by Mises and Hayek, there do appear, however, to be strong and fundamental criticisms of centralized economic planning or government regulation (c.f., Kirzner 1985, 119–49; Lavoie 1985b). The confrontation between the Austrian understanding of knowledge dispersion within a complex industrial economy and the Institutionalists predilection toward economic planning is something I hope will emerge out of this collection and lead to further discussion.

The arguments against planning are informed, as Gonce suggests, by Hitler and Stalin (1989). But, it is not the case that either Mises, Hayek or Rothbard are ill-informed about the American experience. Both Mises and Hayek consider the American experience with democracy as a great, though qualified, 'success.' Rothbard, on the other hand, sees the experience as a missed opportunity for radical libertarianism. The problem with the American revolution is that it did not go far enough, and finally succumbed to the internal contradictions of democracy (1977[1970], 16–7; 189–99). Any theory of collective or public choice must account for the fact that "Government is a mechanism, like markets, through which individuals act collectively to improve their private utility. Government is a vehicle through which is promoted the self-interest of whomever can get into a position to control it" (Samuels 1980, 57). And since we understand that political activity is characterized by the interaction of 'rationally' ignorant voters with special interest groups, the bias toward concentrated benefits and dispersed costs results in a radical critique of the operation of democracy. A critique that suggests that theorists interested in the effect and role of power within the economic system should be greatly concerned with.

This concern with power and its effect on the human condition is fundamental to political economy and can be seen as a major concern of the Austrians. The argument against planning, for example, can be seen as basically taking two interconnected positions. First, the epistemological problem that confronts attempts to centrally plan the economic system manifests itself in the coordination problem—in the absence of markets, how do the planners *know* which goods to produce and what production techniques are economically feasible? Secondly, a totalitarian problem confronts any attempt to centrally plan the economy. The nature of planning requires that discretionary power be put into the hands of a few individuals—would not we expect that, given the nature of political processes, that those with a comparative advantage in exercising discretionary power would capture the institutions of power? This is not just limited to the peculiar personalities of Stalin,

Hitler and Mao, whose experiments in cultural revolution resulted in the cost of some 37 million lives (a modest estimate), but is also true of the abuse of privilege by American businessmen in the 'War Industries Board' and the 'Reconstruction Finance Corporation' (c.f., Cuff 1973; Lavoie 1985b, 174–86).

This concern with the human condition is especially prevalent if we look at issues beyond the economic sphere and concerning foreign policy and the economics of war. The majority of Austrian economists have held the position of radical nonintervention in foreign affairs. This has been informed as much by their classical liberal principles as by their understanding of international division of labor and the humane aspects of trade.[17] Mises, for example, argues that liberalism and pacifism are intimately connected. "In the Liberal Social Philosophy the human mind becomes aware of the overcoming of the principle of violence by the principle of peace," Mises argues. "War," he states, "is harmful, not only to the conquered but to the conqueror . . . the essence of society is peacemaking." "Liberal pacifism is the offspring of the Liberal Social Philosophy" (1981a[1922], 59). These arguments were even more forcefully put foward in Mises's 1927 book *Liberalism*, which is a basic statement of his social philosophy. He argues that, "The goal of the domestic policy of liberalism is the same as that of its foreign policy—peace. It aims at peaceful cooperation just as much between nations as within each nation" (1985a[1927], 105). Such appeals to peaceful cooperation, backed by statements such as; "Let the Russians be Russians," and his policy prescriptions which allow for both free emigration of goods and people, certainly do not sound like the 'paranoid style of rightwing politics' (c.f., Mises 1985a[1927], 153).[18]

Rothbard is even more explicit in his 'leftish' leanings. He advocates liberty across the board, both civil and economic. His concern is not with freedom from a 'nagging wife' or 'garbage' (Gordon 1989), but freedom from oppression. The goal of his political system is not to transform man, though I think there is an emancipatory promise of freedom, but to minimize the opportunities in society for coercive interaction and maximize the opportunities for cooperative behavior. Rothbard's efforts might be shown to be faulty, but it does injustice to both those efforts and their intellectual legitimacy to trivialize them as Gordon, Stanfield, and Dugger do. If these writers are concerned with the freedom of individuals and the betterment of society, then perhaps a more patient and less dismissive treatment of alternative ideas of the 'Good' would produce more fruitful interaction.

VII.   CONCLUSION

Austrian economics is an approach to economics that places a premium on understanding the human condition, both historically and at the present. It is humanistic in its approach, and humanitarian in its concern. As Mises states, "Economics must not be relegated to classrooms and statistical offices and must not be left to esoteric circles. It is the philosophy of human life and action and concerns itself with everybody and everything. It is the pith of civilization and of man's human existence" (1966[1949], 878).

Austrians have a lot to learn from interacting with Institutional economists. I hope that this discussion leads to continuing awareness and appreciation of the work of respective scholars and helps produce some real answers to the tough questions of political economy. And maybe, just maybe, some of us can work together to fight against that formidable enemy that stands in our way—the ahistorical and unrealistic orthodoxy or mainstream economics.

ACKNOWLEDGMENTS

I have benefited greatly from my conversations about this paper with my friends and associates at the Center for the Study of Market Processes; Jack High, Steve Horwitz, Don Lavoie, and Dave Prychitko. A special thanks goes to Dave Prychitko for his helpful comments on an earlier draft of this paper. Responsibility for remaining errors is solely my own.

NOTES

1.   For a more detailed statement on this point addressed to other Austrian economists see Boettke, Horwitz and Prychitko (1986).

2.   Both Hayek (1955;1978, pp. 23–34) and Lavoie (1985b;1986–7) have argued that the same 'pretense of knowledge' that guides the Marxian vision of centralized economic planning and underlies much of Keynesian macroeconomics follows from the dominance of scientistic thinking and the attempt to transform the human or moral sciences into 'social physics.'

3.   I am thinking of the arguments of Oskar Lange, Abba Lerner, and Paul Samuelson. Their arguments resulted in what Caldwell describes in paradoxical fashion, the elimination of both Austrian theoretical arguments and Institutional empirical concerns.

Just as the Austrians insisted that their non-mathematical approach was actually "theoretical," the institutionalists claimed that their holistic, pattern-modelling approach was truly "empirical" because it more accurately reflected reality. Mainstream economists who equated the term 'theory' with mathematical techniques and 'empiricism' with econometric estimation techniques found such claims rather bizzare. But more to the point, such claims could be dismissed as "unscientific" by mainstream practitioners who thought (wrongly, as it turned out) that they were positivists and positivism was an unimpeachable (wrong again) philosophical foundation for the practice of science. Meanwhile the attacks of Austrians and institutionalists against the positivists pretensions of their orthodox counterparts came to sound more and more alike. Though they began as methodological opposites, members of both groups found themselves united against a common enemy, and a formidable one, at that (Caldwell 1989).

Also see Lavoie (1986a;1986b) for similar discussion on the rise of positivism, formalism, the crisis of modernity and its relation to Austrian economics.

4. See Mises (1981b[1933]; 1966[1949]; 1985b[1957]; 1978[1962]; 1984 [1969]), Hayek (1955;1967;1978), Kirzner (1976a[1960]; 1976b), Lachmann (1971; forthcoming), Rothbard (1979), O'Driscoll and Rizzo (1985, pp. 1–70), Lavoie (1986c), Lavoie, edited, (forthcoming), Ebeling (1984;1986), Madison (1986a; 1986b;1987), Selgin (1987a), Prychitko (1986), Prychitko and Boettke (1987) and Boettke (1987).

5. I would like to point out, however, that even at face value these statements are not that absurd given the fact that they come out of well-developed philosophical traditions. For example, if one were to argue that Mises's methodology, as it is understood by mainstream economists, is appalling, then one is not just arguing against Mises, but the philosophy of Kant (or turn of the century Neo-Kantian philosophy to be more accurate) and the economic method of Say, Senior, and Cairnes, as well as Menger and Boehm-Bawerk. Similarly, Rothbard claims to derive his understanding of man's relations to his economic reality as well as 'politics' (in the classical sense) from Aristotelian philosophy. My point is simply that, though it is legitimate to disagree with some of the claims of Mises and Rothbard, such disagreement would have to be against a whole philosophical tradition and not just dismissive of Mises or Rothbard. Moreover, the task of dismissing either Rothbard or, in particular, Mises, is much more difficult if one recognizes the continental context within which their philosophical arguments emerged.

6. Dennis (1989) chides me for calling for a "major re-writing of one significant portion of the history of economic thought." Though he agrees that Menger was more than just one of the three founders of the marginal revolution, and that Austrian economics was misunderstood in the Anglo-American tradition of the history of economic thought, Dennis believes that these msiconceptions have been corrected by recent scholarship and my "correcting process" has gone too far and created new misconceptions. While I welcome the fact that some scholars, for example, William Jaffe (1976) or William Butos (1985), are beginning to recognize that Menger's economics was more than a verbal presentation of the marginal revolution, it is not clear to me that the Austrian paradigm is well understood (a few of the comments in this volume alone testify to the depth of the misunderstanding). For example, on this point of the relationship between theory and history many economists still hold the position that Mises and Austrian economists, in general, are opposed to historical studies. Given the per-

sistence of these misconceptions in the face of conflicting evidence, such as Rothbard's various historical studies and either the work of Lawrence White or Dom Armentano, perhaps a major re-write might be necessary.

7.   For example, Rothbard (c.f., 1979) grounds the action axiom on the historicity of human experience, i.e., the life-world. This is not a "strange, almost a mystical form of empiricism," as Miller suggests, but a phenomenological empiricism (Miller 1989). A radical empiricism that recognizes the primordial fact that we are *thrown in* a social life-world (this is similar to what Rutherford (1988) refers to as "institutional individualism"), conditioned by our language and shared inter-subjective experience with *others*. The fact that man has goals and seeks to achieve those goals, i.e., is a purposive creature, becomes apparent to us through our experiences *with the other*. It is in this sense in which Austrian economists and continental philosophers talk about *knowledge from within*—in the human science we have an advantage over the physical sciences because we are what we study. Through this use of this intersubjective knowledge we can arrive at truth. As Gadamer states, "the certainty that is imparted by the use of scientific methods does not suffice to guarantee truth. This is so especially of the human sciences, but this does not mean a diminution of their scientific quality, but on the contrary, the justification of the claim to special humane significance that they have always made. *The fact that in the knowing involved in them the knower's own being is involved marks, certainly, the limitation of 'method,' but not that of science.* Rather, what the tool of method does not achieve must—and effectively can—be achieved by a discipline of questioning and research, a discipline that guarantees truth" (1985[1960], pp. 446–7, emphasis added).

8.   Economics, it should be pointed out, is not synomous with praxeology. The term praxeology denotes all the human sciences—the study of human action. Mises originally prefered the term sociology, following in the tradition of Max Weber's 'Interpretive Sociology' of *Economy and Society*, but changed the term because he thought that its meaning had been lost. Understanding Mises in terms of Weber is very important, as Lachmann has pointed out, "it is the work of Max Weber that is being carried on here" in Mises's *Human Action* (1977, p. 95). Also see Lachmann (1971) for a further discussion of Weber and praxeology. The influence and respect was not unidirectional—Weber acknowledged Mises's contribution and influence of his ideas. For example, in references to Mises's work in monetary theory Weber states, "The formulation of monetary theory, which has been most acceptable to the author, is that of von Mises" (1978, p. 78). Moreover, Weber acknowledges and accepts Mises's arguments about the problems facing socialists economic organization (ibid., p. 107).

9.   The concept of rationality that is employed by Mises is quite different from that of rational economic action in mainstream economics and lack of familiarity or only casual reading of Mises's writing has lead to confusion—especially evident in some of the comments. Mises rejected Weber's distinction between four views of rationality, and reformulated rationality into a broader concept (1981b[1933], pp. 68–129). Rationality to Mises is action, the opposite of rationality is not irrationality, but non-action. Mises is not arguing that all action is 'correct,' but rather that all action is purposive. (Kirzner's various discussions on the differences between Robbinsian maximizing and Misesian action provide a fuller elaboration on this point). If rationality is instead understood, as it has come to be, in terms of instrumental reasoning (ends-means calculating like the Robbinsian maximizer), then Austrians, it seems to

me, would have to concur with radical critics, such as Jurgen Habermas, who base a large part of the critique of current social forms on their critique of the dominance of instrumental rationality within these social forms—bureaucracy, scientific management, state-capitalism, science, etc..

10. For an example, see Prychitko (1985) who analyzed the origin of 'money' and institutions of trade among the Kwakiutl Indians. Also see the paper by D. Bruce Johnsen (1986) for similar discussion concerning the origin of property-rights. Economic anthropology offers the most striking example of the necessity of "fusing horizons" to get at the meaning structures under analysis and their significance, but whenever one is engaged in historical research this essential task of fusion confronts us if we wish to produce an interesting narrative history. These themes can also be seen in Hayek's examinations of rule formation, legal anthropology and cultural evolution in his recent work (1973;1976b;1979;1988).

11. This debate has been ongoing for over a decade and a substantial literature has developed. The controversy was recently rekindled by the publication of O'Driscoll and Rizzo (1985). For a discussion of the debate among Austrians over the role of equilibrium in economic analysis see Boettke, Horwitz and Prychitko (1986) and the references cited therein.

12. I have benefited greatly from discussion with Jack High and Dave Prychitko on this point about a subjectivist reformulation of marginal productivity theory of distribution. Weakness and flaws in the argument, of course, are may own.

13. I want to point out that in Austrian economics entrepreneurship does not refer to capitalists, investors, speculators, or even risk merchants. Rather, entrepreneurship is an aspect of *all action*, we are all entrepreneurs. Kirzner (1973;1979;1985) has characterized this aspect of action as alertness to opportunities. While I agree essentially with Kirzner's formulation of entrepreneurial activity, I think that Jack High (1982) is correct in pointing out that entrepreneurship is also characterized by the exercising of judgment upon those opportunities.

14. The preceding analysis should be seen as distinct from standard theoretical discussion even in the price searcher model. Within the standard framework everything is essentially still known—there is no role or understanding of the market as the interaction of human minds, consisting of the judgments of other's judgments.

15. It seems appropriate that I lay my biases on the table. My political beliefs derive from the radical libertarian tradition of Lysander Spooner (1973[1870]), Benjamin Tucker (1969[1893]), and Murray Rothbard (1978[1973];1983). In addition, these beliefs have been greatly influenced by writers in the classical liberal tradition, such as Mises (1981a[1922]; 1985a[1927]) and Hayek (1976a[1944];1960;1973), as well as the radical analysis of *state capitalism* found in Rudolf Hilferding (1985[1910]), Gabriel Kolko (1963), James Weinstein (1968) and Jurgen Habermas (1975). I dislike politics, in general, preferring voluntary discourse over human rights and the appropriate social institutions conducive to the flourishing of human potentiality. In this sense, I am a critical utopian who is willing to open up his vision of the better future world to rational analysis.

16. Samuels (1974), for example, has raised some very interesting points against Rothbard's idea of anarcho-capitalism concerning power and private property. Though this is not the time or place for a response, I would like to suggest that Samuels goes too far when he claims that Rothbard's "book is a grotesque distortion of anarchism:

indeed, it is not anarchism but a cleverly designed and worded surrogate for elitist or aristocratic conservatism'' (p. 50). While not defending Rothbard on any particular point, I would like to suggest that his overall vision, like that of Marx, is much more powerful than any of its constituent parts. The relevance of Rothbard is his ability to instill a vision of what the world could be as opposed to what the world is—a vision of society without state violence and power. None of the individual parts, neither his economic or ethical arguments, nor his historical studies, can withstand repeated scholarly criticism, but taken as a whole the Rothbardian system outlines an exciting and powerful research program.

17. Mises and Hayek are both utilitarians of some sort and, therefore, see both the economic arguments for free-trade and political arguments for freedom as interconnected with the consequences that these policies would bring to society. Rothbard, on the other hand, takes a natural rights approach and defends the freedom of trade as a corollary to the defense of private property. All these writers, however, recognize and defend the proposition that political and economic freedoms are inexorably intertwined.

18. It is even proper to refer to Austrians (which assumes a homogenous policy position that is not there) as 'rightwing' or 'conservative' when particular theorists within the Austrian tradition have advocated the *elimination* of: all government restrictions on individual freedom, including the draft and draft registration, taxation, censorship (of any kind), and laws against certain sexual practices or personal consumption of drugs (Rothbard 1978[1973]); government monopoly of note issue (White 1984 and Selgin 1987b); the Federal Trade Commission and antitrust regulation (Armentano 1982;1986); government monopoly of legal services and courts (Barnett 1985;1986), government monopoly of civil and national defense (Rothbard 1977 [1970];1978[1973]), and *all* attempts at central planning for either microeconomic efficiency or macroeconomic stability reasons (Lavoie 1985b;1986–7) ? Perhaps Dugger should re-think his political characterizations and offer a more substantive criticism of the various policies suggested by different Austrians. It certainly would prove more fruitful than merely wonder 'who are the real bad boys of economics.' We could then get on with the important and difficult task of bridging theory with effective and meaningful praxis.

REFERENCES

Armentano, D., (1982) *Antitrust and Monopoly: Anatomy of a Policy Failure*, New York: John Wiley and Sons.

————— , (1986) *Antitrust Policy: The Case for Repeal*, Washington, D.C.: The Cato Institute.

Barnett, R., (1985) "Pursuing Justice in a Free Society: Part One—Power vs. Liberty," *Criminal Justice Ethics*, Summer/Fall, pp. 50–72.

————— , (1986) "Pursuing Justice in a Free Society: Part Two—Crime Prevention and the Legal Order," *Criminal Justice Ethics*, Winter/Spring, pp. 30–53.

Bernstein, R., (1983) *Beyond Objectivism and Relativism*, Philadelphia: University of Pennsylvania Press.

Boehm, S., (1985) "The Political Economy of the Austrian School," *Gli Economisti e la Politica Economica*, a cura di Piero Roggi, Edizioni Scientifiche Italiane, pp. 243–60.

Boehm-Bawerk, E., (1890) "The Historical vs. The Deductive Method in Political Economy," *Annals of the American Academy of Political Science*, July, Vol. 1, pp. 244–71.

Boettke, P., (1987) "Understanding Market Processes: An Austrian View of 'Knowing'," '*Marketing Theory': American Marketing Association Winter Educators' Conference*, Chicago: American Marketing Association, pp. 195–99.

_____ , (1989) "Evolution and Economics: Austrians as Institutionalists," *Research in the History of Economic Thought and Methodology*, Vol. 6.

Boettke, P., Horwitz, S., and Prychitko, D., (1986) "Beyond Equilibrium Economics: Reflections on the Uniqueness of the Austrian Tradition," *Market Process*, Fall, pp. 6–9; 20–25.

Butos, W., (1985) "Menger: A Suggested Interpretation," *Atlantic Economic Journal*, July, Vol 13, No. 2, pp. 21–30.

Caldwell, B., (1988) "Austrians and Institutionalists: The Historical Origins of their Shared Characteristics," *Research in the History of Economic Thought and Methodology*, Vol. 6.

Cuff, R., (1973) *The War Industries Board*, Baltimore: Johns Hopkins.

Dennis, K., (1989) "Ismatically Speaking: Are Austrians Institutionalists?," *Research in the History of Economic Thought and Methodology*, Vol. 6.

Dugger, W. M., (1987) "Democratic Economic Planning and Worker Ownership," *Journal of Economic Issues*, March, Vol. 21, No. 1, pp. 87–99.

_____ , (1989) "Austrians vs. Institutionalists: Who are the real dissenters?," *Research in the History of Economic Thought and Methodology*, Vol. 6.

Ebeling, R., (1984) "A Phenomenological Foundation for Dynamic Subjectivism," paper presented at a Liberty Fund Conference on *The Economics of Time and Ignorance* by Gerald O'Driscoll and Mario Rizzo, Port Chester, NY, November.

_____ , (1986) "Toward a Hermeneutical Economics: Expectations, Prices and the Role of Interpretation in a Theory of the Market Process," in Israel M. Kirzner, edited, *Subjectivism, Intelligibility and Economic Understanding*, New York: New York University Press, pp. 39–55.

Gadamer, H., (1985) *Truth and Method*, New York: Crossroad Publishing, [1960].

Garrison, R., (1984) "Time and Money: The Universals of Macroeconomic Theorizing," *Journal of Macroeconomics*, Spring, Vol. 6, No. 2, pp. 197–213.

Geertz, C., (1979) "From the Native's Point of View," in Paul Rabinow and William M. Sullivan, edited, *Interpretive Social Science: A Reader*, Berkeley: University of California Press, pp. 225–41.

Gonce, R. A., (1989) "Comment on the Comparing of Austrian and Institutionalist Schools of Economic Thought," *Research in the History of Economic Thought and Methodology*, Vol. 6.

Gordon, W., (1989) "Comparing Austrian and Institutional Economics," *Research in the History of Economic Thought and Methodology*, Vol. 6.

Habermas, J., (1975) *The Legitimation Crisis*, Boston: Beacon Press.

Hayek, F. A., (1976a) *The Road to Serfdom*, Chicago: University of Chicago Press, [1944].

_____ , (1955) *The Counter-Revolution of Science*, New York: The Free Press.

————, (1960) *The Constitution of Liberty*, Chicago: University of Chicago Press.

————, (1967) *Studies in Philosophy, Politics, and Economics*, Chicago: University of Chicago Press.

————, (1973) *Law, Legislation and Liberty*, Vol. 1, Chicago: University of Chicago Press.

————, (1976b) *Law, Legislation and Liberty*, Vol. 2, Chicago: University of Chicago Press.

————, (1978) *New Studies in Philosophy, Politics, Economics and the History of Ideas*, Chicago: University of Chicago Press.

————, (1979) *Law, Legislation and Liberty*, Vol. 3, Chicago: University of Chicago Press.

————, (1988) *The Fatal Conceit*, Vol. 1, London: Routledge and Kegan Paul.

High, J., (1982) "Alertness and Judgement," in Israel M. Kirzner, edited, *Method, Process and Austrian Economics*, Lexington, Mass.: D. C. Heath and Company, pp. 161–68.

————, (1986) "Equilibration and Disequilibration in the Market Process," in Israel M. Kirzner, edited, *Subjectivism, Intelligibility and Economic Understanding*, New York: New York University Press, pp. 111–21.

————, (forthcoming) *Maximizing, Action and Market Adjsutment*, Munich: Philosophia Verlag.

Hilferding, R., (1985) *Finance Capital*, London: Routledge and Kegan Paul [1910].

Jaffe, W., (1976) "Menger, Jevons and Walras De-Homogenized," *Economic Inquiry*, December, Vol. 14, pp. 511–24.

Johnsen, D. B., (1986) "The Formation and Protection of Property Rights Among the Southern Kwakiutl Indians," *Journal of Legal Studies*, January, Vol. 15, No. 1, pp. 41–67.

Kern, W., (1989) "Comment on Warren Samuels, 'Austrian and Institutional Economics: Some Common Elements,' and Peter Boettke, 'Evolution and Economics: Austrians As Institutionalists'," *Research in the History of Economic Thought and Methodology*, Vol. 6.

Kirzner, Israel M., (1976a) *The Economic Point of View*, Kansas City: Sheed and Ward, [1960].

————, (1973) *Competition and Entrepreneurship*, Chicago: University of Chicago Press.

————, (1976b) "On the Method of Austrian Economics," in Edwin G. Dolan, edited, *The Foundations of Modern Austrian Economics*, Kansas City: Sheed and Ward, pp. 40–51.

————, (1979) *Perception, Opportunity and Profit*, Chicago: University of Chicago Press.

————, (1985) *Discovery and the Capitalist Process*, Chicago: University of Chicago Press.

Kolko, G., (1963) *The Triumph of Conservatism*, New York: The Free Press.

Lachmann, L., (1978) *Capital and Its Structure*, Kansas City: Sheed, Andrews and McMeel, [1956].

————, (1971) *The Legacy of Max Weber*, Berkeley: Glendessary Press.

————, (1977) *Capital, Expectations and the Market Process*, edited with an introduction by Walter E. Grinder, Kansas City: Sheed, Andrews and McMeel.

————, (1986) *The Market as an Economic Process*, New York: Basil Blackwell.

_____ , (forthcoming) "Austrian Economics as a Hermeneutical Approach," in Don Lavoie, edited, *The Interpretive Turn: Essays in Continental Philosophy and Economics*.

Lange, O., (1970) "On the Economic Theory of Socialism," in Benjamin Lippincott, edited, *On the Economic Theory of Socialism*, New York: Augustus M. Kelley, [1939], pp. 55–143.

Lavoie, D., (1985a) *Rivalry and Central Planning*, New York: Cambridge University Press.

_____ , (1985b) *National Economic Planning: What is Left?*, Cambridge, Mass.: Ballinger Press.

_____ , (1985c) "The Interpretive Dimension of Economics: Science, Hermeneutics and Praxeology," Center for the Study of Market Processes, Working Paper #15.

_____ , (1986a) "Between Institutionalism and Formalism: The Rise and Fall of the Austrian School's Calculation Argument, 1920–50," Center for the Study of Market Processes, Working Paper #21.

_____ , (1986b) "The Present Status of Interpretation in Economics: Bad News with a Glimer of Hope," paper presented at the annual meetings of the Canadian Society for Hermeneutics and Post Modern Thought, University of Manitoba, Winnipeg, May.

_____ , (1986c) "Euclideanism versus Hermeneutics," in Israel M. Kirzner, edited, *Subjectivism, Intelligibility and Economic Understanding*, New York: New York University Press, pp. 192–210.

_____ , (1986–7) "The Political and Economic Illusions of Socialism," *Critical Review*, Winter, Vol. 1, No. 1, pp. 1–35.

Lavoie, D., (forthcoming) edited, *The Interpretive Turn: Essays in Continental Philosophy and Economics*.

Madison, G., (1986a) "Hans-Georg Gadamer's Contribution to Philosophy and It's Significance for Economics," paper presented at Center for the Study of Market Processes conference on "Interpretation, Human Agency and Economics," George Mason University, March.

_____ , (1986b) "Ricoeur and the Hermeneutics of the Subject," Department of Philosophy, McMaster University, mimeo.

_____ , (1987) "Hayek and the Interpretive Turn," paper presented at the annual meeting of the Canadian Philosophical Association, May.

Menger, C., (1985) *Investigations into the Method of the Social Sciences with Special Reference to Economics*, New York: New York University Press, [1883].

Miller, E., (1989) "Comment on Boettke and Samuels: Austrian and Institutional Economics," *Research in the History of Economic Thought and Methodology*, Vol. 6.

Mirowski, P., (1987) "The Hermeneutical Bases of Institutionalist Economics," Tufts University, mimeo.

Mises, L., (1980) *The Theory of Money and Credit*, Indianapolis: Liberty Press, [1912].

_____ , (1981a) *Socialism: An Economic and Sociological Analysis*, Indianapolis: Liberty Press, [1922].

_____ , (1985a) *Liberalism: In the Classical Tradition*, New York: The Foundation for Economic Education, [1927].

————, (1981b) *Epistemological Problems of Economics*, New York: New York University Press, [1933].

————, (1966) *Human Action: A Treatise on Economics*, Chicago: Henry Regnery, [1949].

————, (1985b) *Theory and History*, Auburn, Al.: The Ludwig von Mises Institute, [1957].

————, (1978) *The Ultimate Foundations of Economic Science*, Kansas City: Sheed, Andrews and McMeel, [1962].

————, (1984) *The Historical Setting of the Austrian School*, Auburn, Al.: The Ludwig von Mises Institute, [1969].

O'Driscoll, G., and Rizzo, M., (1985) *The Economics of Time and Ignorance*, New York: Basil Blackwell.

Polanyi, M., (1962) *Personal Knowledge*, Chicago: University of Chicago Press, [1958].

Prychitko, D., (1985) "The Origin of 'Money' and the Institutions of Trade Among the Kwakiutl Indians," Center for the Study of Market Processes, George Mason University, mimeo.

————, (1986) "Interpretation over Prediction: The Case for Hermeneutical Economics," paper presented at the annual meeting of the Eastern Economics Association, Philadelphia, PA., April.

Prychitko, D., and Boettke, P., (1987) "The Pure Logic of Choice or the Phenomenology of Human Action?," paper presented at the annual meeting of the Society for Phenomenology and the Human Sciences, Bellarmine College, Louisville, Kentucky, May.

Rothbard, M., (1970) *Man, Economy and State: A Treatise on Economic Principles*, Los Angeles: Nash Publishing, [1962].

————, (1977) *Power and Market*, Kansas City: Sheed, Andrews and McMeel, [1970].

————, (1978) *For a New Liberty*, New York: Macmillan, [1973].

————, (1979) *Individualism and the Philosophy of the Social Sciences*, San Francisco: The Cato Institute.

————, (1983) *The Ethics of Liberty*, Atlantic Highlands, NJ: Humanities Press.

Rutherford, M., (1989) "Some Issues in the Comparison of Austrian and Institutional Economics," *Research in the History of Economic Thought and Methodology*, Vol. 6.

Samuels, W., (1980) "Toward Positive Public Choice Theory," *Review of Social Economy*, April, Vol. 38, No. 1, pp. 55–64.

————, (1974) "Anarchism and the Theory of Power," in Gordon Tullock, edited, *Further Explorations in the Theory of Anarchy*, Blacksburg, VA: University Publications, pp. 33–57.

————, (1989) "Austrian and Institutional Economics: Some Common Elements," *Research in the History of Economic Thought and Methodology*, Vol. 6.

Selgin, G., (1987a) "Praxeology and Understanding," *Review of Austrian Economics*, Vol. 2, pp. 19–58.

————, (1987b) *The Theory of Free Banking*, Totowa, NJ: Rowman and Allanheld.

Spooner, L., (1973) *No Treason: The Constitution of No Authority*, Colorado Springs: Ralph Myles Publishing, [1870].

Stanfield, J. R., (1989) "Of Paradigms and Discipline," *Research in the History of Economic Thought and Methodology*, Vol. 6.

Tucker, B., (1969) *Instead of a Book*, New York: Haskell House, [1893].

Weber, M., (1978) *Economy and Society*, Vol. 1, Berkeley: University of California Press.

Weinstein, J., (1968) *The Corporate Ideal in the Liberal State, 1900–18*, Boston: Beacon Press.

White, L., (1984) *Free Banking in Britain*, New York: Cambridge University Press.

COMPARING AUSTRIAN AND INSTITUTIONAL ECONOMICS:
RESPONSE

Warren J. Samuels

Notwithstanding the unfortunate absence of commentators from within the Austrian school, I believe that the project has elicited considerable insight into the problem of the relationship between schools of economic thought, insight not always intended by the writers themselves. My response will focus on that problem, the comments, and other pertinent materials.

I. THE PROBLEM OF COMPARING SCHOOLS OF ECONOMIC THOUGHT

Let me make the following points:

1. The meaning of any school, for example, its leading ideas, will differ both between statements from within the school and between

Research in the History of Economic Thought and Methodology,
Volume 6, pages 203-225
Copyright © 1989 by JAI Press Inc.
All rights of reproduction in any form reserved.
ISBN: 0-89232-928-9

these and statements from the perspective of other schools. One school's view of itself (putting aside for the moment the fact that there will be different views of itself from within) will differ from the views of it taken from the perspective of other schools. The view of a particular school held by a representative from another school will be filtered through the ideational system of that other school. It is not possible, I think, unequivocally to establish which view of a school, its own or that of another school, should be given a privileged position as the "correct" statement of the meaning of that school. A matrix thus is formed by the combination of each school's self-perception and the perceptions of each school by representatives of other schools. To the extent that each school of thought is itself heterogeneous, the perceptual and interpretative possibilities are further enlarged and the interpretive matrix rendered more complex, but I want to treat internal heterogeneity separately.

The circumstance of these considerations must affect any treatment of the relationship(s) between Austrian and institutional economics. Neither school need be taken on its own terms. By the same token, neither is necessarily to be seen as others see it, that is, on their other terms.

2.   One key point on which most if not all contributors to this symposium seem to agree is that each of the two schools of thought is heterogeneous. In part because of the unintended predominance of institutionalist commentators, the heterogeneity of Austrian economics is much more prominent here than that of institutional economics, but the latter is no less present in reality, as my subsequent comments (as well as past writings) will evidence, and is not absent from the comments.

One implication is the question quite properly raised by A. W. Coats and Ken Dennis as to the usefullness of the term "school." At the very least, for various reasons but especially that of heterogeneity, the term must be used with care and circumspection.

The heterogeneity of a school means in part that an interpreter has the difficult task of identifying representative figures when no one person is fully representative. The choices of representative figures for purposes of comparison will influence the results; different choices will produce at least somewhat different comparisons. This problem is especially raised by Richard Gonce.

A further problem facing the interpreter is that of identifying the sophisticated in contrast to the naive versions of the doctrines of a school of thought. Naive versions of Austrian and institutional economics can look bad, but it is important to recognize the interpretive problem consequent to the fact that some members of each school do in fact adhere to a so-called "naive" version whereas others have what may be considered to be a much more "sophisticated" version. In a sense there is no problem, because both versions are of the same thing. In another respect there is a problem, because those who lose sight of the arguably sophisticated version can fail to recognize the limits, indeed the fundamental nature, of their position. It is, in any event, a difficult interpretive problem whether a school of thought is to be identified by the arguably more numerous naive statements or by the more sophisticated statements of a relative few. (Is a mass to be designated by its statistical mean or by the substance of one tail of the pertinent distribution?) This is a particular problem, for example, in evaluating neoclassical welfare economics (both Pigovian and Paretian) and its applications. The general intractible problem of the specific identification of the "naive" and the "sophisticated" versions of a body of thought is always a subjective matter, though it may have objective elements to it.

It is my perception that the sophisticated versions of Austrian and institutional economics, or what I consider the sophisticated versions, are much closer than is ordinarily understood to be the case and than is stated by some contributors. I do have some reservations about the matter. This perception, as I shall make clear, requires that one factor out both the ideological driving force behind the two schools (or some of their members) and the consequences generated by the ideology for weighting various considerations. I am fully aware, I think, that ideology and the interests served by ideology are important and that the meaning of the respective schools is profoundly generated by their respective ideologies. Nonetheless, I believe that there is a considerable common positive substance between the two schools and, moreover, that factoring out the ideology—so far from removing it from consideration at all—enables the identification of the different weights given to various considerations. I suggest this below with regard to deliberative versus nondeliberative (rational versus nonrational), spontaneous order, and legal change.

An alternative (but perhaps supplemental) formulation to naive versus sophisticated, raised by Coats, is that of the essential versus inessential elements in the doctrines of a school. Much the same considerations apply.

Both naive versus sophisticated and essential versus inessential elements relate to another question raised by Coats, namely, the identification of any unity and continuity that may exist within a school, that is, the twin problems of the identity and heterogeneity of a school.

3.   Several institutionalist contributors do not like what Boettke has to say about Austrian economics as institutionalism and thus implicitly about institutionalism. Certainly Austrians will not like what several institutionalists have to say about Austrian economics. In part this will be due to differences of ideology but in part it will be due to selective identification of each other's ideas. On the other hand, to the extent that each correctly or adequately knows what the other side is saying (which is *very* limited), they simply will have to agree to disagree.

Each side is partly responsible, however, for the view of it held by others. As indicated above, the view of a school is a function of the perspective from which it is held: the view from within, on its own terms, will be different from the view from without, on the terms of another school(s). When communicating referee reports to authors of submitted papers, I often have had to note that the author should be aware of the more or less extreme reactions which his or her paper elicited. The same is true here. The meaning of a proposition or position derives from both what its advocate and its critic thinks of it.

4.   I should also say that in my view the meaning of a concept, line of reasoning, theory, model, paradigm, doctrine or school resides in both its strengths and its weaknesses, and that the weaknesses are correlative to if not derivative from the strengths: what produces the strengths also produces the weaknesses. We all suffer from a particular myopia, from the preoccupation with the model, theory or paradigm, etc., in which we think and whose limits we tend to sublimate or simply forget.

5.   I also should note that comparison of schools of economic thought is further complicated by two things. The first is their respective mixes of positive and normative content. The second is their respective mixes of two types of work in economics: "economic theory" relating to the allocation of resources, distribution of income, and determination of the level of aggregate income through the market, and "theory of economic order" relating to the organization and control of the economic system as a whole understood to encompass more than the market, especially the structure of power, systemic and/or structural change, and fundamentals of the economic role of government. Notwithstanding the evident positive and normative differences between schools, *all* schools of economic thought have in fact treated both topics (see Samuels 1972).

II.   THE COMMENTS

Given what I tried to do in my original paper, short of producing a vastly longer and more complex document, I am reasonably pleased with it, even after the criticisms from several commentators. Except for minor, basically stylistic changes, the paper has not been revised from what was sent to the contributors. Clearly, certain matters could benefit from more elaborate treatment, for example, the question of the status of macroeconomics within Austrian economics. The large and complex question of the spontaneous-order argument will be addressed in detail in my study of the use of the concept of the invisible hand. What I have to say below will further, albeit briefly, elaborate on some matters from the original paper.

I will not comment on Boettke's paper except to note his emphasis on naive versus sophisticated methodological individualism and methodological collectivism (holism), and that I have mixed feelings about his questioning of A. W. Coats's judgment of the failure of a progressive (in the Lakatosian sense) insitutionalist research program. For one thing, "progressive" is both subjective and heavily influenced by social location (to use Joseph Schumpeter's term) within the discipline or profession. For another, institutionalism has in fact not had the success many institutionalists have wished for it, though it is by no means moribund. For still another, too much institutionalist writing, like too much Austrian writing, is mere ceremonial repetition or restatement, often by epigones, of the doctrines of the great figures of the school— though the works of leading figures inevitably are themselves only rarely fully adequate, which is part of the overall interpretive problem. But, finally, there are in fact increasing numbers of institutionalist writings which do break new ground.

Bruce Caldwell's identification of certain further sociological aspects of the genesis and development of the two schools is useful. Certainly Caldwell is correct that "methodological positions rarely if ever develop in a vacuum." (*Vide* Ken Dennis's stress on the institutionalist emphasis that theory is context-bound and that both schools could accuse one another of parochialism.) His focus on the socialist calculation controversy is suggestive of the degree to which the development of Austrian doctrine has been driven by its continuing effort, especially in the hands of Ludwig von Mises, Friedrich von Hayek, and James M. Buchanan, to erect a useful and effective intellectual fortress in defense of their conception of the market economy and against "socialism" and (certain) forms of governmental activism. It is not inapposite to note that no small amount of institutionalist work has been driven by efforts to reform capitalism, in one way or another. In this respect at least, and somewhat ironically, both schools have evidenced policy activist social engineering; that this is obscured in the case of the Austrian school by certain of their doctrines does not make it any less true. My own perception is that the normative policy-activist social-engineering drive has actually been slightly lower in institutional than in Austrian economics, but that is too complex a question to the taken up here (and probably not a soluble problem). In any event, the ideological element can be factored out for interpretive purposes, or at least efforts in that direction can be made.

A. W. Coat's raising of certain questions—essential versus inessential elements in schools, the coherence of the term "school" itself, and the problem of unity and continuity—have already been noted and affirmed. Inasmuch as Coats again argues that Commons left no theoretical tradition (did not "found a doctrinal school"), I can only cite a fact to indicate that the story is more complex: the work done by Allan Schmid, myself and others in the field of law and economics is directly in and a self-conscious part of the Commons tradition. And there are other examples in economics and agricultural economics.

Ken Dennis's scepticism about hypostatizing "Austrian" and "institutionalist" essences obviously is congruent with my own view, especially in light of his concern with parochialism. His argument that the Hayekian notion of evolution is fundamentally different from that of the institutionalists is well taken, though it may have to be modified by what Malcolm Rutherford has to say. Dennis's emphasis on Austrian universalism is well taken; however, there is a strong element in Ayresian institutionalism of a universalist technological, instrumentalist "transcendent theory of value" (quoting from Ron Stanfield's comment). I also like his identification of the tension between the relativist and reductivist enterprises in the two schools.

William Dugger's comment (and those of several others) certainly raises the critical question as to what is essential in Austrian economics: libertarian ideology, the power structure and interests protected by that ideology, and/or the positive substantive analysis which arguably can be rescued from the ideological analysis? Whether Austrians like it or not, it is obviously perfectly possible to interpret them, following Dugger, as economic fundamentalists, as defenders of the status quo power structure, as elitists, as poseurs. Institutionalism is much more readily perceived as criticism of economic fundamentalism and the status quo power structure. Of course, some Austrians, like some Marxists, may see institutionalism as a half-way house between neoclassicism and radical economics: as seen from the Marxist perspective, sensible enough to appreciate the Marxian critique but not courageous enough to go all the way with radicalism. Some institutionalists are, however, very radical whereas others are quite conservative. But, of course, not every institutionalist is conservative or radical about the same things (and the same point applies to Austrian economists).

This latter matter is suggested by Dugger's affirmation that whereas the Austrians are pro market, the institutionalists are pro planning: "planning is an Institutionalist imperative," he says. Whatever one's feeling about this as a normative issue, empirically this is an overgeneralization: some institutionalists are in favor of planning, others are in favor of the market but not as presently structured. Whereas the Austrians see the market as intrinsically competitive (at least as long as not "interfered" with by government), institutionalists see it as structured by power and accordingly as something of a system of private (or private-public) planning. The difference between institutionalists lies in their reaction to this perception: some take the hierarchic system as inevitable (a technological imperative) and want to democratize, or make responsible, the planning system; others do not accept the perceived existing reality of private power and planning as inevitable, and want to use government to promote a wider diffusion of power and a more effectively pluralistic market. Planning is by no means a universal institutionalist imperative.

Also it is fair to say that, some Austrian writings notwithstanding, the Austrian position on institutions (methodological collectivism) is more complex than outright denial of its existence or usefulness. More on this below.

Richard Gonce systematically tests assertions about similarities and differences through a comparison of the work of von Mises and Commons and reaches findings at variance with those of Boettke and me. He acknowledges the problem of defining the essential attributes of Austrian and institutional economics, particularly in view of the evident heterogeneity of the two schools. He quite properly finds that what Boettke and I consider to be common elements are often only titles of broad categories of ideas, not specific doctrines. *That is a very important point.* He concludes, after a detailed comparison of the specific doctrines of von Mises and Commons that there are fundamental differences between them. With respect to my paper, Gonce confirms the differences and disconfirms the common elements; with respect to Boettke's, he finds that there is no common viewpoint concerning evolution (a view shared by most institutionalist commentators). He stresses, however, that the findings are relative to the selection of von Mises and Commons, and that comparison utilizing the work of other representative figures would likely yield somewhat different findings. The work of von Mises and Commons is, of course, very important to their respective schools, but does not fully comprise their doctrines.

Gonce writes that Commons is "vulnerable to Mises's charge that all institutionalists deny the reality of economic law." I do not think that that is correct. Commons was opposed to an absolutist natural law conception of economic laws, but did understand that economic laws (statements of tendency) operated within the existing institutional and power structures. This, I think, is a false issue (like so many others in both Austrian and institutional economics), arising from partial and incomplete statements of a much more complex position.

Wendell Gordon, as do several other institutionalist commentators, juxtaposes Austrian apriorism to institutionalist pragmatism, instrumentalism and reliance on experience. Early in the paper he remarks about the tendency of persons from within each camp to find totalitarian or dictatorial implications in the other. This is both correct[1] and suggestive of the complexity of the problem of *power* in the real world, something to which economists from both schools could contribute if they would hold their ideology and normative preferences temporarily in abeyance. Authors in each school have acknowledged the possibility of abuse-of-power concerns raised by the other. But this, of course, raises the key question of relative weight—which can be temporarily transcended once the different ideologies with their respective weighting systems are suspended for purposes of objective analysis. And this raises the question, again, as to what is essential: the ideology or the positive substance once the ideology is factored out.

Gordon also notes that both schools seem to emphasize that behavioral norms are generated within the economic process itself, that they are not eternal verities. Still, there are tendencies in the opposite direction in both schools, in some of the Austrian treatment of the status quo norms and arrangements and in some of the institutionalist treatment of technology. Institutionalists have been more conspicuously active in support of changing received norms, though Austrian dismay with the value system of the welfare state and "big government" and efforts to change them must count as logically—of course, not substantively—the same reformist/activist phenomenon. Institutionalists also have been more active in studying the process of valuational change, whereas Austrians seem to worry lest such study lead to social engineering, although Austrian economists are themselves heavily engaged in efforts to change values. Perhaps the difference between the two schools is not in their attitude toward changing norms but the specific norms which they seek to alter.

Perhaps Gordon's most telling argument is that the Austrians, because of their perceived absolutism, apriorism and general identification with the status quo, are unable to rationalize the legal change which their own system, understood in its most sophisticated form, requires. The power of this argument is enormous: Given that the status quo has the privileged status residing in the circumstance that absent a decision to change, it (or its modes of change) will remain in place, the burden on the advocate of change is three-fold: to ground a principle of change, to determine which of all possible changes actively to promote, and to establish that there is a likelihood that the sought-after change has a high probability of realization. The change advocate has especially to determine the criteria of change. Gordon's point, as I interpret his paper, is that these problems pertain to the conservative libertarian Austrians as well and that they suffer the disadvantages consequent to their affection for absolutism, apriorism and the status quo. In Mengerian terms, recognition of the spontaneous genesis of social institutions is accompanied by recognition of the need for deliberative evaluation and often change of received institutions. The sophisticated Austrian position recognizes both elements. But doing so fundamentally weakens what is typically advanced in an absolutist position. Perhaps the most that can be said of the Austrian treatment of the problem of the criteria for change (though this is only rarely evident in their writings because of their apodictic tendencies) is they are themselves in fact engaged in the value-clarification and selection process. This is more evident in the Hayek of *Law, Legislation and Liberty* (1973) and other writings (1967, 1978) than it is in *The Road to Serfdom* (1944). More generally, emphasis on so-called spontaneous-order evolution and on libertarianism has prevented them from analyzing the problem of legal change of legal arrangements in an objective fashion. Austrians seem more interested in advancing a conservative *presumption* rather than objectively analyzing a complex question. An important but incomplete set of facts is elevated to the status of a first principle of policy.

In terms of freedom versus control, they identify (albeit highly selectively) the status quo system with freedom and efforts to change that system (or its structure) with control (coercion), whereas in their technically more sophisticated analyses they agree with the institutionalists (especially the Commons tradition) that freedom is always a matter of a particular structure of freedom and control; thus, as Gordon stresses, they lack the ability to make judgments as to the reasonableness or the desirability of any proposed exercise of control or change of control. Platitudes about "free to choose" and Paretian consent coexist with analyses which demonstrate that freedom of choice is inexorably highly constrained, that there is, as Frank Knight acknowledged, little freedom even in a free society. As Gordon says, the Austrians (not alone, of course) are hung up by wanting "to have it both ways, to impose some value judgments and to venerate the status quo at the same time."

This is a manifestation of the perceived position of the Austrians in which they affirm apriori any change generated by economic entrepreneurs but no other, yet other change, especially legal change (the result of political entrepreneurs and so-called rent-seeking), so much called for by the sophisticated version of their system, is denigrated. Finally, their treatment of entrepreneurship, at its most subtle and sophisticated level, does not necessarily apply to all businessmen or only to businessmen; but at the naive level, that seems typically to be how it is employed. But this, like so many other things touched on in these papers, is another story.

William Kern argues the paradox that the most important differences between Austrians and institutionalists stem from the areas in which they are most alike, that the similarities are epiphenomena, and that the gap between the two schools is likely too large to be bridged. The last two points seem to summarize the views of most, but by no means all contributors. Kern stresses different conceptions of evolution, especially deliberative versus nondeliberative modes of change, about which more below.

I like Kern's distinction between choice within opportunity sets and the formation of the structure of opportunity sets. In their preoccupation with the former, as he says, Austrians are fundamentally neoclassical, whereas the institutionalists are not. Thus, "the sources of dissatisfaction of both schools with [neoclassical] orthodoxy are similar but also widely at odds with one another."

Kern is certainly correct that a fundamental difference between Austrian (and other neoclassical) and institutional economists is that the former see the economy as organized by the market and the latter as organized by institutions. This is a distinction which I have repeatedly made myself, following Ayres and others. But if one perceives that the market is an institution and is formed by institutions, and that the evolution of institutions leads to changes in the markets formed by institutions, as does the sophisticated version of Austrian economics (at least as I envision it), then one can reinterpret some or much Austrian work in a manner much more compatible with institutionalist work than heretofore has been appreciated. This compatibility is made complicated if not fragile by the different attitudes toward institutions within institutionalism: the Veblen-Ayresians tending to understand them as ceremonial bastions of customary rules and power positions, and the Commons tradition seeing them as so many important factors governing economic performance. Of course, a further difference between Austrian and all institutional economists is their different attitudes toward the status quo "free enterprise" system, already noted above.

Edythe Miller takes pretty much the same hard institutionalist position found in several other writings. She finds that any affinities between the two schools are eclipsed by truly fundamental differences, and demonstrates this by comparing them on the basis of their methodologies and their theories of human nature and value. The differences, she affirms, are not of nuance but of essence. That Austrians take the positions she (and the others) attribute to them is beyond cavil; whether these positions fully exhaust the sophisticated Austrian position is another matter. (I am moved to remark that if I had secured a preponderance of Austrian, rather than institutionalist, contributors, my comments might appear quite different, for example, invoking a sophisticated institutionalism rather than a partial or naive one.)

Malcolm Rutherford's comment, I must say, is a gem. As often as I find myself reacting in much the same way as Dugger, Gonce, Gordon, Kern, Miller and (as we shall see) Stanfield to the selective ideological apologetics of the Austrians, I also frequently try to grasp the deeper, more sophisticated, and non-legitimizing substantive content resident in Austrian writings. And this is what Rutherford has, it seems to me, tried to do and page for page has done very well. He concludes that the "observed similarities represent more than merely accidental or superficial resemblances, though this is not to say that their research programs are *identical*."

I should like to underscore Rutherford's point that "It is particularly noteworthy that neither side necessarily rejects the methodological terms used by the other to describe their own position."

Rutherford's interpretive approach is demanding: He seeks to give effect to, or at least to acknowledge, everything present in both schools of thought. Consider, for example, the complex Austrian position on rationalism. It includes: (1) individual choice per se, (2) the necessary rationality of individual choice, (3) the social determination or conditioning of individual choice, (4) favoring nondeliberative ("spontaneous") institutional change, and (5) affirming deliberative legal change when necessary. The first raises the problem of the distribution of choice between individuals. The second and fifth are tautological. All have strong positive elements akin to the recognition by institutionalists of the operation of deliberative and nondeliberative forces, albeit with varying normative emphasis. Furthermore, if institutionalists can be accused of introducing their own preferences into analysis (see also Miller's point that institutionalists insist that not all expenditure decisions and productive efforts are equally legitimate), Austrians do likewise, as Gordon's quotation from von Mises about boxing champions and authors of detective stories illustrates. Once the personal subjective and ideological elements are factored out (to the greatest extent possible), Austrian and institutional economics seem to have much in common with regard to the formation and alteration of institutions, the formation and role of individual choice, and the analytical place of social reform and the relation of science thereto. But these are vast substantive topics and I can only allude to them, and neither demonstrate nor illustrate them, here.

Another respect in which Austrian and institutionalist economics can be compared is their methodological (as contrasted with normative) individualism and collectivism. It seems to me that notwithstanding all the emphasis by Austrians on the methodological individualist nature of their analysis, it is in fact fundamentally methodologically collectivist as well. Both schools represent fundamental blends of methodological individualism and collectivism. With regard to the Austrians, certainly they focus on the subjectively choosing individual. But they also focus on the market and on aggregative, spontaneous-order forces and processes which simply cannot be addressed merely by looking at individual choice. As for institutionalists, their holistic and methodologically collectivist emphases have not prevented their directing attention to the activities of individual economic actors, however much influenced or channeled by larger forces and institutions.

Rutherford quite properly stresses that "the major distinction between reductive methodological individualism and holism . . . is to be found in the primacy given to the individual in the former as opposed to the primacy given to the social or institutional in the latter." But this distinction, which he so accurately draws, is typically (at least in the naive formulations) overdone: *primacy* too often means *total and exclusive reliance* in practice. What Rutherford, after Agassi, calls "institutional individualism" certainly does raise "the possibility that the methodological differences between Institutionalists and Austrians are more rhetorical than real" and that at a more sophisticated level "at least a significant part of the work of Institutionalists and Austrians is *not* as methodologically incompatible as is usually thought." As already indicated, this reasoning applies to the analysis of the origins and evolution of institutions; it also applies to market success and market failure (unless one or the other is absolutistically preempted by tautological formulations), as well as to functional versus dysfunctional institutional evolution.

Ron Stanfield's comment echoes several others in finding the alleged similarities between the two schools to be dubious, forced and much less important than the differences.

Stanfield contrasts the two schools on such questions as the place of the entrepreneur, that only subjective individual preferences count, the place of economy in society, the nature of economic change and process, the central problem of economics, and policy activism. In some respects he is certainly correct. But to say, for example, that the static resource allocation problem is the central problem of Austrian economics is seriously to neglect their enormous attention to the problem of organization and control, perhaps because one does not like their normative, ideological orientation in such matters (I acknowledge that Austrians themselves often, indeed typically, stress static resource allocation, but they too thereby do not give complete effect to their work). Still, Stanfield has a valid point, widely applicable, when he distinguishes between technical acceptance of a point and making it a critical factor, as when he faults Boettke (and by implication me) for not realizing "that it is one thing to accept acculturation in the formation of individual preferences and quite another to make the matter a significant factor in the paradigm." This is absolutely correct. It is the problem of "primacy" again. I would add that factoring out the filtering or weighting role of ideology would make the distinction less significant—though one would still have to engage in weighting individual choice and social acculturation as a factor in one's research.

Apropos of the normative use of his relevant argument, I (1) wonder why a cultural relativist cannot critique existing institutions and power and (2) argue that not all institutionalists affirm a transcendent theory of value encompassing both instrumentalism as an orientation and methodology and a belief in transcendent values. Thus not all institutionalists affirm movement toward a planned society in the sense in which Stanfield uses the term.

Stanfield's most interesting argument is that heterogeneity within each school (and thereby the possibility of apparent similarities between the schools) is due to what he calls "paradigm indiscipline," to "the lack of consensus within the two communities of scholars." Thus he finds that "the similarities, where valid," are "in relatively peripheral areas that are not central to the core interests and *differentia specificae* of the two paradigms." I think that Stanfield is correct here, if one centers of the ideological dimensions of the two schools and on what each accordingly tends to emphasize. But if one factors out the ideological elements and proceeds along the lines of Rutherford's comment, the common substantive content is not insubstantial, however great the differences in nuance and emphasis may be. Finally, I also think that laden within Stanfield's conception of paradigm indiscipline is a dangerous premise of paradigm "discipline," with the implication that there is one and only one true version of institutional and of Austrian economics, respectively. The fact is that, as I have stressed, both schools are heterogeneous and the specific substance of what is "true" institutionalism and "true" Austrian economics is almost always the precise point at issue. Both schools of thought have been wracked by conflicts over what is authentic and inauthentic to them. In these and other respects, some economists can accept ambiguity and inconclusiveness, and others cannot.

III.   FURTHER AND CONCLUDING COMMENTS

1.   Austrian economists paradoxically typically formally define economics very narrowly but practice a much broader conception. Some institutional economists formally define their version of institutionalism very narrowly but both (a) disagree among themselves as to specific details and applications and (b) generally practice a much broader conception, whereas some define institutional economics very broadly but practice a narrower conception.

Additionally, Austrian economists paradoxically promote an ideological libertarianism but also produce research penetrating to some of the fundamentals of legal and nonlegal social control, which in some cases make their libertarianism much more subtle and sophisticated but in others render it quite naive and superficial. Austrian economists also have emphasized the doctrine of unintended consequences but they typically have failed both to appreciate its fundamental inconclusivity when applied to policy (some of Viktor Vanberg's work is a marked exception) and to apply it to their own arguments and policy proposals. Some or many institutionalists, for all their pragmatism and instrumentalism, seem doctrinally wedded to the idea of transcendental values and to certain institutional forms (either in the status quo or in their ideal society). Neither school has produced enough leading figures capable of articulating the realities of the actual processes by which such matters are actually worked out, including the complexities of freedom versus control, continuity versus change, and hierarchy versus equality with subtlety and sophistication, whether in positive or normative analysis.

The great irony of Austrian economics is that the school has strongly tended to narrowly define both its conception of the central problem of economics and its libertarianism while at the same time conducting positive and normative analyses far broader and more sophisticated than its typically narrow formal declarations would lead one to expect. When one makes adjustment for its distinctive ideological position and takes cognizance of its actually quite broad positive substantive content, Austrian economics does have much in common with institutional economics. For example, both have a place for legal and non-legal social control. Austrians tend to stress the latter and institutionalists the former, but both affirm the importance of both types of forces and institutions in society. Moreover, both address the problems of power, power structure, and abuse of power, although each does so within the confines of its own distinctive world view, or myopia.

2. One reader of Boettke's manuscript wrote the following: "On the one hand, he makes a very good point regarding the convergence of the two schools of thought *vis-à-vis* the role of evolution in a useful economic science. Also, I think he is quite correct in his view that Austrian economics has itself evolved since Veblen's day. What I think the paper lacks is a discussion of the important divergencies. Whereas Austrians perceive market processes as central to an understanding of the economy, institutionalists reject the notion that market forces achieve spontaneous order. The underlying technological-ceremonial interaction is what is central. The distinction between technology and ceremony, the linchpin of all theoretical institutionalists, is nonexistant in Austrian expositions. Boettke's paper does not face up to this and other distinctions. Another important question is that of ideology. Nothing could be clearer than the right wing-left wing conflict

between Austrians and institutionalists. By this I mean Austrians are largely laissez faire in their policy espousal while institutionalists are largely interventionist.'' I want to make the following comments.

First, an institutionalist can perceive market processes as central to an understanding of the economy. Where the institutionalist departs from the mainstream is in emphasizing that power structure-institutional structure forms and operates through the market to govern allocative and other performance. This is a fundamental distinction but it is, in my view, largely (not completely) one of emphasis. Factor out ideology and myopia, however, and an institutionalist can share with an Austrian (and other mainstream economists) a view that economic order is *pro tanto* formed by markets and by the institutions which form and operate through markets, insofar as there are in fact markets. Conversely, Austrians (most notably Wieser) can and do go behind markets to power structures.

Second, apropos of spontaneous order, there is a sense in which such an order is achieved, but it too is not unique; it is a function of the existing structure of power and institutions. These latter may themselves have evolved in a spontaneous manner but they also are affected, necessarily and inexorably, by deliberative decisionmaking weighted by power structure and institutional configuration governing whose preferences count not only in the market but in the evolution of institutions and power structure.

Third, the technology-ceremony distinction is a useful tool but not all institutionalists find it alone dispositive of positive and normative questions. And as I have developed elsewhere, the problem of power, that is, the necessity of choice, inexorably pertains to and compromises the heuristic value of the dichotomy (Samuels 1977).

Fourth, the right wing-left wing (laissez faire versus interventionism) conflict at the level of ideology and practical policy is fundamental at that level. But so far as fundamental positive analysis of legal social control and social change is concerned, once one factors out the ideology, there is much in common. Moreover, not all Austrians and not all institutionalists agree on the specifics of their respective putative laissez faire and interventionist policies. Moreover, as I have stressed above, both schools have a place for legal change and both are, or can be understood to be, activist with regard to government, however paradoxical that may be given their usual ideological formulations.

3.   One Austrian-school reader of my paper (who later agreed to but did not write a comment for this symposium) wrote me in 1982 that

it is not adequate to compare institutionalism understood as a broad political economic theory with Austrianism understood as an economic theory; to do so "will inevitably show the narrowness of the latter." He argued that "Austrian economics can be fit into a variety of broader schemes of political economy—from the classical liberalism of Mises and Hayek to the anarchism of Rothbard, and at this level is as broad in scope as Institutionalism." He went on to say that "Austrian economics, narrowly conceived[,] is strictly a theory of how market phenomena work, but it is but a subset of a wider theory of choice which Mises used to call sociology and later refers to as praxeology. Praxeology is itself the strictly *wert frei* analysis of how human action works, and would have to be combined with ethics, political and legal philosophy, psychology and history in order to cover the issues of political economy that concern Institutionalists. Indeed the writing of most Austrian economists does extend beyond narrowly economic issues into these related fields."

I basically agree. Although part of the difference between the two schools at the level of their greatest breadth resides in their respective ideologies, there is no question but that at this level both are political economy rather than narrow, technical economics. Indeed, speaking only of the Austrian school, it is largely (but not completely) their ideological reach which has driven them beyond subjectivist value theory. But, as stressed above, from the very beginning (Carl Menger and later Friedrich von Wieser, to name but two) the Austrians have practiced a much wider and richer economics than they typically technically preached.

This same Austrian writer wrote me that Austrians do not "only admit that preferences are a social product *in private*," citing "Hayek's famous answer to Galbraith on the Dependence Effect."[2] He also stressed that neither school has "said enough yet about processes of learning" but that Austrians "certainly do not neglect this *in principle*. Hayek, Lachmann and Kirzner have written extensively on this . . . ." Once again we have the problem of primacy or of weighting governed by ideology: here, what is stressed versus what is acknowledged in principle.

Similarly this correspondent argues that methodological individualism "is not contrary to the focus on an overall social order but is the name given to the *way* A[ustrians] choose to study the social order: by tracing its elements to individuals' choices," adding that methodological individualism "doesn't mean that you only study Crusoe on his island." That may be, but I, for one, find that the Austrians generally do not acknowledge the methodologically collectivist elements in their analysis but often do allow a selective normative individualism to enter analysis through their ostensible methodological individualism.

He also writes, with regard to my claim that "both schools want to deliberately reshape the economy; they just each offer different agendas for government," that he would "agree with at least some interpretations of the first part of this statement but would insist that at least many A[ustrians] (e.g. Rothbard) do not really offer an agenda for gov't at all but rather deny any legitimate role for gov't. It's true that the Austrians' 'laissez-faire' doesn't mean they are anti-activist, but it's not true that Austrians necessarily think their activism should find its expression in gov't policy. A[ustrians] doubt that gov't can achieve most of the ambitious goals politicians set for themselves but this doesn't imply that we are helpless to change the world we live in. On the contrary it suggests that very serious changes are in order." One of the three[3] main differences this writer sees remaining between the two schools is that Institutionalists "still believe there's a hope for beneficent, activist gov't policy as a cure for social problems; A[ustrians] doubt that gov't can do much of anything right."

My own view is that such a view is more a matter of Austrian ideology than Austrian positive political economy and thus understates the positive legal-economic (including legal-change) fundamentals of the economic system. In addition, the Austrians no less than the institutionalists seek to actively participate in social control, i.e., social engineering, especially but not exclusively through control of the economic role of government. Indeed, it seems to me that a fundamental premise of the central project of each school is that the economy *is* an engineered artifact, and that both furthermore believe that it is produced by both deliberative and nondeliberative decisionmaking, especially the latter. The ideological difference resides in the Austrian policy emphasis on the latter, while recognizing the former, and the institutionalist emphasis on the former, while recognizing the latter.

4.   Another early correspondent suggested that given the important differences between the two schools, one had three possible responses: "(1) I insist on structural simplicity and logical consistency. I am a purist. I want a monolithic body of thought that is elegant and rigorous. Given this view, I will pick either one or the other, but I will not accept both Commons's ideas and von Mises's. (2) I am an eclectic. I'll take both. (3) I am a Hegelian. Here we have a thesis (von Mises's position) and an antithesis (Commons's thought). They represent a contradiction. The contradiction drives my mind toward a higher syn-

thesis incorporating numerous elements of both positions, thereby overcoming the contradiction.'' This writer suggests that von Mises and his disciples would choose the first alternative, whereas Commons would affirm the eclectic position (but whether he was one in practice is, according to this writer, another question).

My own preference is for the eclectic when it comes to gaining insight into and knowledge about substantive topics (for example, institutional adjustment) and, to some extent, also when it comes to ideology. (Let me expand on that last clause very briefly: I concur with the libertarian-anarchist affection for individual freedom; I disagree with uses thereof which constitute defenses of established hierarchic structures (one always has to deal with structures, which govern *whose* freedom is realized); and I disagree with the libertarian-anarchist definition of reality which neglects or obfuscates the effective governance actually found in the political economy (thus when they argue that you can do away with government, to me this is largely semantics, inasmuch as there will be other power structures performing the same functions)). I also think that the dialectical position, as stated, can be absorbed within the eclectic, or vice versa.

This same correspondent, subsequently responding to my paper, suggests (1) that I should make more mention of subgroups, and (2) that "ideology is a big part of each group. On it pivots serious differences and hostilities. Each group . . . has tried to enlist the religious community in its cause.'' I agree with both points.

He also says that *"at its worst"* each school has a bad reputation among many economists: they cannot define themselves; they are sectarian, representing one-sided, narrow, partial viewpoints; they are ideologists; they are sometimes arrogant and intolerant. I agree but add (1) this is only each school admittedly at its worst and (2) mainstream neoclassical economics (presumably the basis for comparison) at *its* worst can be similarly labelled, as indeed can Marxism.

This writer also wonders about my ultimate objectives in writing the paper. ''You suggest several. One is to satisfy idle curiosity, another is to understand the history of economic thought. One that's packed with plutonium and that makes me sit up and take notice is 'to learn about the practice of high priest and social engineering . . .' Another that's crammed with dynamite is that you wish—I surmise this—the members of both schools to not revel in ideology and political action, but to learn from one another 'how the economy operates . . .' (and thereby help advance the scientific understanding of the economy and advance economics as an empirical social science?).'' I agree with all the stated objectives except that about exorcising ideology and political action: Let each economists do his own thing. I am particularly interested in learning about the political economy and the implications of economists' actual practices. As for the possibility of a value- or ideology-free economics (political economy), I have serious doubts whether it can be realized but believe that there is a significant difference in meaningfulness between *is* and *ought* statements.

Interestingly, both this writer and the writer whose letter I quote immediately above found that some statements of similarities "refer to what schools of thought in general do, and . . . don't say anything characteristic of just" Austrian and institutionalist schools. As expressed by the writer quoted above, there are some common features "which it seems to me *any* two living schools of thought must necessarily share, . . . about what one would expect from two minority schools trying to influence a dominant major school." The present writer focused on the presence of rival factors and efforts to maintain internal harmony (apropos of this, vide Stanfield's paper); the writer quoted above focused on the tendency of each school to define itself vis-à-vis neoclassical economics, that each has some outsider paranoia, and that each is preoccupied with methodological, philosophical and political-economic issues, relative to neoclassicists.

The present correspondent cautions that in trying to abstract from ideology I am trying to abstract from a pivotal issue that separates the two schools and thereby have them lose their meanings. My response: I hardly think that my doing so will produce that effect. I would, for certain limited purposes, treat ideology as others treat personal biography when working with or analyzing the theories of an economist: the theories stand on their own, *at least to a point*. Nothing contained in either my original paper or this response should be interpreted as arguing for the complete and permanent suspension (or suppression) of the ideological elements of the two schools when dealing with the schools *qua* schools. But once we focus on particular subject-matter, and not on the schools per se, we need not worry about their respective ideologies but can make adjustments for them, though certainly include ideology as a key variable in the political economy.

This writer also suggests that I might delete the two identifications of myself as an institutionalist. I think, on the contrary, that this is desirable (perhaps not necessary, in light of my past writings and affiliations), so that the reader knows the perspective from which I, for one, come. Of course, too, I am an eclectic institutionalist of the

Wisconsin tradition, who believes that institutional economics is supplementary, not mutually antagonistic, to other schools of economic thought.

5.   Finally I want to call attention to and affirm the findings of Mark Perlman's (1986) investigation of the relation of Austrian subjectivism and American institutionalism.[4] Perlman argues, first, that at least two of the early American institutionalists, Mitchell and Commons, both shared an interest in, applauded and were influenced by the Austrians' subjectivism. Indeed, they criticized Menger et al. "for not incorporating into their theoretical contributions the full measure of subjectivism available to them" (269).[5] In criticizing the Austrian propensity to take preferences and price-elasticities as given and to avoid consideration of the process of valuation (preference formation), says Perlman, "Mitchell, far from rejecting subjectivism, argued that the Austrians . . . did not go far enough. On this point, at least, Mitchell was far more royalist than the king" (273). Veblen similarly treated subjectivism not as a state of mind but as a (potential) description of a mind in action (274).

Perlman argues, second, that some of Hayek's recent work evidences developments along lines followed earlier by Commons, such that "Commons' variant of institutionalism is becoming significantly a pattern for Professor Hayek's work in such form as to be, in truth, an unacknowledged precursor" (269). He says, with particular reference to the development and role of institutions, that "in Professor Hayek's recent work his approach to the way that the mind operates as well as the way that the market operates is strangely consistent with Commons's thinking of a good many decades earlier" (275).[6]

In Perlman's view, "The meaning of the convergence of the two quite different schools of economic thought is not only that they are now trying to deal with the same problem . . ., but also that there was within the Austrian tradition an all but dormant conceptual element, which both Commons and Mitchell perceived as crucial to the 'actual' (meaning *nominalist*) operation of markets . . . 'ignorance,' or . . . *unknowledge*," as well as Commons's concern with "an understanding of how group values that permeated individual decision making . . . were defined and enforced, and what effect that definition had on transaction performance."[7] Hayek, says Perlman, "has come to the same set of concerns,"[8] and "the reason why there is a similarity of conclusion, due allowance being made for both semantic differences and for over 75 years having passed, is that the current question Hayek considers is the same as the one Commons pondered and because Commons' system always incorporated the Austrian contribution of subjectivism'' (276–8).

I take Perlman's article to reinforce my own finding, and that of Rutherford, that, putting their respective ideologies aside, except as is necessary to understand the role of ideology per se in the political economy, there are both important common elements and differences in Austrian and institutional economics.

NOTES

1. Identification of perceived totalitarian tendencies or implications in the thoughts of others may be a rhetorical device in argument, but it may also be a deeply sensed problem. There is certainly enough totalitarian absolutism in the world that one can find it logically if not substantively associated with, if not derivative from, most if not all schools of economic thought.

2. Perlman (1986, p. 269; see also p. 277) writes that Austrian individualism ''in its usual form . . . stresses a social theory favoring free choice and action of individuals. But, it does not, and this is the important point, claim that all values are individually derived, even if a case can be made for the view that individuals may wish to make their own choices from a spectrum of socially influenced values.''

3. The other two have to with the two schools' different positions concerning the employment versus abandonment of, first, macro aggregates and, second, coherent marginalist value theory.

4. Perlman notes both that ''differences between the institutionalists were greater than their similarities'' and that all institutionalists shared ''significant similarities, one of which was to distinguish their work from the orthodoxy of their day'' (1986, p. 270).

5. Appropriately, Perlman says that the shared interest in subjectivism ''should not be stretched to assume that the differences [between institutionalist economists] were less than the similarities'' (1986, p. 271). The point also applies to their relationship with their Austrian ''rivals.''

6. Interestingly, contrary to Gonce's comment, Gunning (1986) argues that von Mises's work on institutions is close to that of the institutionalists.

7. Particularly apposite is Perlman's (1986, p. 275) statement that ''Commons' individual was all but invariably part of a going community, where the community provided institutions which were one and at the same time constraints upon and mechanisms for the realization of certain of most individuals' presumably independent preference schedules.'' Of course, Commons understood that institutions themselves evolved, in large part through the only partly reenforcing behavior of individuals.

8. In my view, not only are the concerns the same but the substantive analyses, once one has made due allowance for ideological differences, are very close.

REFERENCES

Gunning, J. Patrick, (1986) ''The Methodology of Austrian Economics and Its Relevance to Institutionalism,'' *American Journal of Economics and Sociology*, January, *45*, 79–91.

Hayek, Friedich von, (1944) *The Road to Serfdom*. Chicago: University of Chicago Press.

———, (1967) *Studies in Philosophy, Politics and Economics*. Chicago: University of Chicago Press.

———, (1973) *Law, Legislation and Liberty: Rules and Order*. Chicago: University of Chicago Press.

———, (1978) *New Studies in Philosophy, Politics, Economics and the History of Ideas*. Chicago: University of Chicago Press.

Perlman, Mark, (1986) "Subjectivism and American Institutionalism," in Israel M. Kirzner, ed., *Subjectivism, Intelligibility, and Economic Understanding: Essays in Honor of Ludwig M. Lachmann on his Eightieth Birthday*. New York: New York University Press, Pp. 268–280.

Samuels, Warren J., (1972) "The Scope of Economics Historically Considered," *Land Economics*, August, 48, 248–268.

———, (1977) "Technology vis-à-vis Institutions in the JEI: A Suggested Interpretation," *Journal of Economic Issues*, December, *11*, 871–895.

REVIEW ESSAYS

BREMS'S *PIONEERING ECONOMIC THEORY, 1630–1980: A MATHEMATICAL RESTATEMENT*: REVIEW ESSAY

Larry Samuelson

I. INTRODUCTION

This is both an ambitious and unusual book. The first characteristic is not surprising, as no work attempting to examine three hundred and fifty years of recent economic thought could fail to be ambitious. It is unusual because the method chosen for this examination is to translate the important economic ideas which have appeared during the period of its purview into mathematical models. It is further unusual because the period in question ends in 1980, much later than most history of economic thought texts.

To fully appreciate the nature of this work, we begin by considering

Research in the History of Economic Thought and Methodology,
Volume 6, pages 229-237
Copyright © 1989 by JAI Press Inc.
All rights of reproduction in any form reserved.
ISBN: 0-89232-928-9

some basic issues in the history of economic thought. This allows us to place the book in the proper perspective and ascertain its significance.

II. *PIONEERING ECONOMIC THEORY* AND THE HISTORY OF ECONOMIC THOUGHT

Motivation

The first issue of interest concerns the question of why economists study the history of their discipline. Three possible motivations immediately suggest themselves, and we briefly consider each of them.

The first is that we study the history of economic thought out of sheer intellectual curiosity. The discipline of economics includes many elegant theories. One cannot help but be intrigued by the process of their formation and cannot help but admire the pioneers who first formulated these ideas. A foray into the history of economic thought allows one to indulge this curiosity by rubbing intellectual elbows (through their work) with impressive minds and eloquent expositors. While this motivation may be compelling for some, it is unlikely that it alone could account for the amount of energy devoted by economists to the history of their discipline, and we turn to two seemingly more practical motivations.

The second motivation arises out of the observation that studying the history of economics may reveal useful insights into the workings of the discipline of economics. Economists practice their profession according to an intricate and unspecified set of rules. For example, it is not obvious how some assertions or theories come to be widely accepted and others do not. More specifically, it is interesting to note that one of the most serious charges to currently be leveled against a theoretical construction is that it is ad hoc. However, it is virtually impossible to describe how the classification of ad hoc is determined. Why is it often considered ad hoc to specify an aggregate consumption function but not ad hoc to derive a consumption function from a specification of a single, representative consumer? These aspects of the discipline have recently attracted increasing attention, and have been variously characterized as the rhetoric of economics (McCloskey 1983) or the sociology of economics. The history of economics may provide revealing observations on such issues.

Third, we may study the history of economics in order to attain a better understanding of contemporary economics. The history of economics contains a wealth of ideas and theories which are both precursors and alternatives to contemporary thought. Some of these have been developed and then rejected in lieu of seemingly more promising constructions, and a comparison of the prevailing and discarded alternatives often provides insight into the former. Other ideas have simply been neglected, and provide a useful collection of alternatives to contemporary thought. Reconsidering these alternatives may lead to advances in contemporary thought.

Brems' volume will be found compelling by readers who are persuaded by the third motivation and will be less satisfying to those driven by the second motivation. The volume does not generally concern itself with describing how economic theories came to be formulated and accepted. It is also generally not concerned with examining the interactions among various economists of a certain period, nor does it generally describe the relationships between economic thought and the surrounding economic or intellectual environment. However, the volume does provide a clear and concise exposition of a large number of economic theories, taking care to isolate the important elements in each case. The result is an introduction to the central economic insights of the previous three and one-half centuries. A better understanding of current economic thought is one of the results of sampling this collection.

Method

After fixing a purpose for the study of the history of economic thought, one must identify a method. The two primary contenders in this respect are the relativist and the absolutist or positivist approach (Blaug 1978, Introduction). They are distinguished by the perspectives or bases of comparison they use in evaluating economic theories.

The absolutist approach proceeds by expositing an economic theory and then assessing its correctness or usefulness. This assessment invokes a standard which does not vary as the identity of the theory of interest changes (hence the description ''absolutist''), and is presumably given by the current state of economic knowledge. Questions tend to take the form of whether a theory is internally consistent, how the theory compares to contemporary theory, and perhaps how current practice is an improvement over the theory in question. One gets the impression from this approach of a discipline that is progressing by continually supplanting existing theories by better ones, and an impression that the history of economic thought is pursued as an aid to understanding why previous theories have been superseded.

The relativist approach is concerned not so much with evaluating historical theories according to contemporary standards, but with explaining how historical circumstances combined to produce the theories of the day. The important questions involve such issues as how the existing economic and intellectual environment shaped the thinking of economists. Theories that might be regarded as flawed by contemporary standards are often deemed appropriate for the period in which they were formulated. The key is to explore the relationship between the period and the theory.

One who pursues the history of economic thought as a means of giving insight into contemporary theory is most likely to prefer an absolutist approach, while a relativist approach will be most congenial to one seeking insights into the workings of the discipline of economics. It is accordingly no surprise that the present volume generally adopts an absolutist approach. While the author is careful to briefly describe the important economic and intellectual conditions which characterized each period, the volume is primarily concerned with exposing the various economic theories and then scrutinizing them with a rigor characteristic of modern economics. In the process, both triumphs and shortcomings are clearly identified.

Organization

A history of economics requires an organizational structure. The most common approach is to compile a list of prominent economists, and then to examine the contribution of each of these figures. If the study of the history of economic thought can be crudely characterized as an exercise in "who said that," this approach generally places considerable emphasis on the "who" aspect of this question. Particular attention is often paid to the subtleties by which various economists from a particular time period can be distinguished. A common characteristic of such treatment is that prominent economists receive much lengthier discussions than do lesser figures, with an economist's prominence often measured by the economist's influence during his/her lifetime.

A somewhat more sophisticated structure is occasionally achieved by formulating a collection of important ideas from the history of economic thought. The economists to be treated are arranged within this collection according to which ideas are exemplified in their work. This approach emphasizes the "what" portion of our question. Subtleties in the contributions of various figures are often deliberately not treated in order to more effectively isolate major points. The result is that one learns more about economics than about economists. This approach is often less likely to devote disproportionate space to a few very prominent economists, and tends to shift the standard of prominence to influence on contemporary rather than historical economic thought.

The present volume falls into this second tradition. The book opens with the statement that it is a "book about ideas rather than men" (page 9), and the basic ideas around which the book will be organized are presented. A refinement of this basic structure of ideas emerges as the book proceeds, as such concepts as the role of saddle-point theorems in economics become unifying themes within the sections defined by the basic scheme of ideas. The result is only a fleeting acquaintance with any particular economist, but an intimate acquaintance with each important economic idea.

Implications

We have now identified the purpose, method, and organizational structure for the study of history of economic thought that best characterize this volume. What implications can we draw? On the one hand, it might be said that the book has its limitations. It does not provide much in the way of the relativist approach and does not provide a detailed treatment of any one economist. However, limitation is too perjorative a term. Instead, it is more accurate to say that the book has carefully defined its purpose: to use the history of economic thought as an aid to understanding our current body of economic theory. The book does not stray from this purpose. Seen in this light, the limitations of the book are actually its strengths. The sheer scope of the subject matter necessarily imposes limitations on any history of economic thought, and some compromises in coverage must be made. This volume has the advantage of beginning with an explicit conception of what it will and will not attempt. As a result, it does not do everything, but it is able to accomplish what it attempts more effectively than would otherwise be the case.

III. MATHEMATICS AND THE HISTORY OF ECONOMIC THOUGHT

A perusal of the current economics journals reveals both that the use of mathematics has become standard and that the level of mathematical technique has increased. This has been accompanied by a steady

though often ignored stream of protest from those who suspect the
trend toward mathematicization of being a mixed blessing. The history
of economic thought has been one of the last fields to feel the en-
croachment of mathematics and is often viewed as a haven for those
with nonmathematical inclinations. This volume may then be somewhat of a surprise to some historians of economic thought, since its
method of inquiry is to restate each theory in the form of a mathematical model.

Brems' introduction recognizes that this is not the customary practice in the history of economic thought, and he briefly discusses the
question of whether it is advisable. His defense of mathematics rests
upon the conception of mathematics as a language. The use of mathematics is approached as one would approach the use of a language such
as French or German. Ideas can presumably be translated from one
such language into another with their content unaffected while being
rendered more accessible to some readers. Brems' translation actually
goes one step further than most, since his quotations and references to
original sources allow interested readers to check his accuracy.

If the use of mathematics is to be viewed as simply a choice of language, the question arises as to why the original language of each
economist does not suffice. Why is the translation necessary? The use
of mathematics has three possible advantages. First, it allows the economic theories treated in this book to be presented in a common language. This enhances the value of the volume as a reference work.
Readers interested in comparing the theories covered in the volume
will find much of the work involved in such a comparison has already
been accomplished by the translation into a common language. Second, the use of mathematics allows the theories to be presented concisely. This volume covers three and one-half centuries of recent economic thought in a mere 400 pages. This coverage is possible because
one equation can often do the work of several paragraphs of prose.
Finally, a mathematical statement allows the structure of a theory to be
more easily probed. Again, the equation is more efficient than the written word. At the same time, however, the terse and mathematical style
of writing places heavy demands on the reader. This is a book that one
works through rather than reads.

This recital of the advantages of mathematics is not new, and is not
without controversy. The resolution of the mathematics controversy is
likely to be reached not through debate, but through either the general
use or general avoidance of mathematics in the history of economic
thought as well as throughout economics. The present volume could
not have been written without the use of mathematics. It forcefully

illustrates the benefits of mathematics, and will encourage further mathematical studies in the history of economic thought.

IV. DISCUSSION

It is hoped that a coherent characterization of this volume has now emerged. Its scope is prodigious, not so much because of the period of time it covers but because of the number of economic theories presented.[1] The book accomplishes this coverage by deliberately accepting some limitations on the treatment of each theory, presenting relatively little interpretive or historical discussion (though such material is not completely absent), and employing relatively stylized versions of the various theories. Within these rules, the book presents a wealth of information.

Several further comments are in order. In reading this book, one is struck by the author's careful habits of scholarship. Such practices as clearly defining notation, drawing explicit distinctions between variables and parameters, and the explicit identification of assumptions might well be emulated by economists in all fields. The volume is similarly well organized. The brief discussions of the individual economists are tied together by general themes. At the same time, each chapter is self-contained, allowing readers with special interests to easily locate and usefully read pertinent passages in the book.

The primary shortcoming of this volume is the brevity with which some topics and economists are covered. If 57 or more economists are to be examined in only 400 pages, then none can be allocated a very thorough treatment. This is exacerbated by the fact that the final 180 pages of the book are devoted to the period from 1930–1980. The inclusion of this period enhances the ability of this treatment of the history of economic thought to serve as an aid in understanding contemporary economics. At the same time, however, it drastically condenses the treatment of the pre-Keynes era which is the province of most history-of-economic-thought works.

As a result, we find Ricardo treated in only 16 pages and Keynes in nine. The primary treatment of Marshall occupies only two pages. Some examinations are thus so stylized as to be of little help, in spite of the efficiency of presentation allowed by the use of mathematics, and the reader is often left desiring a more complete treatment. In effect, it would have been nice to have a longer book. The potential compensation offered by the book for its brevity is that the volume is well documented, so that the interested reader can pursue further sources.

There is also ample opportunity to quibble with the relative emphasis placed on the various economists. The above-mentioned treatment of Marshall is likely to draw some protests, as are the treatments of Adam Smith and John Stuart Mill. Among more recent economists, one wonders at the brief treatment accorded to Arrow. Schumpeter is mentioned often but is never really discussed. It is undoubtedly impossible to satisfy everyone in this regard, but the choices made in this volume are likely to be especially controversial.

The question arises as to whether certain economists have received an unexpectedly fleeting treatment or have been omitted because their work resists translation into mathematics. It is undoubtedly difficult to capture Smith, Thomas Malthus, or Schumpeter in a simple mathematical model, and they are only briefly treated. The institutional, historical, and socialist schools of economic thought similarly thwart mathematical exposition, and are not treated at all. At the same time, such obviously mathematical economists as Marshall and Arrow are also given little attention, suggesting that amenability to a mathematical treatment alone has not dictated the choice of coverage. It does appear, however, as if the same features which allow a theory to be easily mathematicized, such as its internal consistency, also recommend the theory to the author as important. This is an interesting relationship that warrents further discussion and study.

The preceeding question can be reversed to ask what new insights in the history of economic thought have appeared in this volume because of its mathematical method. The volume's statement that it contains mathematical restatements of economic theories indicates that in most cases we can expect not new results but better statements of existing results. However, some new insights do appear. Perhaps the most notable is the treatment of Cantillon and the land theory of value. Coupled with subsequent discussions of the labor theory of value, the reader is led to an appreciation of both as special cases of single-input theories of value. This provides a useful new perspective on classical economics. In addition, the volume provides an original and much-needed model of Wicksell's dynamic analysis. The exposition also makes it especially easy to compare theories, and previously obscure similarities and contrasts are exposed, such as those between Böhm-Bawerk and Wicksell.

V.   CONCLUSION

On the one hand, this book cannot stand alone as a source in the history of economic thought. There is too much material missing, from interpretation and historical material to additional detail concerning the covered economists. This is no surprise. It is an impossible demand that a single volume should contain a definitive treatment of all aspects of the history of economics. On the other hand, this book successfully addresses a critical gap in the history of thought literature. It will become a standard reference work and guide to the study of the history of economic thought. While no student of the history of economics will be content to rely solely upon the book, none will want to be without it.

It has often been said that if one is to embark on a study of the history of economics, then one would do well to start with a copy of Schumpeter's *History of Economic Analysis* and with the original writings of the prominent economists. This maxim may well have to be revised. A good point of departure is now a copy of Schumpeter, the original sources, and a copy of Brems.

ACKNOWLEDGMENT

The helpful comments and suggestions of Warren Samuels are gratefully acknowledged.

NOTE

1.   An exact determination of the number depends upon some necessarily arbitrary choices as to how theories which receive relatively less attention are to be counted. The book jacket indicates that 57 economists are considered while Brems' introduction identifies 84 pioneers.

REFERENCES

Blaug, Mark, (1978) *Economic Theory in Retrospect* Cambridge: Cambridge University Press.

Brems, Hans, (1986) *Pioneering Economic Theory, 1630–1980: A Mathematical Restatement* (Baltimore: The Johns Hopkins University Press).

McCloskey, Donald N., (1983) "The Rhetoric of Economics," *Journal of Economic Literature* 21, 481–517.

Schumpeter, J. A., (1954) *History of Economic Analysis* (New York: Oxford University Press).

BACKHOUSE'S *A HISTORY OF MODERN ECONOMIC ANALYSIS* AND DASGUPTA'S *EPOCHS IN ECONOMIC THEORY*:

REVIEW ESSAY

Salim Rashid

The two volumes being reviewed here have quite different philosophies and focus upon different periods. While Dasgupta wishes to argue that each era has an economic theory appropriate to itself, a theme that serves to establish the value of classical economics, Backhouse is concerned with tracing the lineage of modern economic analysis, a project that implicitly assumes the value of current economics. Rather than try to set off the two authors against each other, I will deal with each in turn.

Dasgupta states his primary thesis on the relativity of economic truths very clearly in the first few pages.

Research in the History of Economic Thought and Methodology,
Volume 6, pages 239-245
Copyright © 1989 by JAI Press Inc.
All rights of reproduction in any form reserved.
ISBN: 0-89232-928-9

It is of the nature of economic science that it involves events and phenomena which not only change complextion from time to time but do not also occur at all places. Problems that emerge as crucial at one time may turn out to be totally irrelevant at another time in the same economy, and those that are relevant in the context of one economy may well be irrelevant elsewhere. In economics old theories do not die. And they do not die not because one is built on the other but because one is independent of the other (p. 2).

A system of economic theory evolves in response to questions that are provoked by a given set of circumstances in an economy. As circumstances change, or people's attitude to them changes, questions are revised, and a new system springs up. It is wrong to say that the new system is an improvement on an older one; it is different (p. 4).

He believes that the acceptance of such a methodology is not only more accurate but also serves to avoid much needless controversy.

This is not a book on the history of economic theory. Its aim is much more modest; I wish only to suggest a perspective for viewing the development of economic theory. This, I claim, is very important. Much of the controversy which has afflicted the economist's profession over the years could be avoided if it were realized that the different systems of economic theory which the epochs represent were designed to answer different sorts of questions that appeared significant at different points of time (p. 7).

The primary problems that the classical economists tackled involved accumulation, growth and distribution. The treatment of the classicals—Adam Smith, David Ricardo and Karl Marx—takes up the longest part of the book. Dasgupta writes well and the exposition is very lucid. It is a pleasure to read a book so carefully and pleasantly written. The classicals are followed by the marginalist challenge—when emphasis was laid upon the efficient allocation of given resources instead of growth and distribution. Marshall's attempt to synthesize classical concerns with marginalist tools follows and Keynes' questioning of automatic full-employment is the last historical chapter. A short "Overview" concludes the volume. It is clear that Dasgupta has most sympathy for the classicals but this does not mean that the presentation is in any way unfair. The following summary by Dasgupta of the difference between classical and marginalist approaches should be acceptable to all sides.

In classical political economy the central problem is one of production; labour is here supposed to act on material resources, including land, in order to produce commodities. The basic attribute which gives value to commodities is thus supposed to be labour; commodities possess value because they need, for their production, the application of human labour to resources which are given to society by nature; economic activity is supposed to be a struggle of man against nature. The corollary of this approach, let us remind ourselves, is the recognition of surplus as a category over and above the maintenance cost of labour, and of conflict concerning the disposition of this surplus. Marginalist economics shifts the approach, as we have seen, from production to consumption. The central problem in this approach concerns the wants of consumers. Demand is here supposed to be the primary force from which all economic activity proceeds (p. 84).

There are only two points at which I found the exposition questionable. On page 49, where the contradiction in Adam Smith's value theory is presented without indication of how the analysis can be extended to include rents; and on page 85, where the hypothetical nature of profit maximization is obliquely criticized as a "deduction" from the equality of prices and marginal utilities, reversing the usual order of argument.

My difficulties with the Dasgupta exposition are most acute in the first ten and last five pages of the book. I agree so strongly with much of his thesis and it is worth pointing out our difference with some care. That economic analysis does not have a pyramid-like structure and that therefore old theories should not be allowed to fade away because they embody permanent truths is an important and valid claim.

If the view of the development of economic theory suggested here is correct, then it follows that a student of economics, unlike his counterpart in the natural sciences, can ill afford to ignore old theories just because they are old. Since, as we have found, systems of economic theory have grown historically in response to specific situations, each system has its relevance in appropriate contexts; an older theory may indeed turn out to be a more appropriate one in the context of an economy where conditions now are similar to those that had once evoked it (pp. 142–143).

Dasgupta goes on to conclude that each economic theory has validity at a certain historical era. Unfortunately, this is an ambiguous proposition because, at any given time, there are many "economic theories" and many interpretations of what is "really happening" at a given era. For example, Dasgupta claims that Malthus' ideas on general gluts were not accepted in the 1820s because the times were not right but that similar Keynesian ideas were accepted in the 1930s because the time was right. This involves the controversial claim that Keynes and Malthus not only dealt with the same problem but also provided essentially the same solution; furthermore, that Malthus' ideas were not quite relevant in 1820 but that their Keynesian variant was relevant in 1930—the only proof given for this crucial claim is a critical statement of Ricardo! What is entirely missing in Dasgupta's otherwise fine account is due recognition of the fact that ideas rise not only because they are right, but also, perhaps more importantly, because they are pushed. The sociology of economic knowledge is a necessary complement to Dasgupta's account.

The volume by Backhouse is quite frankly one on the history of economic *analysis* (p. 1). He has assimilated a truly vast amount of literature and provided a lucid and readable exposition. Backhouse's aim is to seek out the origins of modern analytical economics. This determines both the selection of economists and the emphasis given to particular topics; in particular, "because the aim of this book is to illuminate contemporary economics as much weight is given to the period after 1939 as to the one before."

The book begins with a section entitled "Background: Political Economy Before 1870" with Adam Smith as the first economist to be discussed. After devoting some 60 pages to the period between 1776 and 1870 and another 60 pages to the 20 years between 1870–1890, Backhouse treats the neoclassical period, 1890–1939, in some 140 pages and the modern period, from 1939–1980, takes up almost as much space as the neoclassical period. In addition to discussing economic thought, Backhouse also provides chapters on British economic policy for both the neoclassical and the modern periods. There is no indication of the intended audience nor is a readers guide provided.

The striking feature of the part that Backhouse intends to provide only as introduction and background, i.e., 1776–1890, is its soundness. The treatment may seem unspectacular but it is quite reliable and this portion can be readily used as a supplement for standard courses in the history of economic thought. A few examples will be indicative:

> Smith provided the vision of the economic system which permeated the whole of classical economics . . . However . . . it would be wrong to see him . . . as the founder of economics (p. 13).

On the relationship between Smith and Ricardo:

> The effect of taking certain features out of Smith's system and constructing from them a model emphasizing only those relationships which were amenable to treatment in terms of simple functional relationships was to transform Smith's theory into something very different (p. 32).

On the implications of Alfred Marshall's desire to be realistic:

> The main price to be paid for this stress on realism, and for the desire to keep theory and fact so close together, was ambiguity. Because Marshall's aim was not to construct a logically precise, abstract model, he would not always commit himself to precise assumptions . . . in his partial equilibrium analysis the *ceteris paribus* clauses were not always adequately specified (pp. 102–103).

While there are occasional misleading statements, these are not very serious. The claim that Samuel Bailey's *Critical Dissertation* "shattered" hopes of consensus among economists gives Bailey unjustified importance; in dealing with Marx's views on surplus value, the links with the Physiocrats and Adam Smith should have been mentioned; while the treatment of neoclassical demand theory does not recognize that the demand theory of the classicals was based on a hierarchy of wants and a potentially infinite commodity space.

In view of the highly technical nature of modern economic theory, it is impossible to deal usefully with more than one aspect of the modern period. The presentation of both Microeconomic Theory (ch. 24) and Welfare Economics (ch. 25) is sound, in that there are no obvious mistakes, but this is hardly the same as saying that the material can be usefully read. There is a great difference between an exposition which correctly states every facet of a technical theory and one which also enables one to *absorb* the leading facets of such a theory. Backhouse's exposition can be credited only with the former virtue. If one does not understand the essentials of say, temporary equilibrium and sequence economics, then the page and a half Backhouse devotes to this topic will scarcely be of help. To be fair, Backhouse explicitly recognizes the difficulty, but this only leads one to question the value of Backhouse's entire approach. The non-theorist will have a hard time understanding what is said, while the theorist will have only a vague idea of the actual issues involved. (I provide some examples below.) Modern economics has become so mathematical in nature that an exposition which does not pinpoint the mathematical difficulties involved has limited value. An exposition can be perfectly sound, and yet fail to indicate the technical problems. Consider, for example the two places where Backhouse deals with Edgeworth and bargaining.

> *Edgeworth's analysis of competition in terms of bargaining.* Starting with a bargain between two individuals he derived the contract curve, showing that the competitive equilibrium was one point on this curve. By gradually increasing

the number of individuals involved in the bargain Edgeworth was able to show
that as the size of the economy increased so the contract curve shrank towards
the competitive equilibrium. Competitive equilibrium could thus be interpreted
as the only feasible outcome in a bargain between an infinitely large number of
individuals (p. 137).

The core, the set of allocations not blocked by any possible coalition, was applied to market equilibrium by Shubik (1959) and proved useful in understanding the nature of competitive equilibrium, for it could be shown rigorously that,
as Edgeworth had argued some 80 years earlier, the core (Edgeworth's contract
curve) contained any competitive equilibria; and that as the number of traders
increased the core shrank until in the limit only competitive equilibria remained.
Competitive equilibria were thus the only feasible equilibria in an economy
where all traders were too small to have any bargaining power (pp. 286–287).

The reader unacquainted with the technical details can be pardoned
for believing that we really do possess fairly general results for the
equivalence between competitive equilibria and cores. However, the
following caveats are in order. First, proofs of Edgeworth's conjecture
proceed by replicating, i.e., the two-person economy of A and B becomes a four-person economy by sprouting twins for A and B so that
the four-person economy consists of (A,A,B,B). We get an eight-
agent economy by having every person in the four-agent economy
sprout a twin again . . . and so on. This is an extremely restrictive way
of increasing the size of an economy. Secondly, Shubik's (1959) proof
used transferable utility, an assumption rarely found acceptable, and it
is actually Debreu and Scarf (1967) who provided the first acceptable
proof of Edgeworth's conjecture (again using replication). Thirdly,
since the identity between cores and competitive equilibria holds only
"at infinity" it should be pointed out that we have difficulty defining
"demand equals supply" for such infinite economies.

Fourthly, given that we need to go to infinite agent economies in
order to obtain the core-equivalence result, it is interesting to note that
we can dispense with all convexity assumptions on preferences in such
economies (Aumann 1964). Finally, the core-equivalence result holds
only when the commodity space is "smaller" (in a sense that can be
made precise) than the space of agents. For example, the result need
not be true with the introduction of public goods.

Not having studied with any care the various other theoretical fields
that Backhouse has exposited, I am unable to say how far they can
guide readers interested in technical results. Off-hand, I would guess
that the entire second half of the book can be read with profit only if
one is ready to follow-up in specialist sources any issue that appears

interesting. Like another history that professes to be analytical (Mark Blaug's *Economic Theory in Retrospect*) this volume becomes most interesting when the author departs from his professed primary aim. The chapters on "Alternative Approaches" (18 and 28) make very good reading. The sections on methodology are also quite good. It would have been very useful if Backhouse had pointed out how mathematization has necessitated the reintroduction of subjectivism at the highest levels. It takes little imagination to prove new results in a mathematical subject—one moves from differentiability to continuity to measurability, or from functions to correspondences, or from two or three to n dimensions and so on. Given the enormous mass of mathematical economics theorems (all perfectly true!) that threaten to strangle us, "theorists" spend a great deal of effort defining publicly, i.e., through seminars, hirings, NFS grants, etc., what are "interesting" problems. A careful study of the waves of fashion overtaking our major theory journals makes for amusement and cynicism. As a practical matter, the philosophy of scientific method has nothing to tell us about the evolution of economic analysis. Backhouse displays a welcome skepticism about the effects of mathematics at several points, e.g., p. 310. It would be nice if he had gathered together and focussed his skepticism into a consistent critique.

REFERENCES

Aumann, R. J., (1964) "Markets with a continuum of traders," *Econometrica*, *32*, 39–50.

Blaug, M., (1985) *Economic Theory in Retrospect*, Cambridge: Cambridge University Press.

Debreu, G., and H. Scarf, (1963) "A Limit Theorem on the Core of an Economy," *International Economic Review*, *4*, 235–46.

Shubik, M., (1959) "Edgeworth Market Games," in R. D. Luce and A. W. Tucker, eds., *Contributions to the Theory of Games*, Princeton University Press, 267–78.

JONES'S *CONFLICT AND CONTROL IN THE WORLD ECONOMY: CONTEMPORARY ECONOMIC REALISM AND NEO-MERCANTILISM:*

REVIEW ESSAY

James P. Henderson

In many respects this book is promising, but in many others disappointing. At issue is the nature and condition of the world economy in light of the "great illusion of indefinite economic well-being and stability fostered during the later 1950s and 1960s," which was shattered by the economic shocks of the 1970s and 1980s (3). Jones adds to the growing chorus of authors disillusioned with the analysis of these events by mainstream economists. Central to this study is the question

Research in the History of Economic Thought and Methodology,
Volume 6, pages 247-251
Copyright © 1989 by JAI Press Inc.
All rights of reproduction in any form reserved.
ISBN: 0-89232-928-9

of "whether the developments of the 1970s were an aberration within an essentially healthy system, or . . . symptoms of an inherently flawed world economic system" (6). What the author proposes to do is both important and timely. Jones specifies two purposes of this study: ". . . to contribute to the general and necessary debate between contrasting views of the global political economy and the most effective forms of economic activities to be adopted by societies" and "to identify the many policies and practices that may actually benefit societies" (17).

The first purpose is handled by an interesting analysis of the shortcomings of "neoclassical or liberal" economics. In Jones' view, the central difficulty with this school is its "problematical fusion of positive analysis with normatively based prescription" (24). Jones holds that the liberal argument is comprised of three basic elements: first, it identifies fundamental aspects of human economic behavior which supposedly operate in all places and at all times; next, it analyzes the implications of these universals under a variety of circumstances; and finally, it invariably comes to the conclusion that an unfettered free market should prevail. What follows is a lengthy critique of the shortcomings and difficulties in the neoclassical, liberal economists' treatment of: rationality, perfect information, perfect competition, barriers to entry, factor mobility, monopoly and oligopoly, the distribution of wealth and income, the methodology of comparative statics, comparative advantage and factor endowments, negative externalities, paradoxes of rationality and collective goods, and finally "zeri-sum" (sic) features and positional goods. Much of this is interesting, though little is original. Yet it was here that I found the work most promising and I looked forward to the author's proposals to rectify these shortcomings and difficulties. I was largely disappointed with the results.

According to Jones, Economic Realism is a much broader, institutionalist approach, willing to draw on both liberal and Marxist analysis. Specifically, "the Realist approach is a broadranging and eclectic perspective developed from a number of basic propositions about human existence, the role of control and influence in human affairs, the nature and significance of communities and their cultures and, hence, the essential character of all relationships between societies, whether 'political' or 'economic' " (65). Jones claims that the roots of Economic Realism are to be found in the writings of Friedrich List (66). A major concern is to bring a turbulent and uncertain world under control by means of such tools as: personal influence, brute force, long standing patterns of association, the proven competence of authorities, well-developed authority roles, and/or mechanisms of social pressure. While the author pays lip service to the valuable lessons of history, he is treading in potentially dangerous territory here. It is one thing, for Friedrich List to offer a variety of schemes to unite the fragmented German states in the nineteenth century; and quite another, to demand "control over a turbulant and uncertain world" in the nuclear age.

Jones notes that the liberal, neo-classical view is based on the assumption of the "atomized individual" who voluntarily enters into relationships of pure exchange with other atomized individuals and firms. Thus "in the world of the liberal model there are no communities, classes, trades unions, oligopolies, monopolies or multinational corporations, or none that can be identified as analytically distinct, or theoretically tolerable, phenomena" (70). In contrast, Economic Realism identifies, "collectivist, non-competitive, and even anti-competitive phenomena as common, natural and, indeed a fundamental feature of all human existence, including economic activity" (ibid.). Unfortunately, Jones then leaps to the conclusion that control "activity has, therefore, to be directed at the level of a whole society" (ibid.). Later he suggests that, "the first principle of Economic Realism is that the world is characterized by inherent uncertainty and turbulence and that this prompts positive action to establish control and, hence, to ensure a necessary minimum of security for its inhabitants" (81). Once again we find the author treading in potentially dangerous territory. This can be interpreted, or misinterpreted, as a prescription for dictatorship or as a call or return to the absolute monarchies of mercantilist days. History teaches us that democracies are "characterized by inherent uncertainty and turbulence" to a much greater extent than either dictatorships or absolute monarchies. While liberal, neo-classical economics can be criticized on many grounds, inattention to issues of freedom and democracy is neither a shortcoming nor a difficulty of that school. The problem here is the author's failure to come to grips with the issues of what limits must be placed on such control activities, and by what principles these controls are to be defined, determined, and implemented. Instead, he merely suggests that there is an important role to be played in the shaping of economic activity by the institutional framework (specifically: culture, politics, government, and the state) as well as historical factors and processes. He tells us that "the view of international cooperation and control taken by the Economic Realist, or the neomercantilist, is one of expectation in general, coupled with pragmatism in detail'' (95). As a guide to policy, this is wholly inadequate.

The author illustrates the conflicts that can arise in economic activities using a number of neoclassical analytical tools: (a) game theory (specifically, the Prisoner's Dilemma), (b) an Edgeworth box diagram, raising some interesting issues concerning the fairness of the distribution of the benefits of trade, and (c) reaction curve analysis, to examine some questions concerning the dynamics of hostility between two independent actors. The analysis is rather superficial, a weakness which flaws much of the book. What follows, in part IV, are several chapters outlining the policies and practices recommended by the Economic Realists, or neomercantilists.

This brings us to the second purpose of Jones' book "to identify the many policies and practices that may actually benefit societies'' (17). The primary neomercantilist policies and practices in the international sphere reviewed by Jones include: Tariffs, Non-Tariff Barriers, Quotas, Bilateral Agreements, and Export Promotion. Several secondary neomercantilist policies and practices in the international sphere are also considered including: "Control" (ranging from imperialism to spheres of influence); Economic Aid; Educational and Cultural Neo-Mercantilism; and the Military-Industrial Complex and International Activity.

Another set of secondary neomercantilist policies and practices, these to be implemented at the domestic level, are also considered. These include: "Economic Policy" (namely, a stable financial system, a stable currency, a sound and supportive legal system, and macroeconomic management); Fiscal Policy; Monetary Policy; Exchange Rate Policy; Industrial and Development Policy (including: planning; the role of nationalized industries and public investment; regulation and control of industry; prices and incomes policy; selective intervention and sectoral support; industrial rationalization; regional industrial and development policy; energy policy; policy towards the financial system; small business support; science, technology, education and training; and finally, "the acquisition of retention of technology" [sic]); Discipline, Restraint, and the 'Work Ethic'; and Health Policy.

It should be noticed that the second purpose of Jones' book is merely intended "to identify the many policies and practices that may actually benefit societies." Throughout these chapters the author relies much too heavily on press clippings as his primary sources of information. This adds to the general impression that the work is superficial. There are no guidelines, nor principles, nor rules for launching or carrying out these "policies and practices" beyond "expectation in general, coupled with pragmatism in detail." This is not an oversight on Jones' part, because, we are told that Economic Realism "lacks, as it must, the deductive and determinate character of neoclassical or, indeed, much of liberal economic thought" (80).

Finally, the book is filled with editorial errors, two of which I have already indicated. Misspellings abound. There are hyphenation rules, but "smoo-thest" (189), "sour-cing" (95), and "divor-ced" (223), fall outside those rules. Obviously, the "wor-st-case" (217), is indeed the worst case!

A classic blunder appears in a table showing "The value of Japan's exports to and imports from selected Advanced Industrial Countries—1983" (Table 6.2, 161). The data is given in "$US billions." We find, for example, that Japanese exports to the United States in that year amounted to "42,829," while imports from the United States equaled "24,647." In the United States where a "billion" is defined as 10^9, Jones is saying that America bought more than $42 trillion from and sold more than $24 trillion to Japan, in a year when GNP was slightly less than $1.7 trillion. But since the author is British, where a "billion" is defined differently ($= 10^{12}$), perhaps he means, in American terms, that the United States bought $42 quadrillion from and sold $24 quadrillion to Japan that year! In a work concerned with "control" in the world economy, one would hope for better editorial control. These kinds of editorial horrors made an otherwise dull and superficial book somewhat interesting to this reviewer, but that is hardly grounds for recommending it to others.

RHOADS'S *THE ECONOMIST'S VIEW OF THE WORLD* AND WHYNES'S *WHAT IS POLITICAL ECONOMY*:

REVIEW ESSAY

William M. Dugger

Whynes defines economics broadly as political economy; while Rhoads defines economics narrowly as neoclassical orthodoxy. One of the authors is a political scientist, the other an economist. Surprisingly, the political scientist uses the narrow definition; the economist the broad.

The Rhoads book is mistitled. It is not about the economist's view of the world. Rather, it is about the view held by U.S. neoclassical microeconomists during a time of retrenchment and reaction. So the book is limited to a parochial view which does not reflect the richness

Research in the History of Economic Thought and Methodology,
Volume 6, pages 253-260
Copyright © 1989 by JAI Press Inc.
All rights of reproduction in any form reserved.
ISBN: 0-89232-928-9

of economics as a more globally-dispersed, multiple-paradigmed discipline. Rhoads wrote the book for the general reader interested in public policy and untrained in economics. But the book will give such a readership the false impression that economics is largely about proselytizing for the free market and about using cost-benefit analysis to justify cutting back public services.

As political scientist, Rhoads does bring some freshness to his task, but his limited reading in the economics literature make his book smack heavily of diletantism. Rhoads does not understand the broad discipline of economics nor does he understand the political context within which economists work. He incorrectly believes that a consensus exists in microeconomics on questions of fact and of theory. Of course, nothing of the sort is the case. Numerous examples of empirical and theoretical controversies immediately come to mind: Are manufacturing prices administered? If so, why? How? Are factor prices determined by marginal productivity? Are most regulatory agencies captured? If so, so what? Has market concentration increased? Do oligopolies face kinked demand curves? Do agricultural prices follow the cobweb theorem? How do political and economic power affect prices? What role is played by economic coercion and by the changing configuration of property rights? Had Rhoads done his homework by reading the literature more thoroughly, he would have found that alternative theories of the firm, of prices, of costs, and of consumer behavior all abound in microeconomics.

Rhoads incorrectly argues that the (nonexistent) consensus in microeconomics is the source of the microeconomist's high repute with contemporary public policy makers. The high repute of the reactionary microeconomists that Rhoads incorrectly uses to represent the whole discipline is due to the dominance of reactionary politicians, not to an alleged consensus of economists. Reactionary public policy makers lend their ears to reactionary economists because such economists tell them what they want to hear. Rhoads mistakes political power for scientific consensus.

Rhoads argues that economists contribute three major concepts to the making of public policy: opportunity costs, marginalism, and economic incentive.

His application of the opportunity cost principle to public policy is thoroughly ideological. Rhoads scapegoats allegedly ignorant, empire-building government bureaucrats for wasting public resources in disregard of the opportunity costs of doing so. These wasteful, free-spending government bureaucrats are, according to Rhoads, ignorant of the opportunity cost principle. Furthermore, according to Rhoads, their empire-building and maximization of public spending are very serious problems. However, wielded with vigor, the opportunity cost principle can help subdue the budgetary excesses of government bureaucrats, according to Rhoads. Of course, he does not mention the multiplier principle, for Rhoads apparently is not aware that government deficits can reduce waste when the economy suffers from unemployment, as his has suffered since World War II.

His application of the marginalist principle to public policy is no better than his application of the opportunity cost principle. Rhoads relies narrowly on the works of Richard McKenzie and Gordon Tullock to beat back empire-building government bureaucrats with marginal costs and marginal benefits. He also relies heavily on public choice theory and cost-benefit analysis in his discussion of government failure and inefficiency. Not surprisingly, he accepts the public choice position that the market is usually much better than the state. With the exception of John Kenneth Galbraith, who Rhoads mentions in order to then dismiss, he totally ignores the works of contemporary institutionalists, Marxists, and other political economists.

Rhoads improves a bit when he discusses the use of economic incentives in public policy. He largely avoids scapegoating public officials and contrasts the license and tax approach with the command and control approach to regulating air and water pollution. The former harnesses economic incentives while the latter does not. He argues that by harnessing the economic incentives of polluters to not pollute, they are encouraged to improve the technology of pollution control. He also explains how the license and tax approach could be used to minimize the total cost of attaining a certain level of pollution abatement. He does not point out, however, that even the license and tax approach would require substantial government regulation in the form of inspection of emission sites and verification of emission quantities.

But after improving his coverage a bit, Rhoads slips back into his parochial view when he discusses public policy toward poverty. He accepts the narrowly neoclassical trickle-down story as a scientific theory of economic growth, rather than as an ideological rationalization of poverty and inequality. In his naive view, poverty is best removed through growth. In the trickle-down story, that means to help the poor, you give the rich more money. War is peace. Black is white. Twiddle, twaddle, tweedle. In his treatment of poverty, Rhoads finds it unnecessary to discuss sexism, racism, or exploitation. Nor does he discuss the growth-reducing and poverty-creating effects of malnutrition, inadequate training, or poor health. Instead, he condemns rent controls and minimum wages for the usual unrealistic reasons. His treatment of voucher programs, aid in kind, and cash subsidies for the poor is somewhat more even-handed. Rhoads even shows some independence of mind when he criticizes economists, as a sociological group, for being more selfish and less concerned with fairness than most people.

Part III of his book, entitled "The Limits of Economics," contains a thoughtful, though ultimately contradictory, critique of the new right limitations of contemporary American neoclassical microeconomics. Rhoads takes a profoundly conservative position in his critique. He focuses his attack on the consumer sovereignty doctrine. But his attack draws heavily on Galbraithian arguments, even though Rhoads dismisses Galbraith himself. Should individual consumer preferences really be sovereign if some consumer preferences reflect habitual, compulsive, or addictive appetites? Rhoads thinks not and criticizes economists for avoiding potentially fruitful discussions of value judgments. But Rhoads is guilty of just such evasion himself. In particular, though he uses the arguments of Veblen and Marx, he avoids confronting institutionalism and Marxism by not acknowledging either.

Rhoads has a split personality. As a conservative, he calls for reinvigorating traditional ethics, good will, and civility. He supports patriotism, respect for law, and religion. But he also wants to help neoclassical economists of the new right support private property and capitalism. However, since his conservative's fear of individualism is not shared by new right neoclassicists, he cannot trust them completely. Rhoads attempts a conservative criticism of the new right, populist tendencies in neoclassical economics, but he is largely unsuccessful. After relying so heavily on the new right's neoclassical defense of the status-quo-supporting market and on the new right's neoclassical attack on progressive government, he finds it impossible to mount an effective defense of any activist government—even a defense of a conservative government.

He is not sophisticated enough to use the new social contract approach of public choice theory to reconstruct a defense of the strong, conservative state. Without resort to the subtleties and subterfuges of public choice theory's new contractarianism, Rhoads, the naive conservative, gets stuck. He is unable to reject neoclassical microeconomics because he would lose most of his arguments against a progressive government of the common man. But he is unable to accept neoclassical microeconomics either because he would have to accept an individualism which implies that the common man could govern himself after all. Rhoads struggles honestly, though ineffectively, against this dilemma faced by conservatives who try to reconcile their conservatism with new right economics. The honesty he brings to the struggle is the major strength of his book. Inadequate study is the major weakness.

David Whynes's book cannot be judged in the same way as the Rhoads book, for the Whynes book is an edited collection of essays written by a number of different scholars, rather than a unified work of one author. Whynes presents a wider spectrum of views than Rhoads, including Marxist, Austrian, Institutionalist, and public choice perspectives. He supplies an introduction and concluding comments himself. Whynes defines political economy as something much broader than the ceteris paribus-bound orthodoxy taught in respectable college courses and found in popular economics textbooks.

Political economy does go beyond ceteris paribus, but it does so in two distinctly different ways. The first essay, "Bread and Circumstances: The Need for Political Economy" by Shaun Hargreaves-Heap and Martin Hollis, is a gem. The authors draw a helpful contrast between the two different ways of going beyond ceteris paribus. They suggest two different slogans: (1) "market relations are social relations" and (2) "social relations are market relations." In the older political economy of Marx, Veblen, and their ilk, the first slogan guides inquiry. That is, Marxists and Institutionalists go beyond ceteris paribus by explaining market relations in the broader historical and social context. In this approach to political economy, individual economic behavior is explained largely as a result of social forces and historical circumstances. This used to be the only approach to political economy. But now a new political economy has arisen in which the inquiry is guided by the second slogan: "social relations are market relations." Both political economies—old and new—go beyond the bounds of ceteris paribus. However, in the new political economy, social forces and historical circumstances are explained largely as results of individual economic behavior. Hence, the new political economy turns the old political economy on its head. Instead of explaining individual economic behavior in terms of social forces and historical circumstances, the new political economy explains social forces and historical circumstances in terms of individual economic behavior. But the new political economy, Hargreaves-Heap and Hollis point out, relies on methodological individualism, which severely hampers the treatment of power and of institutional change, making the new political economy inherently weak as compared to the old political economy.

The second contributed essay in the collection is Norman P. Barry's "The 'Austrian' Perspective." Barry argues that Austrian economics is not just an extreme form of neoclassicism. What makes the Austrians a separate school, according to Barry, is the view that

> the existence of purposive and choosing men interacting in a social environment precludes the reduction of economics to the search for observed regularities or the discovery of mechanical laws from which quantitative predictions may be derived (35).

He does not convince me that Austrian economics is something more than neoclassical fundamentalism, nor will he convince anyone except the Austrians. Granted, Austrian economics is different from the German historical school. But so too is neoclassical economics. Furthermore, it is true that Austrian economics rejects Friedman's positivist methodology, but Friedman's methodological position is not necessary to neoclassical economics. After all, many neoclassicists disagree with Friedman's methodology. Nonetheless, even though Austrian economics does not belong under the expanded rubric of political economy, Barry's description of Austrian economics is lucid and comprehensive. His essay would make excellent student reading.

John E. Elliott's "The Institutionalist School of Political Economy" also would make excellent student reading. Elliott describes the contributions to institutionalism made by Veblen, Commons, Ayres, Myrdal, Galbraith, and Solo. He also explains the continued institutionalist "espousal of a normative political economy." The recent contributions of institutionalists J. Fagg Foster and Marc R. Tool to the construction of a social value criterion are explained. Throughout his essay, Elliott emphasizes both the evolutionary nature and the broad scope of institutional economics. These two characteristics, combined with its explicitly normative thrust, make institutionalism very important to the continued development of political economy. Elliott concludes his perceptive essay with some fascinating speculations about the prospects for a "Grand Union of dissenting perspectives." Such a union, Elliott suggests, might involve an expanded institutionalism with linkages to the dissenting views of Marx, Schumpeter, Kalecki, Robinson, and Sraffa. But Elliott also speculates that the economics profession is not ready for such a development, at least not just yet.

In his essay, "Modern Marxian Political Economy," Arun Bose downplays the importance of the labor theory of value to contemporary Marxian political economy. He stresses, instead, the Marxist conceptualization of capital as a coercive social relation. This social relation involves the ownership of the means of production—capital equipment—by an exploiting class which grants access to the means of production to an exploited class— the proletariat—through wage labor. The social relation is enforced through the state's protection of the exploiting class's property rights in the means of production. So capital, as defined by Marx, is a concept that can only be understood in a broad political economy context. Bose contrasts this Marxist formulation of capital with the neoclassical notion of capital as a measurable quantity of something, that something being a factor of production— something possessed of inherently productive capacities. Bose also discusses Sraffa and some recent controversies surrounding Sraffa's contribution to an amended Marxian theory of value.

Alan P. Hamlin, in "Public Choice, Markets and Utilitarianism," contrasts public choice theory with utilitarianism, but the contrast is not very elucidating. He also discusses the three methodological planks of public choice theory: methodological individualism, subjectivism, and contractarianism. Hamlin incorrectly suggests that the closest relative to the public choice school is the institutionalist school. But public choice theory, of course, has far more in common with Austrian economics than with institutional economics. The public choosers and Austrians share two methodological planks— individualism and subjectivism; while institutionalists share none of the three methodological planks discussed by Hamlin. Institutional economists long ago rejected methodological individualism and subjectivism. Furthermore, institutionalists refer to contractarianism as conjectural history, and find no use for it in their theories or policies. For their part, the public choosers and Austrians share a distrust of the government activism often proposed by institutionalists to counterbalance the power of large corporations. Hamlin misses these points entirely.

In "Modelling Politico-Economic Relationships" Bruno S. Frey introduces "politometrics." Politometrics does for the study of politics what cliometrics does for the study of history. Under the guise of scientific advance, both disciplines are being set back many years by the simplistic application of quantitative methods and reactionary economic hypotheses to profoundly complex questions of fact and theory. Whynes, the editor of this collection of essays, apparently includes politometrics in his extraordinarily inclusive definition of political economy.

But Whynes redeems himself with his essay, "International Political Economy." He contrasts the heterodox and often radical works of the international political economists (IPE) with the orthodox and often conservative works of the neoclassical economists (NC). For example, according to Whynes, IPE generally uses class as a unit of analysis while NC uses the state. That is, in NC all U.S. citizens would be handled as having the same international interests while in IPE all U.S. citizens would not be handled the same—they would be divided into class alliances and analyzed accordingly. In NC, U.S. workers and U.S. capitalists have the same interests. In IPE, they do not—U.S. workers have the same interests as workers in other countries. A number of other contrasts are also drawn by Whynes and he discusses several contemporary issues in IPE.

"Property and the Legal System" by Roger Bowles contains an orthodox discussion of property rights. Bowles explains them in a thoroughly antiseptic, hypothetical, abstract, and unrealistic way. The works of Posner and Coase form the backbone of the essay.

Whynes supplies a few short concluding comments to the collection of essays, stressing the broad scope of political economy and emphasizing its realistic, empirical, pragmatic nature. The volume includes a bibliography and index.

DOW'S *MACROECONOMIC THOUGHT: A METHODOLOGICAL APPROACH*:
REVIEW ESSAY

John Lodewijks

Sheila Dow, in her recent book *Macroeconomic Thought: A Methodological Approach* (1985), argues that there are four distinct schools of thought in macroeconomics—the neo-Austrian, Post Keynesian, Marxian and Mainstream schools. Dow seeks to characterise each of these schools in terms of the distinctive methodological approach that its members use to analyze key macro concepts (such as microfoundations, equilibrium, expectations and money) and policy issues. She largely succeeds in differentiating these schools and presents some very useful literature reviews in the process. Instructors will find the concept chapters handy for teaching purposes and the

Research in the History of Economic Thought and Methodology,
Volume 6, pages 261-268
Copyright © 1989 by JAI Press Inc.
All rights of reproduction in any form reserved.
ISBN: 0-89232-928-9

book should increase the general professional awareness of the contrasting approaches to macro issues and that alternatives do exist.

In such an ambitious undertaking it is not surprising that a number of
criticisms and qualifications can be levelled at the author. My own list
would include the following:

i. Dow makes no attempt to *appraise* the different macro approaches. Weintraub (1985b, 1117) has asked "Why are the numbers
of economists in each school not even roughly equal? Why are there,
in the U.S. at least, 98% mainstream and 2% of all other kinds of economists?" Dow is silent on the appraisal issue. She takes the (convenient?) Kuhnian position that these paradigms are incommensurate and
that one succeeds for other than reasons of scientific rationality. Furthermore, she claims that there is no value-free set of criteria for appraisal and that since there is "little factual basis for choosing between
these abstractions, the choice must derive from values, or ideologies"
(2) But is ideology all or even the main part of the story?

ii. A related point is that nowhere in this book are we presented
with an overview, let alone an evaluation, of empirical work in
macroeconomics. Nor are we presented with any indication whether
the ideas prominent within particular schools have any empirical counterparts. Dow might respond by saying that there are no conclusive
empirical grounds for theory appraisal, that facts are 'theory-laden'
and that each collection of theories is confirmed in some sense by the
evidence. This follows in the 'death to positivism' line that seems to be
fashionable now, but can we so flippantly disregard the huge research
effort that has been undertaken in empirical macroeconomics? Dow's
attitude is hard to understand for she states that "By far the bulk of
methodological discussion within macroeconomics over the last thirty
years at least has centred on the relationship between theory and observed reality"(60).

iii. The mainstream category that Dow employs is far too broad,
combining an amalgam of disparate groups that simply do not fit together cohesively. In an earlier article (Dow 1983) the term 'General
Equilibrium' (GE) was used to classify this group but this is replaced
with 'mainstream' in the book. However, Dow does not give up the
earlier association, claiming that the criterion that differentiates the
mainstream school from the others is the use of some kind of GE
framework, covering any closed system of simultaneous equations
(65). We can question whether this is really the key element that distinguishes mainstream macroeconomists from the others, or even whether

Marx or Kalecki or a number of other nonmainstream economists actually fill this criteria (see Walsh and Gram 1980). But there is a more fundamental problem.

Dow has a very restrictive view of what having a GE framework implies and this is especially noticeable in the policy discussion of Chapter 8. Here she is misrepresenting the policy views of a substantial section of mainstream economists. General equilibrium analysis can not be identified with any *single* GE model. Rather it is an investigative logic and as such can generate a succession of models with contrasting assumptions and implications, with policy conclusions, if any, differing between models. Yet Dow tries to identify a mainstream policy position and in the process combines monetarists, supply-siders and new classical macroeconomists with Keynesians, of both hydraulic and reconstituted varieties. These groups, however, are not compatible in the policy arena. There are just too many variants of the mainstream to be able to generalize. The search for a set of mainstream policy recommendations flowing from a uniform theoretical framework just does not work. Here it is impossible to focus only on differences between the schools, a methodological examination of differences *within* the mainstream is required.

In addition, Chapter 5 needs revision in light of Roy Weintraub's (1985a, 1985c) recent analysis of how the equilibrium concept has changed over time, his contention that the neo-Walrasian program is empirically progressive and with respect to his 'dual appraisal' hypothesis (Weintraub 1985a, 119–120).

    iv.   Finally, more could be said about the role of macroeconomists in the policy-process and how the schools react differently to the active participation of economists in policy-making. In addition, a public-choice perspective on the Post Keynesian view of the role of government would not have gone amiss (pp. 226, 232). The neoclassical theory of politics assumes that politicians are motivated by self-interest. Hence the real purpose and explanation of government macroeconomic policy is the furthering of identifiable private interests and not to benefit the 'public interest'. It should also be noted that some of the groups that comprise mainstream macro share policy views of one or another of Dow's nonmainstream schools. Needless to say there has been no attempt to correlate policy prescriptions with policy performance.

Not withstanding the above qualifications, Dow has presented and elaborated on a useful proposition that a particular world view is associated with a specific technical approach to the subject. Her work, however, provides only one dimension of a broader field of study in the methodology and history of contemporary macroeconomics. The methodological issues can not be examined in isolation from the history of the subject. Yet there has been very little written on the development of macroeconomics from a history of thought perspective. What has been written has been primarily concerned with searching for historical antecedents, attempting to show that modern macro debates have their roots in earlier policy controversies, or is undertaken by macro modellers who attempt to model earlier discussions with modern tools and concepts. Little serious work has been undertaken in examining each historical period on its own terms with respect to problems and issues particular to the period, and to trace and explain the evolution of macro ideas. Such an effort might usefully come to grips with the following sorts of questions:

1. Why do topics (e.g. administered pricing) and methodological tensions (e.g. deduction versus induction) continue to reappear in the literature? For example, can not some of Lucas's attacks on Klein-type Keynesian models be seen as a modern formulation of Koopman's critique of the NBER and Mitchell? Why is this so? Is it because of the intractibility of problems at the aggregate level? I.e. are we dealing with an inherently difficult subject? Or is it 'fads and fashions'? Or the ahistorical nature of contemporary research? Does a study of the past temper the claims and assertions of rival disputants today?

2. A narrative history will reveal surprises and complexities in the macro literature. Can we theoretically explain these findings? Can we answer deeper questions which go beyond describing what happened to examining *why* it happened? Was it simply a steady movement from ignorance to truth, or of settled paradigms that were occasionally disrupted by scientific revolutions? Did we see Popper's vigorous, unceasing testing of new ideas with those ideas surviving that had repeatedly withstood falsification attempts? Can we rationally reconstruct the history of macroeconomics using an internal logic of appraisal? Is Lakatos's notion of competition between rival scientific research programs (SRPs) useful? Here members of a particular SRP adhere to certain methodological rules (heuristics) and are bound by unquestionable acceptance to certain (hard core) propositions/ assumptions. An SRP can be progressive or degenerative depending on its capacity to explain and provide predictions. Does the popularity of

an SRP (e.g. ability to attract followers) depend on the ability to better explain phenomena and provide more accurate predictions than its rivals (see Leijonhufvud 1980, Kamath 1987)?

3.   Is it true, as R. J. Gordon (1980) has claimed, that in macroeconomics "economic ideas rarely lead economic events but usually follow them?" Gordon's 'externalist' approach posits that macro ideas are very malleable in response to contemporary events. Practitioners constantly readjust their theories in light of new data and external events. Does this reflect, as Stigler has alleged in his Nobel Prize lecture, the weak development of the body of macro analysis, or, as Hicks has said, that macroeconomics is not "a good game," meaning that it cannot be just an intellectual exercise because it is too close to the data, to observable and measurable quantities and external pressures (Hicks 1980, viii–ix)?

4.   As a related question, and as an exercise in sub-disciplinary study, why and how did macroeconomic thought develop differently from microeconomics? Is there now appearing to be a convergence of method (e.g. via a game theoretic approach to macro)? Are we seeing a *general* movement toward micro-foundations across all economics, not just macro? Are we now in the early stages of a movement that could change economics as fundamentally as the marginal revolution did?

5.   To what extent do macro textbooks, when they try to cover the history of macroeconomics, disguise the past? Thomas S. Kuhn noted in his *The Structure of Scientific Revolutions* (1970, chap. XI) that each generation of textbooks alters the interpretation of history to conform to contemporary concerns and thereby "truncate[s] the scientist's sense of his discipline's history" and leads to "the depreciation of historical fact" (137). Does this apply to macroeconomics too?

6.   Is there or should there now be a revival of interest in macro thinking during the inter-war period (with the rehabilitation of Pigou, Ronnie Davis's work on early Chicago, burgeoning interest in Kalecki, the Swedes, Hayek, and business cycle research)? Will this work lead to a reassessment of the place of Keynes in the history of the subject?

7.   Do we need to rewrite the history of Institutionalism? Did the movement die away with the passing of the main leaders? Or did something more complicated happen? Have Institutionalist elements survived within the American Keynesian tradition? Can they be discerned in the search for descriptive detail by the model-builders, in the macro

policy discussions, and in the study of labour and product markets? Has this approach become fused with other ideas and statistical techniques? Are practitioners aware that they owe an intellectual debt to earlier Institutionalist thinkers?

8.   What fostered the allocation of substantial academic and financial resources to the construction of ever larger macroeconometric models? Any serious study of the history of macroeconomics must come to grips with this phenomenon. What prompted the search for greater detail and disaggregation in the models?

9.   What about the international transmission of macroeconomic ideas? To what extent and why, for example, did British Keynesianism differ from American Keynesianism? Did there develop a peculiarly American version of Keynes?

10.   Is macroeconomics, as Klamer (1984) claims, the ''art of persuasion'' where the *style* of argument supersedes the evaluation of ideas and theories by formal logic and empirical falsification efforts?

11.   If you take the view that we can give useful advice on macro policy issues, why has our advice often been ignored? Public ignorance? Role of special interests? Or is it because, as Stigler (1976) says, economists don't matter? That ''economists exert a minor and scarcely detectable influence on the societies in which they live.'' Economists hold a variety of views; some appeal to a larger audience than do others. The speakers most in demand provide ideas that the audience wants to hear. Or have politicians by-and-large accepted the ruling macro paradigms of the day? For example, how long did it take, and to what extent were, Keynesian macro ideas implemented into public policy? Is there insufficient attention in the profession placed on problems of policy formulation? Should a new profession be created perhaps called 'economic engineering' with a problem-solving orientation, with a relationship to economics comparable to that between physics/mechanical engineering, bio-chemistry/medicine, and economics/business administration? Does America have a unique group of social scientists (e.g. Okun) who are immersed in the data and very active in public policy issues and who move easily between academia, the think-tanks and government? Do they enrich not only the policy debates but also the profession?

12.   Finally, has there been progress in the science of macroeconomics? What do we mean by 'progress'? Have we increased our understanding of the aggregate economy? Is macroeconomics a settled science? Has the subject become theoretically and empirically

progressive? What have economists contributed to key public policy problems of inflation, unemployment, high interest rates and recession?

As can be seen by this list of of research topics there is plenty of work to do on the history and methodology of macroeconomics; Dow's book is a useful addition to this inquiry.

ACKNOWLEDGMENTS

I have benefited from a discussion with Peter Earl in writing this review. George Argyrous provided useful research assistance.

REFERENCES

Bell, D. and Kristol, I., (ed's) (1981) *The Crisis in Economic Theory*. New York: Basic.

Caldwell, B., (ed.) (1984) *Appraisal and Criticism in Economics*. Boston: Allen and Unwin.

Dow, S. C., (1983) Schools of Thought in Macroeconomics: The Method is the Message. *Australian Economic Papers*, **22**. June. pp. 30–46.

Dow, S. C., (1985) *Macroeconomic Thought: A Methodological Approach*. Oxford: Blackwell.

Gordon, R. J., (1980) Post War Macroeconomics: The Evolution of Ideas and Events, in Feldstein, M. (ed.) *The American Economy in Transition*. Chicago: Chicago University Press, pp. 101–162.

Hicks, J., (1980) *Causality in Economics*. Canberra: Australian National University Press.

Kamath, S. J., (1987) A Rational Reconstruction of the Rational Expectations Revolution, in *Proceedings of the History of Economics Society*. 14th Annual Meeting, **1**. Harvard University.

Klamer, A., (1984) *Conversations With Economists*. New Jersey: Rowman and Allenheld.

Leijonhufvud, A., (1976) Schools, 'Revolutions' and Research Programmes in Economic Theory, in Latsis, S. J. (ed.) *Method and Appraisal in Economics*. Cambridge: Cambridge University Press, pp. 65–108.

Lodewijks, J., (1985a) *Arthur Okun and American Macroeconomics*. Ph. D. dissertation, Duke University.

Lodewijks, J., (1985b) American Macroeconomics in the 1940's—The professional Dialogue, in *Proceedings of the History of Economics Society*, 12th Annual Meeting. George Mason University.

Stigler, G. (1976). Do Economists Matter? *Southern Economic Journal*, **42**, pp. 347–354.

268   JOHN LODEWIJKS

Walsh, V. and Gram, H., (1980) *Classical and Neoclassical Theories of General Equilibrium*. Cambridge: Cambridge University Press.

Weintraub, E. R., (1985a) *General Equilibrium Analysis: Studies in Appraisal*. Cambridge: Cambridge University Press.

Weintraub, E. R., (1985b) Review of Dow (1983). *Economic Journal*, **95**. Dec. pp. 1116–1118.

Weintraub, E. R., (1985c) Appraising General Equilibrium Analysis. *Economics and Philosophy*, **1**, pp. 23–37.

DOW'S METHODOLOGY
AND MACROECONOMICS:
REVIEW ESSAY

Nina Shapiro

The move away from logical positivist conceptions in philosophy has focused attention on methods in economics. This move not only brought into question the methodological tenets of economics, but provided new perspectives on methods and progress in economics. Exploration of these perspectives, and especially those suggested by the epistemological views of Thomas Kuhn and Imre Lakatos, has produced a number of important works on the methodology of economics. One of the most ambitious of these is Sheila Dow's new book, *Macroeconomic Thought, A Methodological Approach*.[1]

Dow examines the connections between methodological positions, conceptual frameworks, and policy positions in macroeconomics. Theoretical and policy disputes are the focus of the examination. Rather than attempting to resolve these disputes, Dow tries to understand their

Research in the History of Economic Thought ànd Methodology,
Volume 6, pages 269-276
Copyright © 1989 by JAI Press Inc.
All rights of reproduction in any form reserved.
ISBN: 0-89232-928-9

persistence. The root of discord in macroeconomics, the source of persistent controversy, is the primary concern.

The methodological approach which Dow adopts towards macroeconomics is a Kuhnian one. Macroeconomic controversies stem from the division of macroeconomics into competing schools of thought. Members of competing schools speak different theoretical languages. The meaning of macroeconomic concepts ("money," "equilibrium" and "expectations") differs across schools, as does the approach to macroeconomic problems and analytical methods.

Facts cannot arbitrate theoretical disputes between the schools. The empirical findings of a school's members are conditioned by the conceptual framework which directs their investigations. Theoretical presuppositions determine the data investigated, its organization and interpretation. Because facts are "theory laden," each school "sees" a different economic world.[2]

Dow's Kuhnian analysis emphasizes the methodological dimensions of paradigms. The methods of a school unite its members and govern its theoretical concerns and practices. Methodology is the key to understanding divisions within macroeconomics and methodological differences stand in the way of the resolution of its controversies.[3]

While theoretical perspective depends on methods, these depend on the "mode of thought" which structures the analysis. A mode of thought is a mode of reasoning, a particular way of understanding reality. One's mode of thought determines how one reasons, the kinds of arguments considered and the way in which arguments are constructed and presented.

Two distinct modes of Western thought are identified, the "Cartesian/Euclidean," and the "Babylonian." The former dominates methodological inquiries and underlies the traditional investigations. New approaches to methodology, and the Kuhnian one in particular, are associated with the Babylonian mode. The modes entail radically different conceptions of knowledge, science, and scientific methods.

A linear and reductionist logic distinguishes Cartesian/Euclidean reasoning. Arguments proceed from first principles or ultimate causes to final consequences. Knowledge is derived through deduction from basic propositions, statements that are either self-evident or "analytic" (true by virtue of the meaning of their terms). Scientific accounts are axiomatic in structure and the axiomatic method defines the theoretic.

Cartesian/Euclidean thought does not preclude empirical investigations. It can incorporate an empiricist epistemology and has done so historically. How induction enters into this mode of thought depends on the cognitive status of the axioms. If these are self-evident propositions, then induction in the form of introspection enters on the ground floor of analysis. Axioms are established by identifying universal dimensions of human experience, such as "scarcity" or the preference for "more goods over less."

When axioms are analytic statements, as they are in the logical positivist version of the Cartesian/Euclidean approach, their scientific status depends on the confirmation of their empirical implications. In this case induction comes at the end of the analysis, after the derivation of the theorems and specification of the empirical conditions under which they hold. Both inductive and deductive methods are employed by Cartesian/Euclidean thinkers and the epistemological problem of induction, of generalizing from facts to universal propositions, is especially important since "true" or certain knowledge is the epistemological ideal.

While Cartesian/Euclidean thought strives for true knowledge, Babylonian thought assumes that true knowledge can never be achieved. The impossibility of certain knowledge is the basic presupposition of Babylonian reasoning. Since the truth of any knowledge claim is necessarily uncertain, Babylonian thinkers "hedge their bets" by offering a variety of different arguments in support of their conclusions. Just as no single piece of circumstantial evidence is decisive, no single account is conclusive. The robustness rather than the certainty of propositions or results is the epistemological ideal.[4]

Babylonian analysis explores the diverse aspects of a situation and highlights the particularity of phenomena and the complexity of their occurence. A system is understood by examining its varied facets and the complex of factors which govern its operation. The facets examined and the factors singled out in the explanation of the system's operation depend on the way the system as a whole is perceived. Babylonian analysis is "holistic" in its approach and its diverse lines of inquiry are bound together by the general perception of the phenomena investigated.

Babylonian thought favors no particular analytical method. Methods are adapted to the problem examined and the same phenomena is analysed in a variety of different ways. Methodological diversity distinguishes Babylonian methodology.

The Babylonian mode of thought is represented in macroeconomics by its post Keynesian school. Mainstream analysis, which includes all general equilibrium approaches to macroeconomics (the monetarist, Walrasian, and traditional or "bastard" Keynesian), embodies the logic of Cartesian/Euclidean thought. This logic also structures neo-Austrian analysis, though its reasoning is not entirely Cartesian. Unlike mainstream thought; neo-Austrian thought has some Babylonian dimensions. The other school examined in Dow's book, the Marxian, incorporates aspects of both modes of thought. Its analytical approach, however, is primarily Babylonian.

I. METHODOLOGICAL PARADIGMS

Dow attempts to "bridge the gap" between methodology and macroeconomics by demonstrating the importance of methodology in theory construction. Modes of thought and methods mold theoretical perspectives and conceptions. While the work establishes significant connections between macroeconomic theories and methods, the primacy of method in theory/methodology connections is not demonstrated. The relation between theoretical conceptions and methods in the mainstream school, and in the other schools also, does not support a methodological interpretation of macroeconomic thought.

As Dow emphasizes, the theoretical perspective of mainstream analysis is neoclassical. Mainstream macroeconomists try to incorporate Keynesian ideas into neoclassical theory. This involves reducing macroeconomics to microeconomics since in neoclassical thought the optimizing behaviour of individuals grounds all economic phenomena. Reductionist methods come with the neoclassical framework, and the mainstream school cannot adopt this framework without adopting a reductionist method.

Dow recognizes the relation between the reductionism of mainstream analysis and its neoclassical framework, but argues that the theoretical perspective of neoclassical economics stems from its Cartesian/Euclidean logic. Neoclassical accounts center on the individual because they employ the axiomatic method. Employment of this method in economics entails the decomposition of the economy and the determination of its operation by the behaviour of its "smallest parts." Smallness, however, has no evident economic meaning, and as Dow herself brings out in the discussion of the microfoundations issue, the way the economy is decomposed depends on how it is conceived. Whereas the constituent elements of the economy are individuals in the mainstream conception, they are classes in the Marxian, and economic "groups," entrepreneurs, rentiers, producers and consumers, in the post Keynesian.

Neoclassical economics certainly strives for indubitable axioms and its reasoning is unmistakably linear and reductionist. Yet, the principles of axiomatic reasoning are too abstract to account for the particularity of the neoclassical conception of the economic. The specific content of this conception, the fact that its axioms are axioms about individual behaviour, cannot be derived from the Cartesian/Euclidean structure of neoclassical thought. Ricardian reasoning is also reductionist, but individuals and their choices have no importance in the Ricardian conception. Ricardian economics grounds the economy in nature, in the fertility of the land and reproduction of the species, not in the preferences and endowments of individuals.

Just as the reductionism of mainstream analysis does not explain its theoretical directions, those of post Keynesian analysis cannot be understood in terms of its holism or other Babylonian dimensions. The "whole" can be conceived in different ways, and the post Keynesian school itself encompasses different conceptions of the system and its logic. Some post Keynesians conceive of the economy in terms of the requirements of output reproduction. Others focus on finance and investment and the whole, for them, is the process of capital accumulation.

The post Keynesian school does stress the uncertainty of economic events and the imperfection of knowledge. Uncertainty is stressed, however, not because of any epistemological judgement on the possibility of achieving true knowledge. Rather, uncertainty is important in a Keynesian world because investment in "long lived equipment" is important. For Keynes and the post Keynesians, it is the irreversibility of investment and its importance in income determination which necessitates an examination of expectations and the rejection of the perfect knowledge assumption. While Keynes may have embraced a Babylonian epistemology, his arguments against the methods of the "classical" school were economic, not epistemological. He emphasized the unsuitability of these methods to the investigation of wealth accumulation and production processes governed by the accumulation goal.[5]

The neo-Austrian arguments against the methods of the "classical" school are quite different. What leads the neo-Austrians away from these methods is not the economic significance of investment and the accumulation drive, but the subjectivity of economic judgments and actions. Neo-Austrian economics emphasizes the uncertainty of economic events because it emphasizes the subjectivity of economic life.

The neo-Austrian school recognizes the impossibility of knowing for certain the results of actions that are wholly subjective, and the Babylonian dimensions of neo-Austrian reasoning stem from this recognition. In the case of the neo-Austrian school, Babylonian views are intertwined with and, in fact, come out of neoclassical conceptions. Neo-Austrian thought is both Babylonian and neoclassical, and on Dow's own account, the macroeconomic views of the neo-Austrian school are even less Keynesian than those of the mainstream one.

This is not to say that methodology is unimportant or that theories and methods are unconnected. As Dow argues, methods are not mere "tools"; they are particular ways of analyzing and thus conceptualizing reality. But the relation between theory and method is not the hierarchical one that Dow emphasizes. Methods depend on theoretical perspectives as much as these depend on methodological principles, and the distinctiveness of a conceptual framework cannot be grasped in terms of its methodological dimensions.

II. THE KUHNIAN APPROACH

In addition to attaching too much importance to the methodological dimensions of macroeconomic thought, Dow also focuses too much on the divisions within macroeconomics. We learn a lot about the differences between macroeconomic theories and methods, but very little about macroeconomics itself, its subject matter, issues, history, and direction. We do not come away from the book with a clear sense of the macroeconomics tradition.

While macroeconomic theories differ, and it is important to recognize the differences between them, they share a common set of problems, those which bring them within the macroeconomics tradition. Macroeconomics traditionally has been concerned with certain kinds of problems (unemployment, inflation, output fluctuations, etc.), and one cannot be a macroeconomist without treating at least some of these problems. Nor can one's treatment of these problems be entirely different from treatments developed in the past. If it were, it would not be a part of macroeconomics, for it would have nothing in common with other macroeconomic investigations.

To become part of the macroeconomics tradition, a theory must relate to both the concerns of the tradition and the theories which compose it. A theory which was unrelated to the theories which comprise this tradition, and could not be understood in terms of its perspectives and directions, would have no recognizable macroeconomic dimensions. Macroeconomists are as concerned with the logic of Keynes's theory as they are with the macroeconomic "facts" because the relation of a theory to the Keynesian one is its relation to macroeconomics. One can criticize Keynes's theory and reject its results, but one cannot ignore it, for one's theory has to either make sense in terms of the Keynesian one or explain its shortcomings and results. In macroeconomics, as in other sciences, the existing theories are an essential part of the field of investigation.[6]

The persistence of controversy in macroeconomics does not itself imply the presence of "incommensurable" macroeconomic perspectives. Indeed, if the conceptual frameworks of the macroeconomic schools were incommensurable, there could be no theoretical disputes between them. Macroeconomic concepts are not arbitrary definitions or subjective notions which only have a meaning to those who adopt them. The meaning of a concept does vary across the schools of macroeconomics, and the members of one school often fail to grasp the meaning of the concepts of another. This, however, does not mean that they could not do so or that the meaning of a macroeconomic concept is indeterminate.

Incommensurable theories are incomparable; they are neither similar nor different. Macroeconomic theories can be compared and are compared by Dow herself. They have a common subject matter and history and can be compared and evaluated in terms of their treatment of this subject matter and their illumination of macroeconomic problems and the macroeconomics tradition. The "theory ladenness" of facts does not mean that the facts can be made consistent with any imaginable conceptual framework or that the relative strengths of different theories cannot be assessed. While the traditional, logical positivist ways of evaluating a theory are not adequate, other kinds of evaluations are possible.[7]

Although Dow's Kuhnian approach weakens her analysis, she does advance our understanding of macroeconomics. The book illuminates the differences between macroeconomic theories and the logic of their concepts. The latter is an especially valuable contribution, since the meaning of concepts rarely is investigated in economics.

NOTES

1. Also see Blaug (1980), Boland (1982), and Caldwell (1982). Developments in the philosophy of science are reviewed in Suppe (1977).
2. The conceptual conditioning of observation and its implications for experiment

and discovery in the natural sciences are investigated by the "Weltanschauungen" philosophers (Feyerabend, Hanson, Kuhn, and Toulmin). See part five of Suppe's introduction to Suppe (1977) and chapters 7, 8, and 12 of Kuhn (1977).

3. The importance of methodological commitments in the determination of research directions is also stressed in Boland (1982).

4. For an extended discussion of this aspect of Babylonian thought see Wimsatt (1981).

5. See Keynes (1937).

6. This is emphasized by MacIntyre (1977). Also see Dudley Shapere's essay in Suppe (1977).

7. See the afterword of Suppe (1977).

REFERENCES

Blaug, Mark, (1980) *The Methodology of Economics*, Cambridge: Cambridge University Press.

Boland, L. A., (1982) *The Foundations of Economic Method*, London: Allen and Unwin.

Caldwell, B. J., (1982) *Beyond Positivism, Economic Methodology in the Twentieth Century*, London: Allen and Unwin.

Keynes, John Maynard, (1937) "The General Theory of Employment," *Quarterly Journal of Economics*, February, 51, 209–223.

Kuhn, Thomas S., (1977) *The Essential Tension*, Chicago: University of Chicago Press.

MacIntyre, Alisdair, (1977) "Epistemological Crises, Dramatic Narrative and the Philosophy of Science," *The Monist*, 60, 452–471.

Suppe, Frederick, ed., (1977) *The Structure of Scientific Theories*, Urbana: University of Illinois Press.

Winsatt, W. C., (1981) "Robustness, Reliability and Overdetermination," in M. B. Brewer and B. E. Collins, eds., *Scientific Inquiry and the Social Sciences*, San Francisco: Jossey Bass.

NEW BOOKS RECEIVED

Arndt, H. W. *Economic Development: The History of an Idea.* Chicago: University of Chicago Press, 1987. Pp. viii, 217. $20.95.

Arthur, C. J. *Dialectics of Labour: Marx and His Relation to Hegel.* New York: Basil Blackwell, 1987. Pp. 182. $39.95.

Beecher, Jonathan. *Charles Fourier: The Visionary and His World.* Berkeley: University of California Press, 1986. Pp. xvii, 601.

Bellamy, Richard. *Modern Italian Social Theory.* Stanford: Stanford University Press, 1987. Pp. 215. $35.00.

Berkowitz, Monroe, and M. Anne Hill, eds. *Disability and the Labor Market.* Ithaca: Cornell Industrial and Labor Relations Press, 1986. Pp. ix, 319. $34.00

Black, R. D. Collison, ed. *Ideas in Economics.* Totowa: Barnes and Noble Books, 1986. Pp. x, 246. $27.50.

Brand, Myles, and Robert M. Harnish, eds. *The Representation of Knowledge and Belief.* Tucson: University of Arizona Press, 1986. Pp. xviii, 368. $39.95.

Brenner, Reuven. *Betting on Ideas*. Chicago: University of Chicago Press, 1986. Pp. xi, 247. $32.00.

Brobeck, John R., et al., eds. *History of the American Physiological Society*. Bethesda: American Physiological Society, 1987. Pp. viii, 533.

Cairncross, Alec. *The Price of War*. New York: Basil Blackwell, 1986. Pp. x, 249. $34.95.

Campen, James T. *Benefit, Cost, and Beyond*. Cambridge: Ballinger, 1986. Pp. xii, 240. $29.95.

Carson, Robert B. *Macroeconomic Issues Today*. Fourth Edition. New York: St. Martin's, 1987. Pp. x, 211. Paper.

Clark, J. C. D. *Revolution and Rebellion*. New York: Cambridge University Press, 1986. Pp. x, 182.

Cooper, David E. *Metaphor*. Oxford: Basil Blackwell, 1986. Aristotelian Society Series, Vol. 5. Pp. 282.

Deutsch, Karl W., et al., eds. *Advances in the Social Sciences, 1900–1980*. Lanham: University Press of America/Abt Books, 1986. Pp. xvii, 460. $39.50, cloth; $23.50, paper.

Dovring, Folke. *Productivity and Value: The Political Economy of Measuring Progress*. New York: Praeger, 1987. Pp. 194. $35.00.

Dumont, *Essays on Individualism*. Chicago: University of Chicago Press, 1986. Pp. x, 284. $27.50.

Edsall, Nicholas C. *Richard Cobden: Independent Radical*. Cambridge: Harvard University Press, 1986. Pp. xiv, 465.

Ettinger, Elzbieta. *Rosa Luxemburg: A Life*. Boston: Beacon Press, 1986. Pp. xv, 286. $24.95.

Feiwel, George R., ed. *Arrow and the Foundations of the Theory of*

Economic Policy. New York: New York University Press, 1987. Pp. lxiii, 758. $75.00.

Feiwell, George R., ed. *Arrow and the Ascent of Modern Economic Theory*. New York: New York University Press, 1987. Pp. liv, 698. $75.00.

Flathman, Richard E. *The Philosophy and Politics of Freedom*. Chicago: University of Chicago Press, 1987. Pp. x, 360. $42.50, cloth; $16.50, paper.

Frank, Robert H. *Choosing the Right Pond: Human Behavior and the Quest for Status*. New York: Oxford University Press, 1985. Pp. xi, 286. $10.95, paper.

Frankel, Boris. *The Post-Industrial Utopians*. Madison: University of Wisconsin Press, 1987. Pp. xii, 303. $35.00, cloth; $12.50, paper.

Freidson, Eliot. *Professional Powers: A Study of the Institutionalization of Formal Knowledge*. Chicago: University of Chicago Press, 1986. Pp. xviii, 241. $20.00.

Frese, Joseph R., and Jacob Judd, eds. *Business and Government*. Tarrytown: Sleepy Hollow Press, 1985. Pp. xii, 233. $25.00.

Frese, Joseph R., and Jacob Judd, eds. *Business Enterprise in Early New York*. Tarrytown: Sleepy Hollow Press, 1979. Pp. vii, 209. $17.50.

Frese, Joseph R., and Jacob Judd, eds. *American Industrialization, Economic Expansion, and the Law*. Tarrytown: Sleepy Hollow Press, 1981. Pp. xv, 251. $20.00.

Geison, Gerald L., ed. *Physiology in the American Context, 1850–1940*. Bethesda: American Physiological Society, 1987. Pp. viii, 403. $55.00.

Ginsberg, Benjamin. *The Captive Public: How Mass Opinion Promotes State Power*. New York: Basic Books, 1986. Pp. xi, 272. $18.95.

Gray, John. *Liberalism*. Minneapolis: University of Minnesota Press, 1986. Pp. xi, 106. $25.00, cloth; $9.95, paper.

Helburn, Suzanne W., and David F. Bramhall, eds. *Marx, Schumpeter, Keynes*. Armonk: M. E. Sharpe, 1986. Pp. xii, 343. $35.00, cloth; $16.95, paper.

Heller, Thomas C., et al., eds. *Reconstructing Individualism*. Stanford: Stanford University Press, 1986. Pp. xiv, 365. $39.50.

Hinde, Wendy. *Richard Cobden*. New Haven: Yale University Press, 1987. Pp. xii, 367. $30.00.

Hogarth, Robin M., and Melvin W. Reder, eds. *Rational Choice: The Contrast Between Economics and Psychology*. Chicago: University of Chicago Press, 1987. Pp. ix, 332. $30.00, cloth; paper.

Hoy, David Couzens, ed. *Foucault: A Critical Reader*. New York: Basil Blackwell, 1986. Pp. vii, 246. $45.00, cloth; $14.95, paper.

Hsieh, Ching-Yao, and Stephen L. Mangum. *A Search for Synthesis in Economic Theory*. Armonk: M. E. Sharpe, 1986. Pp. xii, 268. $35.00, cloth; $14.95, paper.

Joyce, Patrick, ed. *The Historical Meaning of Work*. New York: Cambridge University Press, 1987. Pp. 320.

Kanth, Rajani K. *Political Economy and Laissez-Faire*. Totowa: Rowman and Littlefield, 1986. Pp. vii, 200. $34.50.

Kelly, Aileen. *Mikhail Bakunin*. New Haven: Yale University Press, 1987. Pp. 320. $14.95, paper.

Klausner, Samuel Z., and Victor M. Lidz. *The Nationalization of the Social Sciences*. Philadelphia: University of Pennsylvania Press, 1986. Pp. xiv, 296. $34.95.

Klay, Robin Kendrick. *Counting the Cost: The Economics of Christian Stewardship*. Grand Rapids: Eerdmans, 1986. Pp. ix, 187. $9.95, paper.

Langer, Gary F. *The Coming of Age of Political Economy*. Westport: Greenwood, 1987. Pp. xv, 224. $35.95.

Levine, David O. *The American College and the Culture of Aspiration, 1915–1940*. Ithaca: Cornell University Press, 1986. Pp. 281. $29.95.

Lincoln, Yvonna S., and Egon G. Guba. *Naturalistic Inquiry*. Beverly Hills: Sage, 1985. Pp. 416.

Lowry, S. Todd, ed. *Pre-classical Economic Thought*. Boston: Kluwer, 1987. Pp. x, 271. $47.50.

Marcus, Alan I. *Agricultural Science and the Quest for Legitimacy*. Ames: Iowa State University Press, 1985. Pp. x, 269. $22.50.

Mayr, Otto. *Authority, Liberty and Automatic Machinery in Early Modern Europe*. Baltimore: Johns Hopkins University Press, 1986. Pp. xviii, 265. $30.00.

McLellan, David. *Ideology*. Minneapolis: University of Minnesota Press, 1986. Pp. viii, 99. $25.00, $9.95, paper.

Mirowski, Philip, ed. *The Reconstruction of Economic Theory*. Boston: Kluwer, 1986. Pp. 266. $42.50.

Nisbet, Robert. *Conservatism*. Minneapolis: University of Minnesota Press, 1986. Pp. x, 118. $25.00, cloth; $9.95, paper.

Pearce, David W., ed. *The MIT Dictionary of Modern Economics*. 3rd ed. Cambridge: MIT Press, 1986. Pp. 462. $12.50, cloth.

Peden, G. C. *British Economic and Social Policy: Lloyd George to Margaret Thatcher*. Oxford: Philip Allan; Atlantic Highlands: Humanities Press, 1985. Pp. xiii, 239. $29.50.

Powers, Charles H. *Vilfredo Pareto*. Newbury Park: Sage, 1987. Pp. 166. Paper.

Rayack, Elton. *Not So Free to Choose: The Political Economy of Milton Friedman and Ronald Reagan*. New York: Praeger, 1987. Pp. xi, 215.

Reddy, William M. *Money and Liberty in Modern Europe*. New York: Cambridge University Press, 1987. Pp. xii, 264. Paper.

Reich, Robert B., and John D. Donahue. *New Deals: The Chrysler Revival and the American System*. New York: Penguin, 1985. Pp. 359. $7.95, paper.

Resnick, Stephen A., and Richard D. Wolff. *Knowledge and Class*. Chicago: University of Chicago Press, 1987. Pp. vii, 352.

Ricoeur, Paul. *Lectures on Ideology and Utopia*. George H. Taylor, ed. New York: Columbia University Press, 1986. Pp. xxxvi, 353. $35.00.

Riha, Thomas. *German Political Economy: The History of an Alternative Economics*. Bradford, England: MCB University Press, 1985. Pp. 252. International Journal of Social Economics, vol. 12 (1985)

Robyn, Dorothy. *Braking the Special Interests*. Chicago: University of Chicago Press, 1987. Pp. xii, 295. $24.95.

Samuelson, Paul A. *Collected Scientific Papers*. Vol. 5. Kate Crowley, ed. Cambridge: MIT Press, 1986. Pp. xii, 1052. $65.00.

Sass, Steven A. *The Pragmatic Imagination: A History of the Wharton School 1881–1981*. Philadelphia: University of Pennsylvania Press, 1982. Pp. xxiii, 351. $26.50.

Schneider, Louis. *Paradox and Society: The Work of Bernard Mandeville*. New Brunswick: Transaction Books, 1987. Pp. vii, 248. $39.95.

Sher, Richard B. *Church and University in the Scottish Enlightenment*. Princeton: Princeton University Press, 1985. Pp. xix, 390. $47.50

Smelser, Neil J. *Contemporary Classics in the Social and Behavioral Sciences*. Philadelphia: ISI Press, 1987. Pp. xxiv, 361. $39.95.

Stephen, Frank H. *Essays in Reappraisal*. Bradford: MCB University Press, 1986– Journal of Economics Studies, vol. 13 (1986). Pp. 62. Paper.

Stocking, George W., Jr. *Victorian Anthropology*. New York: Free Press, 1987. Pp. xvii, 429.

The Review of Austrian Economics. Vol. 1, 1987. Lexington: Lexington Books, 1987. Pp. xiii, 246. $30.00

Unger, Roberto Mangabeira. *The Criticial Legal Studies Movement*. Cambridge: Harvard University Press, 1986. Pp. 128.

Warner, John Harley. *The Therapeutic Perspective*. Cambridge: Harvard University Press, 1986. Pp. x, 367.

Wiley, Norbert, ed. *The Marx-Weber Debate*. Newbury Park: Sage, 1987. Pp. 206. Paper.

Wolff, Richard D., and Stephen A. Resnick. *Economics: Marxian versus Neoclassical*. Baltimore: Johns Hopkins University Press, 1987. Pp. xiv, 279. $32.50, cloth; $12.95, paper.

Young, Warren. *Interpreting Mr. Keynes: The IS-LM Enigma*. Boulder: Westview, 1987. Pp. xii, 218. $37.95.

Research in the History of Economic Thought and Methodology

Edited by

Warren J. Samuels

Department of Economics
Michigan State University

This annual series will publish research in the history of economic thought and in methodology. Contributions will be accepted from all points of view in these resurgent fields but must make substantive contributions to either field or to their interaction. Contributions will be selected through a referee process. Occasional volumes will comprise, in their entirety or in part, symposia or collections on cognate topics.

Volume 1, The Craft of the Historian of Economic Thought
1983, 275 pp. $58.50
ISBN 0-89232-328-0

Action, *A.W. Coats, University of Nottingham.* **Frank Hyneman Knight and the History of Economic Thought,** *Richard S. Howey, University of Kansas.* **T.W. Hutchinson as an Historian of Economics,** *A.W. Coats, University of Nottingham.* **G.L.S. Shackle as an Historian of Economic Thought,** *Brian J. Loasby, University of Sterling.* **G.L.S. Shackle as an Historian of Economic Thought,** *Mark Perlman, University of Pittsburgh.* **G.L.S. Shackle as a Historian of Economic Thought,** *Arnold Heertje, University of Amsterdam.* **Joseph J. Spengler: The Institutional Approach to the History of Economics,** *Irvin Sobel, Florida State University.* **George J. Stigler as an Historian of Economic Thought,** *Ingrid Rima, Temple University.*

Volume 2, 1984, 246 pp. $58.50
ISBN 0-89232-476-7

CONTENTS: List of Contributors. Acknowledgements. "Just Notions of Political Economy", George Pryme, the First Professor of Political Economy at Cambridge, *James P. Henderson, Valparaiso University.* The Attitude to Political Economy of Writers in the Working-Class Press, 1816-1834, *N.W. Thompson, University College of Swansea, England.* John Stuart Mill and India, *Karl de Schweinitz, Jr., Northwestern University.* Three Essays on Ricardo and Ricardiana. Ricardo and the Provident Institutions, *John P. Henderson, Michigan State University.* The Political Economy Club: Robert Torrens and the Decline of Ricardo's Influence, *John P. Henderson, Michigan State University.* Malthus and the Edinburgh Review, *John P. Henderson, Michigan State University.* Symposium on Recent Work in Methodology, Is Economics Methodology Special? *Timothy J. Brennan, U.S. Department of Justice.* Methodological Diversity: Recognition, Responses, and Implications, *William Guthrie, Appalachian State University.* On the Current State of Methodology in Economics, *Royall Brandis, University of Illinois.* Views of Economic Ignorance, *Ian M.T. Stewart, University of Nottingham, England.* On the State of Economic Methodology, *Lawrence A. Boland, Simon Fraser University.* Current Thinking on the Role of Value Judgements in Economic Science: A Survey, *Charles K. Wilber, University of Notre Dame and Roland Hoksbergen, Calvin College.* Economic Methodology in the Postpositivist Era, *Bruce J. Caldwell, University of*

North Carolina at Greensboro. **Comments on McCloskey on Methodology and Rhetoric,** *Warren J. Samuels, Michigan State University.* **The Sociology of Knowledge and the History of Economics,** *A.W. Coats, University of Nottingham, England.* **Book Reviews, Russell Keat and John Urry, Social Theory as Science,** *Bruce J. Caldwell, University of North Carolina at Greensboro.* **Mark Blaug and Paul Sturges, Eds., Who's Who in Economics: and Justin Wintle, Ed., Makers of Nineteenth Century Culture, 1800-1914,** *Warren J. Samuels, Michigan State University.* **Books Received.**

Volume 3, 1985, 295 pp. $58.50
ISBN 0-89232-616-6

CONTENTS: List of Contributors. Editorial Board. Acknowledgements. The Economics of Johann Von Thunen, *Mark Blaug, University of London.* **Richard Cantillon and Adam Smith: A Reappraisal,** *Edwin G. West, Carleton University.* **On the Market as a Game: Hayeek vs. Knight,** *William S. Kern, Franklin and Marshall College.* **Hypothesis Testing and Data Interpretation: The Case of Milton Friedman,** *Paul Diesing, State University of New York, Buffalo.* **In Search of a Method: The Nature and Evolution of the Categories of Political Economy,** *Michael Perelman, California State University.* **SYMPOSIUM OF THE AUSTRIAN SCHOOL. Introduction,** *Mark Perlman, University of Pittsburgh.* **Lionel Robbins, The Austrian School and the LSE Tradition,** *Jack Wiseman, University of York.* **Schumpeter and the German and Austrian Socialization Attempts of 1918-1919,** *Wolfgang F. Stolper, University of Michigan.* **Schumpeter's Ediface on Schaffle's Foundation: A Raised Eyebrow,** *Nicholas Balabkins, Lehigh University.* **Wicksell and the Austrians,** *Carl G. Uhr, University of California, Riverside.* **From the Knowledge of Economics to the Economics of Knowledge: Fritz Machlup on Methodology and on the "Knowledge Society",** *Richard N. Langlois, University of Connecticut.* **Comment on R.N. Langlois, "From the Knowledge of Economics to the Economics of Knowledge: Fritz Machlup on Methodology and on the 'Knowledge Society'",** *Israel M. Kirzner, New York University.* **Machlup on Knowledge: Science, Subjectivism and the Social Nature of Knowledge,** *Warren J. Samuels, Michigan State University.* **THREE REVIEWS. Karl Pribram, A History of Economic Reasoning,** *S. Todd Lowry,*

Washington and Lee University. **Louis Dupre, Marx's Social Critique of Culture,** *Michael Perelman, California State University.* **M.L. Meyers, The Soul of Modern Economic Man,** *William O. Thweatt, Vanderbilt University.* Books Received.

Volume 4, 1986, 376 pp. $58.50
ISBN 0-89232-678-6

CONTENTS: Editorial Board. List of Contributors. Acknowledgements. Keynes as a Historian of Economic Thought: The Perspectives of the General Theory, *Donald A. Walker, Indiana University of Pennsylvania.* Sir William Petty on Value: A Reconsideration, *Glenn Hueckel, Purdue University.* Nicholas Barbon and the Origins of Economic Liberalism, *Tyler Cowen, Harvard University.* Essentialism and Socialist Economic Planning: A Methodological Critique of Optimal Planning Theory, *David F. Riccio, University of Notre Dame.* Monetarist and Anti-Monetarist Causality, *J. Daniel Hammond, Wake Forest University.* Rhetoric at the Expense of Coherence: A Reinterpretation of Milton Friedman's Methodology, *Uskali Maki, University of Helsinki.* Symposium on the Sociology of Economics. The Rise of Modern Finance Theory: Its Characteristics as a Scientific Field and Connections to the Changing Structure of Capital Markets, *Richard Whitley, Manchester Business School.* The Structure and Context of Economics as a Scientific Field, *Richard Whitley, Manchester Business School.* Public Science and Public Knowledge, *Brian J. Loasby, University of Stirling.* The Orthodoxy and Professional Legitimacy: Toward a Critical Sociology of Economics, *Jeffrey Burkhardt and E. Ray Canterbery, Florida State University.* Paradigmatic Growth of Knowledge Explaining Responses to Criticism in Economics, *Guy Ahonen, Swedish School of Economics and Business Administration.* The Crisis in Economic Theory: A Sociological Perspective, *Vincent J. Tarascio, University of North Carolina.* REVIEW ESSAYS: Peter C. Sederberg. The Politics of Meaning, *Malcolm Rutherford, University of Victoria, Jack L. Amarglio, Merriack College, E. Ray Canterbery, Florida State University and John B. Davis, University of Dallas.* Morton Deutsch, Distributive Justice: A Social-Psychological Perspective, *H. Scott Gordon, Indiana University and Stephen T. Worland, University of Notre Dame.* Books Received.

Volume 5, 1987, 248 pp. $58.50
ISBN 0-89232-832-0

CONTENTS: Editorial Board. List of Contributors.
Acknowledgements. Justice and Freedom in Marx's Moral
Critique of Capitalism, *John E. Elliott, University of
Southern California, Los Angeles.* Marx's Conception of
Ethics in Capitalist Society, *John B. Davis, University of
Dallas, Irving.* The Alternative First Chapter of Schumpe-
ter's "History of Economic Analysis", Some Questions of
Principle, *Joseph A. Schumpeter; Loring Allen, editor.*
New Lights on J.A. Schumpeter's Theory of the History
of Economics? *Hans E. Jensen, University of Tennessee.*
Two Transcripts and Afterwords of Panel Discussions.
What Aspects of Keynes's Economic Theories Merit
Continued or Renewed Interest? *Edwin Burmeister, Robert
W. Clower and Warren J. Samuels. Donald A. Walker,
editor, Indiana University of Pennsylvania.* A Rhetorical
Interpretationof the Panel Discussion on Keynes, *Arjo
Klamer, Wellesley College.* Methodological Diversity in
Economics, Bruce J. Caldwell, editor, University of North
Carolina, Greensboro. Books Received.

Volume 6, 1989, 283 pp. $58.50
ISBN 0-89232-928-9

CONTENTS: List of Contributors. Editorial Board.
Acknowledgements. Herbert Simon's Human Rationality,
Brian J. Loasby, University of Stirling. Aspects of Austrian
Economics in the 1920s and 1930s, *Peter Rosner and Georg
Winckler, University of Vienna.* J. M. Keynes and D. H.
Robertson: Three Phases of Collaboration, *John R.
Presley, Loughborough University.* SYMPOSIUM ON
AUSTRIAN AND INSTITUTIONAL ECONOMICS.
Introduction, *Warren J. Samuels, Michigan State
University.* Austrian and Institutional Economics: Some
Common Elements, *Warren J. Samuels, Michigan State
University.* Evolution and Economics: Austrians as
Institutionalists, *Peter J. Boettke, George Mason
University.* Austrians and Institutionalist: The Historial
Origins of Their Shared Characteristics, *Bruce J. Caldwell,
University of North Carolina.* Reflections on the Austrian/
Institutionalism Symposium, *A. W. Coats, Duke
University.* Ismatically Speaking: Are Austrians Institu-
tionalists, *Ken Dennis, University of Manitoba.* Austrians
vs. Institutionalists: Who Are the Real Dissenters?, *William*

Volume 7, In preparation, Fall 1989
ISBN 0-89232-040-3 $58.50

Ahonen, *Swedish School of Economics and Business Administration.* **Voluntary Exchange and Economic Claims,** *Timothy J. Brennan, George Washington University.* **SYMPOSIUM ON THE METHODOLOGY OF RATIONAL EXPECTATIONS. Rational Expectations in the Light of Modern Psychology,** *Malcolm Rutherford, University of Victoria.* **Implicit Contracts, Rational Expectations, and Theories of Knowledge,** *James R. Wible, University of New Hampshire.* **Rationality, Expectations, and Relevance in Economic Analysis: Implications of the Methodological Gyratopms of Monetary Theory,** *Will E. Mason, Pennsylvania State University.* **Grunberg and Modigliani, Public Predictions and the New Classical Macroeconomics,** *D. Wade Hands, University of Puget Sound.* **Poster's Foucault, Marxism and History and Barnes's About Science: Review Essay,** *Jack L. Amariglio, Merrimack College.* **White's When Words Lose Their Meaning: Review Essay,** *Arjo Klamer, University of Iowa.* **Johnson's Research Methodology for Economists: Philosophy and Practive: Reivew Essays,** *Bruce J. Caldwell, University of North Carolina and Lewis E. Hill, Texas Tech University.* **Woo's What's Wrong with Formalization in Economics? An Epistemological Critique: Review Essays,** *Bruce J. Caldwell, University of North Carolina, Don Lavoie, George Mason University, Philip E. Mirowski, Tufts University, and Larry Samuelson, Pennsylvania State University.*

JAI PRESS INC.
55 Old Post Road - No. 2
P.O. Box 1678
Greenwich, Connecticut 06836-1678
Tel: 203-661-7602